SEPHARDIC TRAJECTORIES

ARCHIVES, OBJECTS, AND THE OTTOMAN JEWISH PAST IN THE UNITED STATES

T0079685

Koç University Press: 237

HISTORY | MIGRATION STUDIES | CULTURAL STUDIES

Sephardic Trajectories: Archives, Objects, and the Ottoman Jewish Past in the United States
Editors: Kerem Tınaz, Oscar Aguirre-Mandujano

Copyeditor: Matt Hanson
Proofreader: Tara A. Ingman
Coordinating editor: Defne Karakaya
Book design: Gökçen Ergüven
Cover design: Emre Çıkınoğlu
Cover photo: Clipping from newspaper or magazine of interior of Cozy Corner restaurant, Seattle. University of Washington Libraries, Special Collections.

Print: A4 Ofset

Otosanayi Sitesi, Donanma Sk. No: 16 Seyrantepe/İstanbul

Certificate no: 44739

+90 212 281 64 48

Koç University Press

Rumelifeneri Yolu 34450 Sarıyer/İstanbul

kup@ku.edu.tr • www.kocuniversitypress.com • www.kocuniversitesiyayinlari.com

Certificate no: 18318

+90 212 338 1000

Koç University Suna Kıraç Library Cataloging-in-Publication Data

Sephardic trajectories: archives, objects, and the Ottoman Jewish past in the United States / editors Kerem Tınaz, Oscar Aguirre-Mandujano ; copyeditor Matt Hanson ; coordinating editor Defne Karakaya. -First Edition.- İstanbul : Koç University Press, 2021.

256 pages; 16,5 x 24 cm. Koç University Press 237 ; History/Migration Studies / Cultural Studies

Includes bibliographical references and index.

ISBN 978-605-7685-36-0

1. Sephardim--Turkey--History. 2. Jews--Turkey. 3. Sephardim--Material culture--Turkey. 4. Jews, Turkish--Material culture. 5. Turkey--History--Ottoman Empire, 1288-1918. 6. Turkey--Ethnic relations. I. Tınaz, Kerem. II. Aguirre-Mandujano, Oscar. III. Hanson, Matt. IV. Karakaya, Defne.

DS135.T8 S47 2021

Sephardic Trajectories

Archives, Objects, and the Ottoman Jewish Past in the United States

EDITORS: KEREM TINAZ, OSCAR AGUIRRE-MANDUJANO

KUP

Table of Contents

List of Figures

Acknowledgements

This book has had its own trajectory. It began as a small research project for a graduate student assistantship at University of Washington (UW), evolved into a museum exhibit, and before it could materialize, it transformed into a conversation about archives and history, the results of which we present here. During the process, we acquired many debts to the people who believed in this project and did all they could to see it bear fruit. First and foremost, we should thank the contributors to this volume: colleagues, mentors, and friends, who discussed with us the nature of *Sephardic Trajectories* since its inception and who later agreed to put those reflections, work, and research into written form. We are particularly thankful to Devin Naar, who became the unofficial academic advisor of this project.

Sephardic Trajectories originated from conversations we had when both of us were junior fellows at Koç University Research Center for Anatolian Civilizations (ANAMED) in 2014–15 and it would not have been possible without the encouragement of Buket Coşkuner, ANAMED's manager, as well as its director and team: Chris Roosevelt, Şeyda Çetin, Ebru Esra Satıcı and Alican Kutlay. Similarly, we would like to specially acknowledge the help, vision, and support we received from the UW's Stroum Center for Jewish Studies and the Sephardic Studies Program, home to the collection. In particular, Ty Alhadeff's knowledge and generosity helped us navigate the collection and become familiar with its holdings. We also want to thank the executive director of Koç University Press, Rana Alpöz, who supported this project since we first turned to her with the idea of editing a volume from what was originally the catalogue of a museum exhibit.

We are also thankful to those who helped us shape the project throughout the last few years: Nisya İşman Allovi, Tyler Babbie, Nicholas Foretek, Aimee Genell, Naim A. Güleryüz, Reşat Kasaba, Selim S. Kuru, Ali Kemal Öztürk, Pınar Tınaz and Joel Walker. A word of thanks, if mostly in terms of inspiration, we own to Carlos Modragon with whom one of us (Oscar) co-curated years ago two exhibits on material culture: Moana: Culturas de las islas del Pacífico and the Museo Nacional de las Cultura's Pacific Hall in Mexico City. Working on ethnographic materials raised questions about history and collecting that prompted us to put together an exhibition and an edited volume.

Trajectories, such as this, also require material support, and we are grateful to those who helped this happen. In this regard, we would like to thank the Stroum Center for Jewish Studies at UW, the Koç University ANAMED, the Mitchell F. and Sophie Wise Ehrlich Student Support Fund in Jewish Studies, and the Mickey Sreebny Memorial Scholarship.

Last but not least, we would like to express our deepest gratitude to Seattle's Sephardic community and the *Ladineros*. Through the Stroum Center, they have supported this project and welcomed it. Their enthusiasm in being part of the Sephardic Studies Collection, not only as donors but as active members, has been an inspiration to us throughout the entire project.

Note on Names and Transliteration

The trajectories of the individuals and families discussed in this volume linked geographies and spaces where a variety of languages were used. Many Ottoman Sephardi Jews operated with some level of fluency in Ottoman and Modern Turkish, Ladino, French, Greek, Hebrew, and English, among other languages. However, as much as some of them were multilingual, many of the people they interacted with were not. Consequently, words that were not easily translated, such as given names, family names, and names of religious holidays, were often adapted. Elia was at times Eliya, A-Levi was Halevi or Levy, and Carmona could be spelled as Karmona. This is most evident in the sources used throughout the volume, wherein a person's name can appear in different orthographies, depending on the time and place in which the document was written. We believe this is also part of the history of the trajectories studied in this volume. For that reason, we decided to respect each authors' preference of names and transliterated words, respecting the usage in the sources they used. Thus, chapter 8 discusses the life of Avram Galanti in the Ottoman Empire and Turkey, while chapter 9 mentions him as Abraham Galante, the way he was known in English and French. We have indicated the varied orthographies in the Index.

In addition to proper names, whenever a non-English word is used in the American context and has entered English dictionaries, we have preferred the English orthography (e.g., Hazzan, Rosh Hashanah, and Yom Kippur). However, when words were used in Ladino in the original context, we have respected the Sephardic pronunciation (e.g., Rosh Ashana). For terms in Ottoman Turkish, we use the Modern Turkish orthography.

We decided to sacrifice some of the clarity provided by standardization, for we believe the many orthographies, languages, and usages reflected in the names of people, places, religious holidays, and other terms approximate better and more accurately the historical context of the trajectories we have aimed to narrate here.

Introduction

OSCAR AGUIRRE-MANDUJANO, KEREM TINAZ

On December 16, 1928, *The Massacre of the Jews in Russia: A Drama in Three Acts* premiered at Washington Hall, Seattle. The actors were members of Seattle's Sephardic community, as were the sponsors of the event and most likely the majority of the play's audience. The play's program offers a revealing combination of Sephardic family names (Alhadeff, Calderon, Franco, and Reina) and local Seattleite businesses (Palace Fish and Oyster Co. and Broadway Shoe Cleaning) who supported the production, juxtaposed with the names of fictional Jewish and Russian characters (Olga, Dimitri, and Dr. Jack).[1] The contents of the program reflect the circumstances of the Sephardic community in Seattle in its early phase. This and other plays were directed towards a recently formed Sephardic community, which was trying to connect to the local Ashkenazi community.[2] The overlap of past, present, and fiction is even more palpable in the surviving photographs from *The Famous Dreyfus Drama*, which depict local men dressed in military uniforms and heavy Ottoman style mustaches.[3] Only the stage curtain betrays the illusion, letting the viewer know this was in fact a fictional scene (FIGURE 0.1).

Between 1922 and 1928, the Seattle Sephardic Theater also staged *The Famous Joseph Drama with his Eleven Brothers, Genoveva, The Jewish Captive,* and *Love and Religion,* all directed and performed by community members who had immigrated

---

1   *Program: The Massacre of the Jews in Russia,* 1928, Sephardic Studies Digital Collection, University of Washington, ST01092.

2   See Marc D. Angel, "The Sephardic Theater of Seattle," *American Jewish Archives Journal* 5, no. 2 (1973): 156–7.

3   Alfred Dreyfus was a Jewish artillery officer in the French army who was unjustly arrested and condemned in Paris in 1894. Since the end of the nineteenth century, retelling Dreyfus's life story became a popular theme in Jewish literature. The story functioned as an allegory of injustice against a loyal Jewish citizen. In 1898, for instance, Ottoman Sephardi intellectual Shemuel a-Levi published an article in *La Epoca* about the gradual public recognition of the injustice inflicted on the "honorable Captain Dreyfus;" the same year, a-Levi published in Belgrade a monograph on Dreyfus' life, "Hestoria del capitán Alfred Drayfus;" in 1904, Dreyfus's memories were translated into Ladino and published in Salonika. See Michael Molho, *Literatura Sefardita de Oriente* (Madrid: Instituto Arias Mondano, 1960), 326, 353–4.

FIGURE 0.1. The cast portrait of *The Famous Dreyfus Drama*, directed by Leon Behar on March 1922. ST00943, Sephardic Studies Digital Collection, University of Washington. Courtesy of Rochelle Romano.

from Ottoman lands at the turn of the twentieth century.[4] All of the play programs were printed in English and Ladino[5] in modern Hebrew script.[6]

The programs for these and other plays are held at the University of Washington's Seattle Sephardic Collection (UWSSC).[7] The UWSSC is the result of an initiative to collect, preserve, and make public the heritage of Ottoman Sephardic Jews in

---

4   Angel, "The Sephardic Theater of Seattle," 156–160.

5   Also known as Judeo-Spanish, Ladino is the language that Sephardic Jews brought with them from the Iberian Peninsula to the Ottoman Empire in the sixteenth century. Ladino remained an important language among Sephardic communities up until the twentieth century. For a detailed discussion of Ladino and its significance for Sephardi Jews, see Aron Rodrigue, "The Ottoman Diaspora: The Rise and Fall of Ladino Literary Culture," in *Cultures of the Jews: A New History,* ed. David Biale (New York: Schocken Books, 2002), 863–885. See also Olga Borovaya, *Modern Ladino Culture: Press, Belles Lettres, and Theatre in the Late Ottoman Empire* (Bloomington: Indiana University Press, 2012).

6   See for instance, the two different brochures for *The Dreyfus Affair* in English and Ladino. *The Dreyfus Affair Advertisement,* 1922, Sephardic Studies Digital Collection, University of Washington, courtesy of University of Washington's (UW) Libraries Special Collection, ST01091.

7   The UWSSC is an umbrella project that includes the UW's Seattle Sephardic Digital Collection, which is the result of the digitization of documents and objects lent to or held

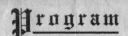

Program

Given by the

CONGREGATION EZRA BESSAROTH
SUNDAY, MARCH 19, 1922

✦ ✦ ✦

THE LITTLE MAN of MYSTERY
Played by BEN FRANKLIN

✦ ✦ ✦

The FAMOUS DREYFUS DRAMA
IN FIVE ACTS

Directed by Mr. **LEON BEHAR**

❖ ❖ ❖

CAST

DREYFUS	NENASHE ISRAEL
MRS LUCY DREYFUS	MISS ALEGRA ALHADEFF
FABRIS	JACK ALMELEH
ESTERHAZY / DIRECTOR	JACK AZUZE
CRATINION / GARCON	BEN FRANKLIN
PICARD	MORRIS ISRAEL
RECHARDON / GENERAL	PINHAS ALMELEH
CHIEF OF POLICE / MINSTER OF WAR	MORRIS ALHADEFF
CAPTAIN / GENERAL OF GENDARMERIE	ISAAC BENVENISTE
LAWYER / INSPECTOR	JOSEPH SOURIANO
DREYFUS GUARD / DETECTIVE	JOSEPH CHAPELOTO

♭ ♭ ♭

I.
The tragedy of Fabris and Esterhazy. The document of the traitor sent to Germany and caught by Colonel Picard. The suspicion against Dreyfus.

II.
The newspaper against the Jews. The quarrel between Colonel Richardon and Cretinion. The arrest of Dreyfus.

III.
Dreyfus in temporary prison. Dreyfus attempts suicide. The sentence of Dreyfus and degradation.

IV.
Picard finds Esterhazy's documents. The quarrel between Picard against Cretinion and Fabris. Picard proving Dreyfus' innocence to the Minister of War. Picard defeated.

V.
Dreyfus on Devil's Island. Dreyfus Prayer. The guard attempts to kill Dreyfus. Emin-Zola, Dreyfus' best friend and lawyer, comes to prison. Dreyfus' salvation and home again.

THE END

MONOLOGUE	MORRIS ISRAEL

FIGURE 0.2. Program for *The Dreyfus Drama* featuring Leon Behar as director. ST01060, Sephardic Studies Digital Collection, University of Washington. Courtesy of UW's Libraries Special Collection.

Seattle and the United States, launched by the University of Washington's Sephardic Studies Program in collaboration with Seattle's local Sephardic community.

Based on the play programs and other documents donated to the UWSSC, largely from local Jewish communities in Seattle, it is evident that the community continued using Ladino, also known as Judeo-Spanish, Djudyo, and Judezmo, as an important language for communal activities for many years, although younger generations used it less. Consequently, in 2010, Mrs. Josie Agoado, hoping to understand her family's past, brought what she thought was another "Ladino notebook" to the University of Washington (UW). The fragile notebook with blue covers belonged to her father, Yehuda Leon Behar (1900–1970), who was the director of all the plays noted. To her surprise (and ours), the "Ladino notebook" was written in Ladino but were mainly in Ottoman Turkish—the literary and bureaucratic language of the empire.[8] Unlike the official documents donated to the UWSSC, such as passports or identity cards, the "blue notebook," as we began calling it, was a personal item written in Ottoman Turkish not by a state official, but by an active member of Seattle's Sephardic community.[9]

Since Mrs. Agoado donated the blue notebook in 2010, its contents have triggered many conversations about the multiple links between Seattle and the Ottoman Empire. Filled with notes in Ottoman Turkish and Ladino, the blue notebook was a perfect example of an object that connected the many lives and trajectories

---

at the UWSSC. Some of the documents have been digitized in collaboration with the UW's Libraries Special Collections.

8   *Leon Behar Notebook: Poetry in Ladino and Ottoman Turkish*, Sephardic Studies Digital Collection, University of Washington, courtesy of Josie Agoado, ST00011.

9   Behar's apparent fluency in Ottoman Turkish was interesting to us, since most Ottoman Sephardim preferred to write in Ladino, rather than the imperial language. That being said, while Behar's choice of writing his personal notes in Ottoman Turkish seems unusual for a personal notebook, it must be noted that some Ottoman Sephardi intellectuals wrote in Ladino, Ottoman Turkish, French, and other languages. In this vein, see Stein's remarks on Thessalonian editor and journalist Shemuel a-Levi and his fluency in Ottoman Turkish: Sarah Abrevaya Stein, *Family Papers: A Sephardic Journey Through the Twentieth Century* (New York: Farrar, Straus and Giroux, 2019), 38. See also Devin Naar, *Jewish Salonica: Between the Ottoman Empire and Modern Greece* (Stanford: Stanford University Press, 2016), 146–150. For a brief discussion of the work of Ottoman Sephardi intellectuals in Turkish, see Laurent Mignon, "Türkçe Yahudi Edebiyatının Doğuş Sancıları: İsak Ferera Efendi ve Mirat Dergisi," in *Ana Metne Taşınan Dipnotlar: Türk Edebiyatı ve Kültürlerarasılık Üzerine Yazılar* (Istanbul: İletişim Yayınları, 2009), 11–24; Laurent Mignon, "From İshak to İsak The Birth Pangs of Jewish Turkish Literature," in *Turkish Jews in Contemporary Turkey*, eds. Rıfat N. Bali and Laurent-Olivier Mallet (Istanbul: Libra Kitapçılık ve Yayıncılık, 2015). Also see Kerem Tınaz's chapter in this volume.

of Ottoman Sephardic Jews in the United States. As a graduate student, one of us, Oscar, began a preliminary transcription and translation of Behar's notebook into the Latin alphabet in 2013 as part of a research project at the Stroum Center for Jewish Studies at UW.[10] Together with colleagues in Istanbul, we realized the verses in the notebook that Oscar had initially understood to be Behar's original poems were in fact his adaptations of Turkish songs popular during the first decades of the twentieth century.[11] The combination of Turkish songs and Ladino notes, as well as the history of the notebook, were revealing. The verses in the notebook told a story of change and adaptation, of military pride and patriotism. After looking at other sources related to Leon Behar, it became clear that the notebook was just one among many other objects in the UWSSC that expressed an Ottoman afterlife in Seattle.

For us, it was fascinating to see the large number of objects brought to the university by community members interested in discovering their own past. What other stories could researchers discover by studying objects and family papers held at UWSSC? How does the interaction between the university and the local community help historians to study the Ottoman Sephardic past in the United States? And how does the emergence of new collections, the use of new media, and the increasing involvement of the local Sephardic community shape the ways we write history? *Sephardic Trajectories* is inspired by the sheer number of objects that Ottoman Sephardic Jews brought from the Ottoman Empire to Seattle, which are today housed in the UWSSC. This volume brings together scholars of Ottoman and Jewish history to discuss some of the collections and to explore their shared significance in the United States and in former Ottoman lands. This book aims to highlight the interconnected histories of migration represented by the objects and the processes of their collection. But *Sephardic Trajectories* does more than that: it also provides a series of reflections to think about how access to private collections and the growing role of new media in engaging universities with local

---

10   The original was written in Ottoman cursive, typical of the nineteenth century. Turkish underwent a reform in 1928 that changed the script from Arabic to Latin, as well as modified some words, grammar, and usage. The difference between Ottoman and Modern Turkish has led to the scholarly practice of transcribing the Ottoman text into the Latin alphabet. Furthermore, since the Arabic script is not used for writing, handwritten documents often require paleographic work to be deciphered. The transcription of the blue notebook was possible thanks to the Sephardic Studies Program at UW, the Mitchell F. and Sophie Wise Ehrlich Student Support Fund in Jewish Studies, and the Mickey Sreebny Memorial Scholarship.

11   We are thankful to Akın Sefer (Koç University), who first recognized some of these songs while discussing the contents of the blue notebook.

communities and their histories change the ways historians research the past. The history of these objects is not limited to their Ottoman origins. The book traces their path from the Balkans and the Eastern Mediterranean to America, as well as their more recent transformation from household objects into digitized historical artifacts. Furthermore, following the paths of these objects allows us to examine the influence and transformation of Ottoman Sephardic material culture beyond the territorial and periodical limitations of the Ottoman Empire. We see this book as another station of their ongoing journey.

Sephardic Trajectories: A Historical Sketch

At the turn of the twentieth century, the world was on the move. Between 1891 and 1910, more than 11 million people emigrated from continental Europe to the United States.[12] Significant numbers of Ottoman subjects were part of this wave of unprecedented human mobility. It is estimated that 1.2 million Ottomans departed for the Americas between 1861 and 1914.[13] While the majority of these emigrants were Christians from the Syrian provinces, a considerable number were Muslims and Jews from different parts of the Ottoman Empire. In addition to internal factors that pushed emigrants to leave their homes—political transformations, the rise of nationalism, war, and natural disasters—socioeconomic opportunities in the "New World" constituted an important "pull" factor. According to the U.S. Immigration and Naturalization Service, between 1893 and 1924, over 50,000 Jews immigrated to the United States from the Ottoman Empire and its successor states.[14]

The location of established Jewish communities across the globe, personal networks, economic expectations, local languages, and political dynamics significantly influenced how immigrants chose their final destinations. Some Ottoman Jews

---

12 The U.S. Immigration and Naturalization Service calculates the number of immigrants from Europe to be 11,611,392. *Statistical Yearbook of the Immigration and Naturalization Service, 2000* (Washington, D.C.: U.S. Government Printing Office, 2002), 20.

13 Kemal H. Karpat, "The Ottoman Emigration to America, 1860–1914," *International Journal of Middle East Studies* 17, no. 2 (May 1985): 185.

14 Aviva Ben-Ur, *Sephardic Jews in America: A Diasporic History* (NY: NYU Press, 2009), 193–196. Rifat N. Bali, *Anadolu'dan Yeni Dünya'ya Amerika'ya İlk Göç Eden Türklerin Yaşam Öyküleri* (Istanbul: İletişim Yayınları, 2004), 86–87. Also, for an examination of demographic features of the Ottoman Jewry and the mobility trends of the community in the late Ottoman Empire, see Yaron Ben-Naeh, "Jews on the Move During the Late Ottoman Period: Trends and Some Problems," in *A Global Middle East*, eds. Liat Kozma, Cyrus Schayegh, Avner Wishnitzer (London: I.B. Tauris, 2015), 134–162; Justin McCarthy, "Jewish Population in the Late Ottoman Period," in *The Jews of the Ottoman Empire*, ed. Avigdor Levy (Princeton: The Darwin Press, 1994), 375–397.

settled in France. Others preferred to move to Central and South America. An important portion of immigrants decided to sail to the United States. Some of the first Ottoman Jews arrived in the United States to represent the Ottoman Empire at the Chicago World's Fair in 1893 and the St. Louis World's Fair in 1904.[15] As Devin Naar discusses in chapter 1, Ottoman Jews introduced American consumers to "Oriental rugs," halva, Turkish delight, and baklava. Along with Ottoman Greeks, they played an instrumental role in transforming the tobacco industry in the United States. While many of those who participated in the fairs returned home, permanent Jewish immigration increased after the Young Turk Revolution of 1908. Then, not only merchants, but also families began to settle in the United States. The flow of migration continued through World War I, but ceased in 1924 when the United States implemented immigration restrictions that targeted people from southern and eastern Europe, as well as the Middle East.[16] The majority of Ottoman Sephardic immigrants in the U.S. settled in New York. However, smaller numbers of these migrants built their new lives in cities like Philadelphia, Atlanta, Los Angeles, and Seattle. By the start of the First World War, Seattle was home to the second largest Ottoman Jewish community after New York.[17]

The study of Ottoman migration to the Americas in the late nineteenth and twentieth centuries necessitates engagement with sources beyond traditional state archives.[18] Attitudes towards migrants, both in the homeland and the diaspora, changed as migrants participated in local and international politics.[19] The interac-

---

15 Devin E. Naar, "*Turkinos* beyond the Empire: Ottoman Jews in America, 1893 to 1924," *The Jewish Quarterly Review* 105, no.2 (Spring 2015): 174–205. Rifat N. Bali, *Anadolu'dan Yeni Dünya'ya Amerika'ya İlk Göç Eden Türklerin Yaşam Öyküleri* (Istanbul: İletişim Yayınları, 2004), 57–86.

16 Naar, "*Turkinos beyond the Empire*," passim. See also Chris Gratien and Sam Negri's contribution to this volume.

17 See Devin Naar's chapter in this volume.

18 Recent scholarship has expanded our view of archival practices, including the type of questions we ask from sources and where we find these sources. For instance, historical anthropologist Camila Pastor has recently written a global history of migration to Mexico from the Ottoman Empire and the French Mandate using both state and family archives, as well as ethnographic materials. *The Mexican Mahjar: Transnational Maronites, Jews, and Arabs under the French Mandate* (Austin: University of Texas Press, 2017).

19 Historians studying the transnational histories of migration from Ottoman lands to America have raised questions about the role of non-archival sources, shifting identities, and strategies of political adaptation in understanding individual and communal experiences of migration. For example, see Devi Mays, *Forging Ties, Forging Passports: Migration and the Modern Sephardi Diaspora* (Stanford: Stanford University Press, 2020).

tions Ottoman migrants had with their communities, as well as their families, left myriad documents scattered in community and family archives, as well as private collections.[20] These sources tell a story about a shifting sense of belonging and the formation of old and new identities, but also about the intimate connections between past and present. Repositories like the UWSSC facilitate research on migration history by bringing together objects and documents that would otherwise be scattered, and sometimes lost, among the possessions of Ottoman descendants in the United States.

Several chapters in this volume show that there was already a vibrant Sephardic community in Seattle in the first decades of the twentieth century, as evidenced through Ladino prints, plays, notebooks, and other objects held at the UWSSC. The titles and content of the plays, for instance, speak to a strong communal identity, a shared past, and reflect the vicissitudes of forging a new life among other American Jews. At the same time, the official papers, personal notebooks, photographs, and other objects at the University of Washington document the Ottoman past of those young members of the Seattle Sephardic community who migrated from Rhodes, Istanbul, Salonika, and other Ottoman cities and villages at the turn of the twentieth century.

As we will see in chapters 1 and 2, research conducted by faculty and students at the UW has begun to unearth the trajectories of the local Sephardic community and its links to the Ottoman world. The intersection between the local community and the university clearly shows the research possibilities of new digital collections and community-led archives. The authors reflect on the nature of the collection, which is so different from the organization and shape of official state archives. To begin with, the collection is still in the making, as members of the local community discover family papers, photographs, and books left behind by their parents and grandparents in attics and basements. Eager to learn more about their past, local Jewish families brought and continue to bring these objects to the university for analysis. The UWSSC collection is composed of loaned and donated objects, some

---

Stacy D. Fahrenthold, for instance, shows precisely this complex history of Ottoman migration into the Americas by following different types of documentation (personal correspondence and newspapers) of Syrian activists in South America. *Between the Ottomans and the Entente: The First World War in the Syrian and Lebanese Diaspora, 1908–1925* (New York: Oxford University Press, 2019).

20   Recently, Sarah Abrevaya Stein wrote an account of one of the most prominent families in Ottoman Salonica and their different paths to exile in Europe and Latin America. Stein's monograph on the family papers of the a-Levi family shows the rich possibilities of research using family documents and personal archives, much in the way we hope this volume will. Stein, *Family Papers.*

from individuals and some from entire families. The nature of the donations varies and includes everything from official documents to religious phylacteries (*tefillin*) and music records, as well as books acquired or printed in Istanbul, Rhodes, Salonika, Livorno, Vienna, Amsterdam, and New York. Laurent Mignon, in chapter 4, uses books in the UWSSC to reconstruct Ottoman Sephardic reading practices, while, Naar, Alhadeff, and Pressman, in chapters 1, 2, and 9, respectively, show that many of the donated objects still have strong family and personal value to the donors and other members of the Seattle Jewish community. In this sense, the UWSSC functions almost as an ethnographic collection, ranging from household objects and sacred items to family papers and memorabilia.

Collections, Objects, and Migration

Access to new media has led to the rapid growth of digitized archival materials, which subsequently extended the reach of historical works beyond academia and increased the university's interactions with local communities. Thanks to these transformations, the UWSSC is today one of the larger repositories of Ladino books, as well one of the premier hubs for the study of Ottoman Sephardic material cultures in the United States. The collection's numerous published and unpublished materials offer opportunities to researchers to explore the intellectual, social, and cultural journey of the Ottoman Sephardim and allows them to understand the stories of families and individuals. These opportunities also pose new challenges, which are explored in this volume by Ty Alhadeff, Chris Gratien, and Sam Negri, as well as Hannah Pressman, as they each embark upon unearthing family history through new media, archives, and digital collections.

The UWSSC's potential and promise dovetails with a rich and growing scholarly interest in memory, trust, and violence in relation to the material culture borne of population movements throughout the twentieth century.[21] Simultaneously, the increasingly important place of Sephardic history in this scholarship, particularly in the Ottoman Empire, has led to the publication of Ladino sources in English translation.[22]

---

21   See, for instance, Leora Auslander and Tara Zahra, eds., *Objects of War: The Material Culture of Conflict and Displacement* (Ithaca: Cornell University Press, 2018). See especially Auslander and Zahra's "Introduction," 1–21; and chapter 9, Jeffrey Wallen and Aubrey Pomerance, "Circuitous Journeys: The Migration of Objects and the Trusteeship of Memory," 248–276.

22   In 2012, for instance, Sarah Abrevaya Stein and Aron Rodrigue made available a translation of Sa'adi Besalel a-Levi's memoir. Aron Rodrigue and Sarah Abrevaya Stein, eds., *A*

Since we began working on *Sephardic Trajectories*, we have learned of projects similar to the UWSSC led by scholars and institutions in the Unites States. Aron Rodrigue launched the Sephardi Studies Project at Stanford's Taube Center for Jewish Studies.[23] The Sephardi Studies Project is a digitized Ladino library with several works, both secular and religious, offered in translation. Similarly, Sarah A. Stein spearheaded an important project in 2015 that seeks to preserve materials from local community archives by involving the UCLA Special Collections in the acquisition, cataloguing, and safeguarding of documents and other materials from local institutions, such as the Sephardi Temple Tifereth Israel.[24]

As Ty Alhadeff explains in chapter 2, all these projects, however similar they may be, differ from the UWSSC in the way that UW's collection is a hybrid of documents loaned for digitization and physical objects held at the university. While each project is unique, they all resonate with our interest in the potential benefits of combining new media and community engagement to make connections between collected objects and their histories tangible to researchers and community members. These newly formed archives and collections allow us to reflect on the possibilities, challenges, and the ethical considerations inherent to the repositories themselves. They also grant some access to the lives of those who owned the objects they hold and the history of their trajectories from Ottoman to American contexts.

In recent years, a rising number of digitization projects have made the preservation and dissemination of entire repositories possible, expanding the kinds of documentation collected by institutions. In order to show the potentially novel ways in which archives can be constructed through digitized media, it is worth mentioning some initiatives that aim to preserve non-traditional sources, such as *Gharamophone*, led by Christopher Silver, which preserves and documents the sounds and music of North African Jews.[25] Similarly, Zemirot.org is a community-

---

Jewish Voice from Ottoman Salonica: The Ladino Memoir of Sa'adi Besalel a-Levi (Stanford: Stanford University Press, 2012).In 2014, Stein, together with Julia Philips Cohen, co-edited *Sephardi Lives: A Documentary History 1700–1950,* a volume containing over a hundred translations of documents related to Sephardic history from the eighteenth to the mid-twentieth century. Julia Philips Cohen and Sarah Abrevaya Stein, eds., *Sephardi Lives: A Documentary History, 1700–1950* (Stanford: Stanford University Press, 2014).

23   "Sephardi Studies Project," Taube Center for Jewish Studies, Stanford University, accessed July 12, 2020, https://jewishstudies.stanford.edu/sephardi-studies-project.

24   "UCLA Sephardic Archive Initiative," Alan D. Leve Center for Jewish Studies, UCLA, accessed June 15, 2015, https://www.cjs.ucla.edu/ucla-sephardic-initiative/.

25   For the details of the project, see Christopher Silver, "About," *Gharamophone*, accessed July 18, 2020, https://gharamophone.com/about/.

led digital archive that preserves the sound of Sephardic and Romaniote liturgical traditions from communities from former Ottoman territories with full recordings of prayers from these traditions.[26] Thanks to these initiatives, tapes of family interviews, voice-recordings of recipes, recording of prayers, and the music that people listened to have become part of the cultural landscape now available to historians and people interested in their own past and heritage. In addition to sound and daily practices, new archives also document different moments in the life cycle of Ottoman Sephardic Jews, such as marriage and death. For instance, the Goldstein-Goren Diaspora Research Center of Tel Aviv University launched a database project documenting 61,022 Jewish tombstones located in Turkey. Titled, "A World Beyond: Jewish Cemeteries in Turkey, 1583–1990," the computerized database stands out as, in their own words, "the largest academic tombstone database of its kind in the world."[27] Another example is the National Library of Israel's recently launched website that provides access to over 4,200 *ketubot* from around the world.[28]

A Moment of Reflection

Sephardic Trajectories aims to give the reader a sense of the contents of the UWSSC as an archive of Ottoman Sephardic history and to draw attention to the challenges posed by producing history, while at the same time producing a digitized archive. With initiatives such as the UWSSC, scholars are piecing together a story about the past not only by writing, but also by collecting, sorting, and organizing a constant flow of objects produced and donated by the very community whose history they hope to write. Indeed, the importance of taking a reflective and critical approach to collecting practices is precisely what links these new forms of historical preservation and historical writing to the complex history of ethnographic collections. The production of histories, like the production of ethnographies, is in many ways

---

26 The archive is available at https://zemirot.org/, accessed July 30, 2020.

27 "A World Beyond: Jewish Cemeteries in Turkey, 1583–1990," Goldstein-Goren Diaspora Research Center of Tel Aviv University, accessed July 21, 2020, https://jewishturkstones. tau.ac.il.

28 A *ketubah* (pl. ketubot) is a marriage contract, often crafted from handmade objects with complex decorations and calligraphy, clarifying the groom's obligations and rights of the bride with reference to rabbinic law and social customs. See "Ketubot," The National Library of Israel, accessed July 22, 2020, https://web.nli.org.il/sites/nli/english/collections/ jewish-collection/ketubbot/pages/default.aspx. For a discussion about *ketubah* tradition and designs with a focus on Ottoman Jewry in Istanbul, Salonica, Rhodes, Izmir and Edirne in the nineteenth century see Shalom Sabar, "Decorated Ketubbot," in *Sephardi Jews in the Ottoman Empire: Aspects of Material Culture*, ed. Esther Juhasz (Jerusalem: The Jerusalem Publishing House, 1990), 219–237.

determined by the logics of collecting and preserving material culture. One of the differences between archival or institutional collections, sometimes simply understood as repositories of art, manuscript volumes, or documents, and ethnographic collections, is the definition of the culture whose objects are collected. An ethnographic collection often constitutes material objects from a culture different from one's own. For instance, daily objects are turned into museum items, exhibited as visual representations that document or accompany the information of anthropological, ethnographic, and sociological discourses. The ethnographic approach is different from the state archive in that materials in the archive are the first clues to reconstruct the past. In contrast, ethnographic collections are often arranged as to be representative samplings of a whole, be that of a culture, a people, or a religion. Collections like the UWSSC are located precisely at the intersection of these two theories of collection, in that many of the objects are vestiges of material culture extracted from their actual context in which they were created with an aim other than to preserve information, with varied purposes and materials. The collection stands in contrast to archival documents that, even if not written for the historian, were produced with the aim of documenting an event for administrative or bureaucratic purposes. At the more material level, many of these objects were produced with less of an interest in long-term survival than of an immediate practical need. By contrast, the traditional contents of an archive or a museum, such as a piece of art, a section of a building or an official document were produced with the expectation that they will last for long periods of time, generations at the very least, to ensure the continuity of their value. Objects in this collection are, on the other hand, more quotidian in their intent, some created only for the eyes of someone's children, like a *boreka* recipe produced by a mother hoping her sons would remember her cooking, but most certainly not as evidence of the Mediterranean influence in the traditional cooking of Sephardic Americans (**FIGURE 0.3**).[29]

Similar to recent and much-needed discussions about the archive, most debates about ethnographic collections have revolved around the question of colonialism and the violence which dispossessed cultures of their material objects. Anthropologists, in particular, have reflected on the implications of exhibiting objects obtained as part of ethnographic and collecting enterprises, as well as the knowledge produced

---

29   For more information about this recipe, see Ty Alhadeff, "The Flavor of Rhodes: Paradise Lost, Recipe Saved," Stroum Center for Jewish Studies, University of Washington, December 2, 2016, https://jewishstudies.washington.edu/sephardic-studies/rhodes-boreka-recipe-saved/. For a discussion on the role of family recipes as authoritative voices of the past among migrants from the French Mandate to Mexico, see Pastor, *Mexican Mahjar*, 176–212.

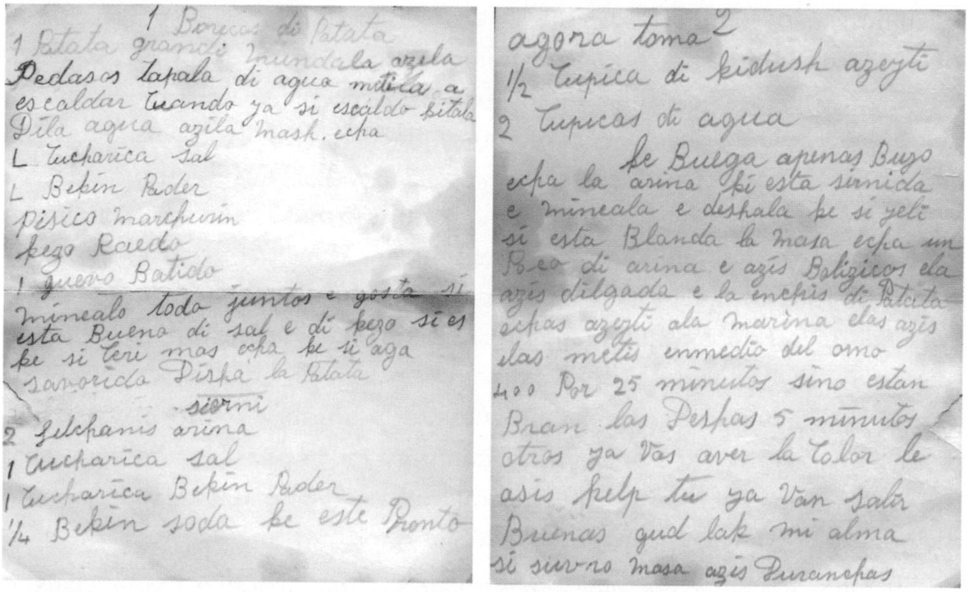
1 Borecas di Patata
1 Patata grandi Inundala azila
Pedasos tapala di agua metela a
escaldar cuando ya si escaldo pitala
Dila agua azila mash. echa
L cucharica sal
L Bekin Poder
pisico marchurin
kezo Raedo
1 guevo Batido
mincalo todo juntos e gosta si
esta Bueno di sal e di kezo si es
ke si keri mas echa ke si aga
savorida Dispa la Patata
sierni
2 felchanis arina
1 cucharica sal
1 cucharica Bekin Poder
1/4 Bekin soda ke este Pronto

agora toma 2
1/2 cupica di kidush azeyti
2 cupicas di agua
ke Buelga apenas Buyo
echa la arina ki esta sernida
e mincala e deshala ke si yeli
si esta Blanda la masa echa un
Poco di arina e azis Bolizicos ela
azis dilgada e la enchis di Patata
echas azeyti ala marina elas azis
elas metis enmedio del orno
400 Por 25 minutos sino estan
Bran las Peshas 5 minutos
otros ya vas aver la color ke
asis help tu ya van salir
Buenas gud lak mi alma
si sierno masa azis Puranchas

FIGURE 0.3. *Boreka* recipe by Rachel Shemarya. ST00674, Sephardic Studies Digital Collection, University of Washington. Courtesy of Al Shemarya.

around them, as prizes of Western progress in Euro-American museums and galleries.[30] Recent scholarship has shown that the auto-critical approach of this literature provides new pathways to further problematize collecting.[31] Indeed, as

30 Maybe the most renowned example of this revision of the archive and its logics is Ann Stoler's *Along the Archival Grain: Epistemic Anxieties and Colonial Common Sense* (Princeton: Princeton University Press, 2010). For the Ottoman Empire, see Wendy Shaw, *Possessors and Possessed: Museums, Archaeology, and the Visualization of History in the Late Ottoman Empire* (Berkeley: University of California Press, 2003). In the case of ethnographic collections and the museum, Nicholas Thomas's work has put at the forefront of the discussion the colonial project prevalent in the act of collecting. See, for instance, *Entangled Objects: Exchange, Material Culture and Colonialism in the Pacific* (Cambridge: Harvard University Press, 1991). Thomas's analysis aims to show the many dimensions of colonial power in the acquisition of objects in the Pacific, not only as an act of violence and dispossession but also as it was embodied in ethnographic practices and scientific discourses. Thomas, however, also emphasizes the agency of islanders and local structures of power in the process of material exchange. In this sense, Thomas offers an instance of how the logics behind the act of collecting, even if identified as a neutral scientific project, embed the resulting collection into larger phenomena of power, representation and, in the case of the Pacific, imperial dominance. For this discussion, see, in particular, *Entangled Objects*, 167–74, 177–84.

31 See, for instance, the volume edited by Michael O'Hanlon and Rober Louis Welsch, *Hunting the Gatherers: Ethnographic Collectors, Agents and Agency in Melanesia 1870's-1930's* (New York: Berghann Books, 2000). See especially O'Hanlon's introduction to the vol-

we find the opportunity to write history that also accompanies the production of a quasi-historical archive and quasi-ethnographic collection of sorts, it is worth considering the ethics of exhibiting the pasts of the people we write about. Should we think of the limits of our own professional practice as historians when browsing documents and objects that were meant for private eyes only? Are we responsible to the community that donated them and their efforts to understand their communal past? Questions about unexpected dimensions not known by donors arise as we consider the many trajectories of the given objects: through war and dispossession; exile, self-imposed or forced; and, family separation. How are we to account for the voices of those who did not leave behind traces as we closely examine the objects left by prior generations when engaging the community's history? Are we inadvertently producing too limited a picture of the community and its past? How are we to hear the remembrances of members of the community as we weave our stories around their objects, involving them in the process of history-writing?

The present volume does not intend to answer those questions as much as to raise them. Yet, the chapters herein can be seen as practical answers to those questions, either by reflecting upon the histories of the collection itself or by writing a history using the objects themselves. The volume thus includes case studies and reflections that hope to participate in a constant conversation over methods, heeding the advice of anthropologists. We must continue this conversation as we keep using, creating, and producing archives and histories.

Sephardic Trajectories consists of three main sections. The first, comprising chapters 1 and 2, is devoted to a discussion of the migration of Ottoman Sephardic Jews to Seattle at the turn of the twentieth century. Devin Naar's chapter provides a short history of Ottoman Sephardic Seattle, and Ty Alhadeff narrates the subsequent formation of the UWSSC. The second section is dedicated to exploring aspects of Ottoman Sephardic culture in the Ottoman Empire and the United States, and it is inspired by the material from the UWSSC and Seattle's Sephardic community. In chapter 3, Maureen Jackson focuses on Ottoman Sephardic music and its heritage in America. Chapter 4, written by Laurent Mignon, reconstructs reading practices among Ottoman Sephardim through the Ladino books brought from the Ottoman Empire to Seattle. In chapter 5, Özgür Özkan provides a reflection on compulsory military conscription among the Ottoman Jewish population. The third section offers a series of reflections on new methodologies and sources

---

ume, 1–34. On the relation of art, the museum, and colonialism, see Nicholas Thomas, *Possessions: Indigenous Art/Colonial Culture* (New York: Thames & Hudson, 1999).

study of Ottoman history in general and the Ottoman Sephardic past in particular. Based on his work on Ottoman special operations officer Kuşçubaşı Eşref Bey, Benjamin Fortna begins this section by reflecting on how personal archives allow us to challenge the premises of grand narratives in official histories and extend the scope of our perspective on Ottoman history. In chapter 7, Chris Gratien and Sam Negri discuss the role of new media, such as investigative podcasts, in shedding light upon the lives of Ottoman Americans through the study of deportation in the early twentieth century and their impacts on contemporary perspectives towards the past. Focusing on the fate of Ottoman Sephardic intellectual Avram Galanti's personal notes and paper, Kerem Tınaz reflects in chapter 8 on how the available documents allow us to better understand the Ottoman intellectual world at the turn of the twentieth century, as well as to discuss preservation practices among the Jewish community in Turkey. Last but not least, Hannah S. Pressman uses family documents brought by her mother to the US in order to reconstruct the journeys of her great-grandmother, Estrella Leon, and her great-grandfather, Haim Galanti, Avram Galanti's brother.

Afterword

An earlier draft of this introduction began with the story of how this book came to be, for we believe it reveals the richly layered contexts of the UWSSC's objects and their trajectories, objects that demand special attention and careful handling both in the collection itself and in scholarship. In 2015, we decided that working on a gallery exhibition to showcase the contents of the collection was the best way to reflect on its dual nature—ethnographic and archival—and to venture research possibilities for researchers and students at the UW and beyond. The project began formally in 2016 at Koç University Research Center for Anatolian Civilizations (ANAMED), and, as we progressed, it became evident that we were ourselves working on the history of a new type of collection. The UWSSC is led by the engagement of over eighty community members—individuals, families, and local institutions—rather than the efforts of a single organization, such as the state or a foundation. As the reader will discover in chapters 1 and 2, the UWSSC was created out of the interest and curiosity of the local community in its own past and was facilitated by the strong link between the community and the university, with both working together to produce historical knowledge. This also meant that the collection was a new type of entity, even within the university.

Due to the collection's complicated legal status, the exhibit was cancelled a few months before its opening. Both of us as curators, together with the UW and Koç

University ANAMED, were primarily motivated to ensure the preservation of the objects of the collection, and we carefully considered whether it was secure to move them across continents. Indeed, we realized some of the objects had complex histories of ownership, and transporting them could endanger their integrity. In an ironic turn of events, we were dealing with a collection of objects whose earlier circumstances made them move across the globe, while their current circumstances forced them to stay put. The hybrid nature of the objects at hand, with strong family value and yet ready for historical research and study, challenged us, as curators, with the need to balance these two aspects of the collection. Ultimately, we had to abandon the project. This setback helped us, however, to re-imagine *Sephardic Trajectories*. Immediately after the exhibit was cancelled, we began having conversations with colleagues who had considered writing for the exhibit's catalogue, as well as with colleagues who were familiar with the UWSSC or who had worked with similar repositories. This was also part of the history of the collection and was an important consideration when thinking how we, as historians, can use and benefit from the formation of community-led archives. The present volume is the result of those reflections.

Bibliography

"A World Beyond: Jewish Cemeteries in Turkey, 1583–1990." Goldstein-Goren Diaspora Research Center of Tel Aviv University, accessed July 21, 2020, https://jewishturkstones.tau.ac.il.

"Ketubot." The National Library of Israel, accessed July 22, 2020, https://web.nli.org.il/sites/nli/english/collections/jewish-collection/ketubbot/pages/default.aspx.

"Sephardi Studies Project." Taube Center for Jewish Studies, Stanford University, accessed July 12, 2020, https://jewishstudies.stanford.edu/sephardi-studies-project.

"UCLA Sephardic Archive Initiative." Alan D. Leve Center for Jewish Studies, UCLA, accessed June 15, 2015, https://www.cjs.ucla.edu/ucla-sephardic-initiative/.

Alhadeff, Ty. "The Flavor of Rhodes: Paradise Lost, Recipe Saved." Stroum Center for Jewish Studies, University of Washington, December 2, 2016, https://jewishstudies.washington.edu/sephardic-studies/rhodes-boreka-recipe-saved/.

Angel, Marc D. "The Sephardic Theater of Seattle." *American Jewish Archives Journal* 5, no. 2 (1973): 156–160.

Auslander, Leora and Tara Zahra, eds. *Objects of War: The Material Culture of Conflict and Displacement*. Ithaca: Cornell University Press, 2018.

Bali, Rifat N. *Anadolu'dan Yeni Dünya'ya Amerika'ya İlk Göç Eden Türklerin Yaşam Öyküleri*. Istanbul: İletişim Yayınları, 2004.

Ben-Naeh, Yaron. "Jews on the Move During the Late Ottoman Period: Trends and Some Problems." In *A Global Middle East*, eds. Liat Kozma, Cyrus Schayegh, Avner Wishnitzer, 134–162. London: I.B. Tauris, 2015.

Ben-Ur, Aviva. *Sephardic Jews in America: A Diasporic History.* New York: NYU Press, 2009.

Borovaya, Olga. *Modern Ladino Culture: Press, Belles Lettres and Theatre in the Late Ottoman Empire.* Bloomington: Indiana University Press, 2012.

Cohen, Julia Phillips and Sarah Abrevaya Stein, eds. *Sephardi Lives: A Documentary History, 1700–1950.* Stanford: Stanford University Press, 2014.

Fahrenthold, Stacy D. *Between the Ottomans and the Entente: The First World War in the Syrian and Lebanese Diaspora, 1908–1925*

Karpat, Kemal H. "The Ottoman Emigration to America, 1860–1914." *International Journal of Middle East Studies* 17, no. 2 (May 1985): 175–209.

Mays, Devi. *Forging Ties, Forging Passports: Migration and the Modern Sephardi Diaspora.* Stanford: Stanford University Press, 2020.

McCarthy, Justin. "Jewish Population in the Late Ottoman Period." In *The Jews of the Ottoman Empire*, ed. Avigdor Levy, 375–397. Princeton: The Darwin Press, 1994.

Mignon, Laurent. *Ana Metne Taşınan Dipnotlar: Türk Edebiyatı ve Kültürlerarasılık Üzerine Yazılar.* Istanbul: İletişim Yayınları, 2009.

———"From İshak to İsak The Birth Pangs of Jewish Turkish Literature." In *Turkish Jews in Contemporary Turkey,* eds. Rıfat N. Bali and Laurent-Olivier Mallet, 257–282. Istanbul: Libra Kitapçılık ve Yayıncılık, 2015.

Molho, Michael. *Literatura Sefardita de Oriente.* Madrid: Instituto Arias Mondano, 1960.

Naar, Devin E. "*Turkinos* beyond the Empire: Ottoman Jews in America, 1893 to 1924." *The Jewish Quarterly Review* 105, no. 2 (Spring 2015): 174–205.

———*Jewish Salonica: Between the Ottoman Empire and Modern Greece.* Stanford: Stanford University Press, 2016.

O'Hanlon, Michael and Rober Louis Welsch. *Hunting the Gatherers: Ethnographic Collectors, Agents and Agency in Melanesia 1870's-1930's.* New York: Berghahn Books, 2000.

Pastor, Camila. *The Mexican Mahjar: Transnational Maronites, Jews, and Arabs under the French Mandate.* Austin: University of Texas Press, 2017.

Rodrigue, Aron. "The Ottoman Diaspora: The Rise and Fall of Ladino Literary Culture." In *Cultures of the Jews: A New History,* ed. David Biale. New York: Schocken Books, 2002.

Rodrigue, Aron and Sarah Abrevaya Stein, eds. *A Jewish Voice from Ottoman Salonica: The Ladino Memoir of Sa'adi Besalel a-Levi.* Translated and transliterated by Isaac Jerusalmi. Stanford: Stanford University Press, 2012.

Sabar, Shalom. "Decorated Ketubbot." In *Sephardi Jews in the Ottoman Empire: Aspects of Material Culture*, ed. Esther Juhasz, 219–237. Jerusalem: The Jerusalem Publishing House, 1990.

Shaw, Wendy. *Possessors and Possessed: Museums, Archaeology, and the Visualization of History in the Late Ottoman Empire*. Berkeley: University of California Press, 2003.

Silver, Christopher. "About." *Gharamophone*, accessed July 18, 2020, https://gharamophone.com/about/.

Stein, Sarah Abrevaya. *Family Papers: A Sephardic Journey Through the Twentieth Century*. New York: Farrar, Straus and Giroux, 2019.

Stoler, Ann. *Along the Archival Grain: Epistemic Anxieties and Colonial Common Sense*. Princeton: Princeton University Press, 2010.

Thomas, Nicholas. *Entangled Objects: Exchange, Material Culture and Colonialism in the Pacific*. Cambridge: Harvard University Press, 1991.

———*Possessions: Indigenous Art/Colonial Culture*. New York: Thames & Hudson, 1999.

U.S. Immigration and Naturalization Service, *Statistical Yearbook of the Immigration and Naturalization Service, 2000*. U.S. Government Printing Office: Washington, D.C., 2002.

Wallen, Jeffrey and Aubrey Pomerance. "Circuitous Journeys: The Migration of Objects and the Trusteeship of Memory." In *Objects of War: The Material Culture of Conflict and Displacement*, eds. Leora Auslander and Tara Zahra, 248–276. Ithaca: Cornell University Press, 2018.

PART ONE

Histories: The Formation of a Community-Led Archive

CHAPTER ONE

Ottoman Imprints and Erasures among Seattle's Sephardic Jews

DEVIN E. NAAR[1]

Despite his longstanding family roots in Bursa (Prousa)—the bustling north-western Anatolian town fifty miles from Istanbul that served as the first capital of the Ottoman Empire—Rabbi Abraham Maimon embarked on a journey that propelled him across three continents and ultimately brought him six thousand miles away from his place of birth over the course of a dozen tumultuous years (1912–1924).[2] Leaving behind the sulphur baths, hot springs, and silk industry that made Bursa famous, Maimon embarked on an itinerary that coincide with the final paroxysms that precipitated the collapse of the Ottoman Empire: the Balkan Wars (1912–1913), the Great War (1914–1918), the Greco-Turkish war and the exchange of populations (1919–1923), the declaration of the Republic of Turkey (1923), and the abolition of the Caliphate (1924). Amidst the turmoil and the redrawing of political boundaries, the trajectories of many of the empire's Jews, like Maimon, moved in new and unexpected directions as they participated, by choice or by force, in one of the most extensive population movements in human history.[3]

Maimon's first move was symbolically dramatic as he transplanted himself from Asia to Europe when he crossed the Sea of Marmara in 1912, on the eve of the Balkan Wars, to serve as the rabbi of the Jewish community in the seaside Thracian town of Tekirdağ (Rodosto). More than a decade later—in the wake of continuing war that resulted in the bombing of the Jewish quarter of Tekirdağ, a grain shortage that threatened famine, a two-year Greek occupation, and the ultimate dissolution of the Ottoman Empire—Rabbi Maimon, along with his family, embarked from Istanbul in the autumn of 1924, traversed the Mediterranean with stops in

---

1   Generous support for this project came from the University of Washington Royalty Research Fund and the Isaac Alhadeff Professorship in Sephardic Studies.

2   See the recollections of Rabbi Maimon's son: Sam Bension Maimon, *The Beauty of Sephardic Life* (Seattle: MAIMON IDEaS, 1993), 44–50.

3   Reşat Kasaba, *A Moveable Empire: Ottoman Nomads, Migrants, and Refugees* (Seattle, 2009).

FIGURE 1.1. Maimon family passport photo, 1924. ST001817, Sephardic Studies Digital Collection, University of Washington. Courtesy of Albert S. Maimon.

Marseilles and Le Havre, and crossed the Atlantic over the course of two weeks. Finally reaching New York harbor, they were promptly detained at Ellis Island for more than a week and nearly excluded.[4] Ultimately freed, they traveled by train across the American continent to the far corner of the Pacific Northwest, to the expanding port town of Seattle, Washington, so that Rabbi Maimon could answer a call to serve as the spiritual leader of Congregation Sephardic Bikur Holim.[5]

One of the major challenges to bridging those two worlds that Maimon likely encountered upon his arrival in Seattle in 1924 was that Ottoman-born Jews in his new city of residence were already embarking on a process of self-transformation. Ottoman-born Jews found themselves in a vulnerable position in the United States not only as "Hebrews" and as speakers of a language that sounded similar to Spanish, but also as natives of the "Orient" and representatives of the "Terrible Turk," affiliations that rendered them targets both of new immigration restriction laws and of race-based restrictive covenants that limited the neighborhoods in which they likely could live in Seattle.[6] As a strategy to maneuver a system that sought to

---

4   Although those who arrived at Ellis Island and were not admitted into the country were technically the target of "exclusion," in the Ladino press they were referred to with the terms *deportasion* and *deportado*.

5   Maimon, *The Beauty of Sephardic Life*, 48–49.

6   Districts in Seattle such as Sandpoint, South Park, View Ridge, Mercer Island, and Clyde Hill all contained clauses specifically excluding Jews, or, in the racial language of the era,

exclude or limit their participation, Ottoman-born Jews across the United States, including in Seattle, distanced themselves from their empire and region of origin and recast themselves as "Spanish Jews" or "Sephardic Jews" in an effort to gain greater legitimacy and status in general American, as well as broader Ashkenazi-dominated Jewish, society shaped by racial and civilizational hierarchies that both explicitly and implicitly positioned Europeanness, Christianity, and whiteness at the top.[7] But even once widely adopted, the terminological shift did not liberate "Spanish Jews" from their liminal position, as evidenced by a 1925 editorial in *The Seattle Times*, which drew on the logic of "race science" en vogue at the time to classify "Spanish Jews" among the "intermediate types," along with "Arabians" and "Turks," who, as inferior races, were viewed as not quite European, yet not quite Asian.[8] In short, Ottoman-born Jews claims to being white—and therefore "American"—in Seattle, as across the country, remained precarious.[9]

This chapter seeks to draw attention to the broader political, legal, and cultural contexts that shaped the first decades of the Ottoman Jewish experience in Seattle and the conditions that molded the Maimon family's trajectory—including that of their library, along with hundreds of other books, letters, postcards, and photographs from other Ottoman Jewish families who settled in Seattle and which now constitute the Sephardic Studies Collection at the University of Washington. Furthermore, as home to an unusually large Ottoman Jewish population—by World War I, 3,000 of the 15,000 Jews in Seattle (i.e., 20 percent) hailed from the Ottoman Empire,

---

"Hebrews." The language of the covenant on a property in Madison Valley is representative: "That no part of said property shall ever be used or occupied by any Hebrew or by any person of the Ethiopian, Malay, or any Asiatic race." See the Seattle Civil Rights & Labor History Project: https://depts.washington.edu/civilr/covenants.htm. On the "Terrible Turk," see John M. Vander Lippe, "The 'Terrible Turk:' The Formulation and Perpetuation of a Stereotype in American Foreign Diplomacy," *New Perspectives on Turkey* 17 (1997): 39–57

7   On the campaign that emerged in the Ladino press in New York in 1915 to convince Ottoman Jews to stop calling themselves "Turks," "Levantines," and "Orientals" and instead designate themselves as "Spanish" or "Sephardic," see Devin E. Naar, "'Sephardim Since Birth': Reconfiguring Jewish Identity in America," in Saba Soomekh, ed. *The Sephardi and Mizrahi Jews in America* (Purdue University Press, 2016), 75–104.

8   W. A. Evans, "Daily Health Talk: Types of Mankind," *The Seattle Times*, June 23, 1925, 6. The editorial endorsed the views of the two most notorious American white supremacists, Madison Grant (author of *The Passing of the Great Race: Or, The Racial Basis of European History* [1916]) and Lothrop Stoddard (author of *The Rising Tide of Color: The Threat to White World Supremacy* [1920]).

9   Annie Lewis, "Precarious Whiteness: Reimagining the Seattle Sephardic Origin Story," University of Washington, 2018: https://digital.lib.washington.edu/researchworks/handle/1773/41904.

in comparison to less than 5 percent nationally[10]—Seattle serves as a particularly rich site for exploring the Sephardic experience in the twentieth century. Some scholarship and popular writing has focused on the tale of Seattle's Sephardic Jews, with particular attention to the establishment of the main synagogues, struggles for unity, early uneasy relations between Sephardic and Ashkenazi Jews in the city, and the processes of "Americanization."[11] Rather than conceptualize "immigration" as a single, discrete, unidirectional act that brought the Ottoman Jewish "pioneers"—as they are often called in a celebrated yet unsettling evocation of a term associated with popular tales of exploration and conquest in the American West—from the "old world" to the "new world," this chapter explores Ottoman Jewish migration to Seattle (and back) as a prolonged, ambivalent, and precarious process.[12]

Drawing on source materials that Ottoman Jewish families brought with them to, or created in, Seattle, in addition to reportage from Ladino newspapers published in New York and Istanbul, as well as English-language American newspapers, U.S. government immigration and naturalization documents, private correspondence, memoirs, and oral history, this chapter argues: the first Ottoman Jews who came to the United States conceptualized themselves in relationship to, and as an extension of, the Ottoman Empire as encapsulated in their preferred self-designation as *Turkinos*; the

---

10   Albert Adatto, "Sephardim and the Seattle Sephardic Community" (M. A. Thesis, University of Washington, 1939), 31; Aviva Ben-Ur, *Sephardic Jews in America: A Diasporic History* (New York, 2009), 188–192.

11   See Adatto, "Sephardim and the Seattle Sephardic Community"; Marc Angel, "Notes on the Early History of Seattle's Sephardic Community," *Western States Jewish Historical Quarterly* 7, no. 1 (October 1974): 22–30; Marc Angel, *La America: The Sephardic Experience in the United States* (Philadelphia, 1982), 158–161; Joseph M. Papo, *Sephardim in Twentieth Century America: In Search of Unity* (San Jose, Calif., 1987), 285–293; Howard Droker and Jacqueline B. Williams, *Family of Strangers: Building a Jewish Community in Washington State* (Seattle: University of Washington Press, 2003), esp. 60–76; Rifat Bali, *From Anatolia to the New World: Life Stories of the First Turkish Immigrants to America* (Istanbul, 2013), 110–113; Taryn Harris, "Sephardic Jews in Washington," *History Link* (2014): https://www.historylink.org/File/10778. See also Ellen Eisenberg and Ava Fran Kahn, *Jews of the Pacific Coast: Reinventing Community on America's Edge* (Seattle: University of Washington Press, 2009).

12   This chapter develops themes from my earlier work, now with Seattle as the primary setting: Devin E. Naar, "From the 'Jerusalem of the Balkans' to the 'Goldene Medina': Jewish Immigration from Salonika to the United States," *American Jewish History* 93.4 (2007): 435–473; idem., "*Turkinos* beyond the Empire: Ottoman Jews in America, 1893–1924," *Jewish Quarterly Review* 105, no. 2 (Spring 2015): 174–205. On the figure of the "pioneer" in Seattle and more broadly, see Coll-Peter Thrush, *Native Seattle: Histories of the Crossing-Over Place* (Seattle: University of Washington, 2007); Greg Grandin, *The End of the Myth: From the Frontier to the Border Wall in the Mind of America* (New York: Metropolitan Books, 2019).

first *Turkinos* in Seattle likewise understood themselves as part of a shared Ottoman American diaspora, inclusive of Greeks and Armenians, until the First World War, during which efforts to distance themselves from their empire of birth and to reimagine themselves as "Spanish" Jews first crystalized; and, U.S. government officials' persistent identification of Sephardic Jews with the Ottoman Empire and Turkey—if not as Turks—continued to pose obstacles for them with regard to the processes of immigration and naturalization and to the development of a public image.

The present chapter constitutes part of an ongoing project to reframe the narratives of Sephardic Seattle and of Sephardic America, more generally. Taken together, the sections of this chapter, each of which begins with an illustrative vignette related to Rabbi Maimon and his family, demonstrate the centrality of the "Ottoman" dimensions of the Sephardic Jewish experience, as well as the previously unrecognized significance of the broader American legal, racial, and political dynamics that deeply shaped the ways in which Sephardic Jews have left their imprint on Seattle.

The Making of Turkinos and their Diaspora

Rather than imagine an unbridgeable chasm separating their new places of residence from those of their birth, Jewish migrants from the Ottoman Empire and its successor states who arrived in the United States during the early twentieth century often kept their native communities and relatives close at heart while seeking to navigate their new environments, whether New York City or other locales where they established *kolonias* ("colonies") of *Turkinos*, as they called themselves, with Seattle home to the second largest colony in the country by the start of World War I. Links maintained between *Turkinos* abroad and their metropole facilitated the arrival of Rabbi Maimon and his family to Seattle in the first place. Those from Tekirdağ numbered among the first Ottoman Jews in the Puget Sound region. After establishing their own congregation, initially called the Oriental Bikur Holim Society of Rodosto, they invited Rabbi Maimon, whose *hazanuth* (cantorial style) and "charming personality" they fondly remembered, to serve as their spiritual leader.[13] Lay leaders among Seattle's Ottoman Jews hoped that Rabbi Maimon would ultimately serve as the spiritual leader for all of the city's *Turkinos*, regardless of specific place of origin, whether Tekirdağ, Marmara, or Rhodes, and the particular customs, practices, and personalities associated with each locale. Maimon soon presided over joint services at Congregation Ezra Bessaroth for the Jewish holiday of Sukkot, during which he gave wildly popular sermons that commented not only

---

13   Maimon, *The Beauty of Sephardic Life*, 44–46.

on relevant passages from the Torah but also advocated for "harmony" and "union" among Seattle's "colony."[14] One of the main Ladino newspapers in New York at that time, *La Vara*, enthusiastically endorsed the aspiration for Maimon to "centralize all the societies of Seattle and create a united community, strong and well-founded."[15]

The plan for an institutionally unified *Turkino* community in Seattle ultimately did not materialize—and the leaders of the city's Sephardic institutions continue to discuss this merger today, nearly a century later. While Maimon's arrival marked a new beginning with hopes for institutional consolidation, it also marked the end of more than two decades of movement of people, ideas, and goods back and forth between the Ottoman Empire and Ottoman Jewish "colonies" across the world. Just as *El Tiempo* in Istanbul advertised steamship lines that would take passengers (and goods and mail) from Istanbul to Naples, Marseilles, Liverpool, Buenos Aires, and New York, *La Amerika* in New York advertised the "Ottoman American Line" that embarked on return trips to Istanbul, Naples, Varna, and Constanza.[16]

While precise numbers are not available, it is estimated that nearly a third of Ottoman Jews left the region in the decades bracketing the turn of the century.[17] From the late nineteenth century until 1924, when the U.S. Congress solidified strict immigration quotas for those from eastern and southern Europe, as well as the Middle East, at the initiative of Washington State congressman Albert Johnson, perhaps around 50,000 Jews from the Ottoman Empire and its successor states arrived in the United States. Compared to the 2.5 million Yiddish-speaking Eastern European Jews, the 500,000 Syrians (mostly Christians) from Ottoman Lebanon, and the 400–500,000 Greek Orthodox Christians, the numbers of Ottoman (and former Ottoman) Jews were relatively small, similar to the number of Armenians (around 80,000), although larger than the roughly 35,000 Ottoman Muslims who arrived in the U.S. during the same period.[18]

---

14 Shabetai Naon, "Korespondensia de Siatli. Rabi Avraam Maimon ala ovra," *La Vara*, November 7, 1924, 4. *The Jewish Transcript* of Seattle also reported on Maimon's popularity as an orator: "Rabbi Maimon to give address on Sunday, April 12," *The Jewish Transcript*, April 10, 1925, 1.

15 "Nota de la redaksion," *La Vara*, October 31, 1924, 7.

16 For an advertisement for the Cunard Line in *El Tiempo*, 1919, see Sarah Abrevaya Stein, *Making Jews Modern*, 197–198; "Ottoman American Line," *La Amerika*, July 1, 1921, 2.

17 Devi Mays, "'I Killed Her Because I Loved her Too Much': Gender and Violence in the 20th Century Sephardi Diaspora," *Mashriq & Mahjar* 3 (2014): 4–28, esp. 5

18 For perspectives on Jews, Greeks, Turks, and Armenians, see Bali, *From Anatolia to the New World*.

That dispersed Ottoman and formerly Ottoman Jews referred to themselves as *Turkinos* and to their new communities as "colonies" demonstrates the extent to which they continued to see themselves as connected to "Turkey" (the colloquial name for the Ottoman Empire en toto). They embraced imperial metaphors to conceptualize their new communities as outposts of their empire of birth. The resulting *kolonias* in the Americas established links with each other: New York, Seattle, Rochester, NY, New Brunswick, NJ, Atlanta, GA, Montgomery, AL, Indianapolis, IN, Los Angeles, and Portland, OR; with each *sivdad madre* (mother city) in Istanbul, Salonica, Izmir, Rhodes, Tekirdağ, Gallipoli, Monastir, and elsewhere; and, with other Ottoman Jewish diasporic hubs across Europe, the Americas, and beyond, such as Paris, Marseilles, Brussels, London, Tel Aviv, Jerusalem, Haifa, Buenos Aires, Mexico City, Havana, São Paolo, Elisabethville in the Congo, and elsewhere.

The Ladino term *Turkino* was not coined in the context of diaspora, but rather emerged as a neologism during the *Tanzimat,* the era of Ottoman state reform (1839–1876) that sought, among other goals, to transform the diverse subjects of the empire into citizens with equal rights and obligations, regardless of religious affiliation. In the 1858 Ladino translation of the *Ceza Kanunname-i Hümayun* (Ottoman imperial penal code), for example, the Ottoman Jewish journalist and judge Yehezkel Gabbay translated the expression *tebaa-yı Devlet-i Aliye* ("subjects of the Sublime State") into Ladino as *suditos Turkinos*: "Ottoman subjects" or "citizens," regardless of religion.[19] The French translation of the penal code, in contrast, rendered the expression as *sujets de l'Empire* ("subjects of the Empire").[20] Although a different phrase, it nonetheless points to the imperial nature of the expression of belonging and also reveals the sui generis status of the term *Turkino*.

The civic, imperial, and more inclusive meaning of *Turkino*, in contrast to an ethnic signifier like *Turko*, was made clear in public spaces and in the Ladino press across the Ottoman Empire.[21] When Sultan Abdulmecid I visited Salonica in 1859, a local writer composed Ladino songs in his honor and declared his arrival a "festive day" for "every

19 Isaac Jerusalmi, ed., *Kanun Name de Penas* (Cincinnati, Ohio: 1975), 9; Naar, *Turkinos,* 178–179.

20 George Young, ed., *Corps de droit ottoman; recueil des codes, règlements, ordonnances et lois* (Oxford: Clarendon Press, 1906), v. VII, 9 (art. 48, 49, 50); Tobias Heinzelmann, "The Ruler's Monologue: The Rhetoric of the Ottoman Penal Code of 1858," *Die Welt des Islams* 54 (2014): 292–321.

21 The sentiment captured by the distinction between *turko* and *turkino* echoes in modern Turkish with the terms *Türk* (ethnic Turk) and *Türkiyeli* (citizen of Turkey). Ioannis Grigoriadis, "Türk or Türkiyeli? The Reform of Turkey's Minority Legislation and the Rediscovery of Ottomanism," *Middle Eastern Studies* 43, no. 3 (May 2007): 432–438.

turkino," by which he meant all Ottomans.[22] The newspaper *El Nasional* of Istanbul referred, in 1877, to *todo el puevlo turkino, sea turko o judio* ("all of the Turkino people, whether Turk or Jew"), suggesting again that *Turkino* captured a more inclusive sense of civic rather than ethnic or religious belonging.[23] Notably, however, the usage of the term *Turkino* in 1877 did not encompass Christians, likely a sign of mounting tensions over the position of Greeks, Bulgarians, and Armenians in the context of the Russo-Ottoman War (1877–1878) and of the desire of the newspaper to align itself with the Ottoman state, both out of a sense of genuine loyalty as well as fear.[24]

In the context of trans-Atlantic migration in the early twentieth century, the term *Turkino* took on an even more precise meaning and, especially in Ladino newspapers published in the United States, became associated with Ottoman and formerly Ottoman Jews living abroad.[25] Unlike those leaders among other non-Muslim communities from the Ottoman Empire who emigrated and sometimes adopted nationalist stances that positioned them at odds with their empire of origin, Ottoman Jewish elite—both those in the empire and those abroad—largely eschewed nationalist separatism, including political Zionism, until well into World War I.[26] Further due to the relatively small numbers of Ottoman Muslims in their new places of settlement (there do not appear to have been any who settled in Seattle during the early twentieth century), Ladino-speaking Jews embraced the term *Turkino* as an distinguishing moniker for themselves and in so doing

22   Aron Rodrigue and Sarah Abrevaya Stein, eds., *A Jewish Voice from Ottoman Salonica* (Palo Alto: Stanford University Press, 2012), 142–147; Elena Romero, *Entre dos (o más) fuegos: Fuentes poéticas para la historia de los sefardíes de los Balcanes* (Madrid, 2008), 283–286; Devin E. Naar, *Jewish Salonica: Between the Ottoman Empire and Modern Greece* (Palo Alto: Stanford University Press, 2016), 20.

23   Naar, *Turkinos,* 178–179; Marie-Christine Varol, "Du bon usage des langues dans une communauté plurilingue: les histoires drôles des judéo-espagnols d'Istanbul," *Langage et societé* 61 (1992): 31–54.

24   Julia Phillips Cohen, *Becoming Ottomans: Sephardi Jews and Imperial Citizenship in the Modern Era* (New York: Oxford University Press, 2014). Salomon Cherezli defined "Turkino" and "Turko" as synonymous: "turc." (p. 112). See Aitor García Moreno, "Salomon Israel Cherezli's Nuevo chico diccionario judeo-español–francés (Jerusalem 1898–1899) as a Judeo-Spanish Monolingual Dictionary," in Saul Mahir Saul and José Ignacio Hualde, eds., *Sepharad as Imagined Community. Language, History and Religion from the Early Modern Period to the 21st Century* (New York: Peter Lang, 2017), 192–211.

25   Naar, *Turkinos,* 186–189.

26   On Syrian and Lebanese diasporas, see Akram Khater, *Inventing Home: Emigration, Gender and the Making of a Lebanese Middle Class, 1861–1921* (Berkeley: University of California, 2001); Stacey Farenthold, *Between the Ottomans and the Entente: The First World War in the Syrian and Lebanese Diaspora, 1908–1925* (New York: Oxford University Press, 2019).

revealed their continued preference for imperial affiliation in an age of intensifying, exclusionary nationalism.

Economic factors initially provoked *Turkinos* to leave the Ottoman Empire and to seek out new opportunities in the United States during the late nineteenth and early twentieth centuries. Jewish merchants played key roles as representatives of the Ottoman Empire at the Chicago World's Fair in 1893—and then again at the St. Louis World's Fair in 1904 and the Portland World's Fair in 1905—that prompted them to showcase "Oriental" products for an American consumer market, including Oriental rugs and tobacco, as well as yogurt, halva, Turkish delights, and baklava. These first Ottoman Jewish merchants in the United States presented themselves as "Ottomans"—even drawing upon Orientalist imagery in their advertisements—as they sought economic gains; they often returned home.[27]

Working class Ottoman Jews who began arriving in the United States in greater numbers in the first years of the twentieth century similarly followed the established pattern of seeking their fortune and then returning home. As the editor of *La Amerika*, the first Ladino newspaper published in the United States, Moise Gadol observed in 1910 about his fellow *Turkinos*: "Most of them work in various factories here in America, and their concern is to send money back to their families in Turkey and later they return to their country [to be] beside their beloved ones."[28] Although born along the Danube River in Rusçuk (Ruse) in 1874 while the region remained part of the Ottoman Empire (until 1878), Gadol came to the United States as a Bulgarian citizen.[29] That Gadol appealed to the category of *Turkinos*—regularly invoking the phrase *muestros turkinos* ("our Turkinos") in his columns to refer to his newspaper's readers—reveals the extent to which he saw himself as part of a dispersed Ottoman and post-Ottoman Jewish collective that could include those from post-Ottoman Bulgaria, Greece, Rhodes (which became part of the Italian Empire in 1912), and elsewhere. Gadol's conceptualization

---

27 Julia Phillips Cohen, "Oriental by Design: Ottoman Jews, Imperial Style, and the Performance of Heritage," *American Historical Review* 119, no. 2 (April 2014): 364–398.

28 "Por la emigrasion de Turkia en Amerika," *La America*, November 11, 1910, 1.

29 On the ship manifest documenting Gadol's arrival at Ellis Island in 1910, under "nationality," he was first listed as "Bulgarian," but that was crossed out and above was written "Turk" (his "race" was listed as "Hebrew"). In contrast, in his petition for naturalization filed in 1913, he indicated that he was a Bulgarian citizen. Moise Gadol, List or Manifest of Alien Passengers for the United States Immigration Officer at Port of Arrival, S. S. La Lorraine, July 16, 1910, in "New York, Passenger and Crew Lists (including Castle Garden and Ellis Island), 1820–1957," via Ancestry.com; Moses Solomon Gadol, Declaration of Intention no. 18260, July 25, 1913, in "New York, State, and Federal Naturalization Records, 1794–1943," via Ancestry.com.

resonated with that of another *Turkino*, who defined the group as "our Ladino friends."[30] In this context, speaking Ladino became a key marker of one's Ottoman Jewish affiliation, regardless of one's formal citizenship or place of birth.

Political transformations and the decade of war that ravaged the eastern Mediterranean provoked new waves of emigration and mitigated the prospects of return: young men and later nuclear and extended families increasingly intended to stay permanently in the United States. In response to the introduction of compulsory military service for all male Ottoman citizens in 1909 following the Young Turk Revolution—part of the new regime's effort to ensure uniform rights and duties for all citizens, regardless of religion—young Jewish men began to leave in greater numbers, with the United States, including Seattle, among the destinations. *La Amerika* in New York lamented the new dynamic in a poem: "A sin bit the Turk/ who sought to conscript the non-Muslims into the army/ and for this reason, many Jews from Turkey emigrated, / most of whom settled in America."[31] Notably, however, Jewish men did serve in the Ottoman military, and new research suggests that emigration as a strategy to avoid military conscription among Ottoman Jews has been exaggerated.[32] The Balkan Wars (1912–1913), the devastating mass violence of the Great War (1914–1918), and then the Greco-Turkish war (1919–1922) resulted in the violent dissolution of the Ottoman Empire and the emergence of successor nation-states in the Balkans and European colonial regimes in the Middle East that provoked further waves of refugees and migrants.

Those *Turkinos* who settled in the United States forged their own sense of communal space in cities across the country. *La Bos del Pueblo*, a Ladino newspaper published by Salonican immigrants, observed in 1916 that on New York's Lower East Side, Eldridge Street served as the *sentro Turkino* ("*Turkino* center"), where the offices of the Ladino newspapers, important social clubs, and a commercial hub comprised of shops, cafes, and other businesses owned and frequented by *Turkinos* could be found.[33] When the Oriental Progressive Society hosted a New Year's Eve party, the

---

30 As quoted in Tracy Harris, *Death of a Language: The History of Judeo-Spanish* (University of Delaware Press, 1994), 233. Reinforcing the link between one's status as *Turkino* and speaking Ladino, an article in *El Tiempo* of Istanbul, in 1893, referred to "*Turkinos* who speak our jargon" living in Romania, quoted in Elena Romero, "La polémica sobre el judeoespañol en la prensa sefardí del imperio otomano: más materiales para su estudio," *Sefarad* 70, no. 2 (July-Dec. 2010): 435–473, esp. 456.

31 Moise Soulam, "Nuestro Ahi," *La America*, Jul. 31, 1914, 3.

32 Naar, "From the 'Jerusalem of the Balkans' to the *Goldene Medina*," 443–445.

33 "Eldrige Street sentro turkino," *La Bos del Pueblo*, August 4, 1916, 2.

organizers framed it as a "Turkino ball."[34] The Tivka Tova Society advertised a social gathering along the water at North Beach—known as the Coney Island of Queens—as a "Turkino picnic" for "all those from the various countries of Turkey, Greece, Romania, etc."[35] The invocation of the ecumenical category of *Turkino*—embracing Jews from Ottoman and extra-Ottoman contexts—remained explicit and part of a strategy of uniting Ladino-speaking Jews across political borders.

Advertisements for business enterprises published in the Ladino newspapers further reinforced the sense of connection among *Turkinos* by invoking the term to signal their legitimacy to prospective clients. Some advertisements included images of the star and crescent (sometimes alongside the American flag) or of the sultan.[36] Café Jerusalem on Allen Street, Café Smyrna on Chrystie Street, and Café Constantinople on Eldridge Street each advertised as a "Turkino restaurant and café."[37] A "Turkino cabaret" on Forsyth Street advertised "songs and dances in the Turkish and Greek style."[38] Help wanted ads sought employees for a "Turkino restaurant"[39] or for a "Turkina girl" to serve as a housekeeper for a "Turkina family."[40] An array of businesses and products included: "The best Turkino barber;"[41] "Turkino shaving salon;"[42] "the best and cheapest Turkino wine and raki";[43] "Turkino liquor merchant"[44] "Turkino [insurance] agent;"[45] "Turkino shop" selling Jewish ritual items;[46] "Turkino movers;"[47] "Turkino haberdashery;"[48] and, an ad for Sultan Rechad's Coffee: "Buy coffee where all Turkinos do."[49]

---

34   "No vos olvidesh," *La Amerika*, December 29, 1911, 1. Established in 1904, this society included Ashkenazi Jews from Istanbul among its founders and members. Papo, *Sephardim in Twentieth Century America*, 301.

35   "Venid todos este alhad al pik-nik turkino," *La Amerika*, July 19, 1912, 1.

36   "Panaderia Palestina," *La Amerika*, July 12, 1912, 4.

37   "Nuevo kafe i restaurante turkino," *La Amerika*, April 2, 1915, 2

38   "Nuevo kafe i kabaret turkino," *La Amerika*, November 3, 1916, 1.

39   "Se bushka," *La Amerika*, September 1, 1916, 1.

40   "Se bushka," *La Amerika*, May 22, 1914, 1.

41   "El mijor berber turkino," *La Amerika*, June 30, 1922, 3.

42   "S. Aguado i Abrevaya ermanos," *La Amerika*, November 11, 1910, 4.

43   "Los mijores i mas baratos vino i raki turkino," *El Progresso*, September 1, 1916, 3.

44   "Yayin gefen kasher le-Pesah," *La Amerika*, April 18, 1913, 1.

45   "Asiguradvos la vida," *La Amerika*, September 7, 1917, 2.

46   "Protejad vuestros kompatriotes," *La Amerika*, September 20, 1912, 3.

47   "Si keresh transportar," *La Amerika*, July 22, 1918, 1.

48   "Los mas nuevos sortes de chapeos," *La Amerika*, June 14, 1912, 4.

49   Naar, *Turkinos*, 188; Cohen, *Becoming Ottomans*, 135–137.

As central as the concept of *Turkino* was to articulating a sense of communal cohesion among readers of New York's Ladino newspapers, invocations of the term in advertisements and other contexts appear to have decreased—although by no means disappeared—especially beginning in 1917: once the United States declared war on Germany that year—and by extension the Ottoman Empire became an American "enemy"—Ottoman and former Ottoman Jews sought to subdue both their public and even private expressions of affiliation with the Ottoman Empire and the broader "Orient." The wartime conditions compounded the nativism, racism, and orientalism in American culture and politics and provoked Ladino newspapers in New York to initiate a wide-spanning campaign to displace terms like *Turkino*, "Ottoman," "Turkish," and "Oriental" from the names of synagogues, clubs, and publications and replace them with designations like "Spanish" or "Sephardic" that would link them more closely to Europe and to whiteness, as well as the protections afforded by those categories of belonging. The process of recasting *Turkinos* as Sephardic or Spanish Jews was not limited to New York but also played out across the continent, including in the country's second largest colony in Seattle.

Forging and Recasting the *Turkino* Imprint on Seattle

Considering how frequently the main New York Ladino newspapers like *La Amerika* and *La Vara* referenced Seattle, an uninformed reader could have imagined Seattle as a borough of New York City (although some *Turkinos*, when they first arrived in New York, did make the mistake of getting on a train to Washington D.C., rather than Seattle, in Washington state!).[50] In 1935, Rabbi Maimon's son, Bension, began serving as the Seattle agent and correspondent for *La Vara*—a particularly important role, considering the status of Seattle as the flagship *Turkino* colony on the West Coast. Thanks to the younger Maimon's close relationship with *La Vara*'s editor, Albert Levy, who directed Seattle's Sephardic Talmud Torah (Hebrew school) from 1931 to 1934, dialogue between Seattle's colony and the newspaper remained strong.[51] Subscribers to *La Vara* located across the country and beyond—surpass-

---

50   While Ladino newspapers in New York carried frequent reports on major activities in Seattle, they also published mundane Seattle news, such as notices when local businesses changed address: e. g., "Avizo interesante," *La Amerika*, June 3, 1921, 6. For mistaking Washington D.C. for Washington state, see the case of Jacob Aroghetti from Rhodes, in Marc Angel, "The Sephardim of the United States: An Exploratory Study," *American Jewish Yearbook* 74 (1973): 85.

51   Letters from Albert Levy, New York, to Bension Maimon, Seattle, 1935–1937, Sephardic Studies Digital Collection (SSDC), University of Washington, ST-1835–1842. *La Vara*

ing 16,000 at its height[52]—awaited the arrival of the weekly issue of the newspaper with great anticipation. As Seattle philanthropist Becky Benaroya recalled, when she tried to tell her mother (who had fled her native Rhodes during the Balkan Wars in 1913) that she was pregnant with her first child in 1943, she initially failed to get her attention because she was so engrossed in *La Vara*'s columns![53]

But by the time Bension Maimon, a grocer whose 24th Avenue Market served as a meeting place for Ottoman-born Jews and their kin in Seattle, had taken on his role with *La Vara*, and certainly by the time Becky Benaroya shared the news of her pregnancy with her mother nearly a decade later, the terms of discussion had changed: seldom did *La Vara* continue to refer to "*Turkino* colonies" dispersed across the country and beyond, but rather increasingly to "Sephardic communities." That shift was accompanied by another, as those in Seattle not only referred to their adopted city in the Pacific Northwest as *Siatli*, but also to themselves as *Siatelinos* (a linguistic construction that paralleled and competed with *Turkinos*).[54] As in New York, in Seattle, too, the initial affinities that Ottoman-born Jews expressed for their empire of origin would be transformed, even undermined, during World War I. Through a concerted effort of Ladino journalists and leaders, a new way of framing a sense of collectivity emerged that emphasized "Spanish" and "Sephardic" identity of the more rooted and permanent "community" in Seattle, as across the country. The new phrasing sought to assure the position of Ottoman-born Jews within an American political, legal, and cultural framework that provided privileges and protections for those who could demonstrate their status as civilized, European, and, ultimately, white—categories that entailed distancing themselves from the Ottoman Empire and the Orient.

The tales of the "pioneers" of Seattle's colony nonetheless reveal an initial sense of connection between not only *Turkinos* and their empire of origin, but also with other Ottoman-born migrants in Seattle. While available accounts occasionally disagree on who the first Ottoman Jews in Seattle were or when precisely they arrived, all recognize that the first Ottoman Jews came to Seattle in 1902 or 1903 thanks to their connections with other Ottomans—namely, Ottoman Greeks, who began

---

announced Maimon's official appointment as the newspaper's Seattle representative in: "A los abonados de Siatli," *La Vara*, July 31, 1936, 9.

52   Aviva Ben-Ur, "In Search of the American Ladino Press: a Bibliographic Survey, 1910–1948," *Studies Bibliography and Booklore* 21 (Fall 2001): 11–51, esp. 31.

53   Roz Bornstein, oral history with Rebecca Benaroya, "Weaving Women's Words," Nicki Newman Tanner Oral History Archive, Jewish Women's Archive, July 17, 2001.

54   "Un banketo en Siatel [sic]," *La Bos del Pueblo*, July 14, 1916, 2.

settling in Seattle in the late nineteenth century to work at lumber and sawmills, in the fish industry, and to pursue opportunities arising from the 1897 Klondike gold rush.[55] Invited by Greek friends from their native island of Marmara who had already been to Seattle and shared alluring descriptions of economic opportunities in the fish business, Solomon Calvo and Jacob Policar left via Istanbul, traversed the Mediterranean and the Atlantic, arrived in New York, and then took the train across the country: Seattle had become the terminus of the transcontinental Great Northern Railway in 1893.[56]

These two Ottoman Jews, both of whom spoke Greek in addition to Ladino and likely Turkish, socialized at Greek-owned cafes, drank Turkish coffee together, and perhaps even sang together with their Greek friends: at least some Jews from Marmara who came to Seattle were versed in Greek folk songs, *tragoudia*.[57] At one of the Greek cafés in Seattle in 1904, Calvo and Policar met the first Jew from Rhodes to come to the city, Nessim Alhadeff, likewise introduced to Seattle by a Greek friend from the nearby Aegean island of Leros.[58] So close was the association between the two groups, that in 1913, *The Seattle Times* even referred to a squad of mostly Ottoman Jewish bootblacks in downtown Seattle as "Greeks."[59] Social connections between Ottoman Jews and Ottoman Greeks—and their children and grandchildren—in Seattle continued throughout much of the twentieth century, as several marriages between members of both communities took place, and socialization, especially at cafes and via dancing at Greek clubs in downtown Seattle, continued through the 1970s and beyond.[60]

---

55   Dorothea Mootafes et al., *A History of Saint Demetrios Greek Orthodox Church and Her People* (Seattle, 2007), 57–59.

56   Adatto, "Sephardim and the Seattle Sephardic Community," 55–56.

57   Rina Benmayor, "A Greek *Tragoúdi* in the Repertoire of a Judeo-Spanish Ballad Singer," *Hispanic Review* 46.4 (1978): 475–479. Calvo spoke Greek and Turkish, in addition to Ladino, as documented in Adatto, "Sephardim and the Seattle Sephardic Community," 184.

58   Adatto, "Sephardim and the Seattle Sephardic Community," 194; Howard Droker, interview with Charles Alhadeff, Seattle, May 3, 1982, Washington State Jewish Historical Society Oral History Collection, University of Washington. The café that served as the meeting spot was likely the first one in the city known to be owned by Greeks, namely by James C. Angel (Angelo) (d. 1907), from the island of Leros, as recorded in Mootafes, *A History of Saint Demetrios Greek Orthodox Church and Her People Greeks in Seattle*, 57.

59   Eddie Boyden, "Negro patriot routes Greeks, saving flag," *The Seattle Times*, September 2, 1913, 4.

60   Video interview with David Behar, March 2016, for "Greeks and Jews Together," The Greek-American Historical Museum of Washington State, https://greeksinwashington.org/jews-and-greeks-together/.

FIGURE 1.2. Madras Kirkor, proprietor of Kirkor's Grocery, 1621 Yesler Way, Seattle, approximately 1925–1929. University of Washington Libraries, Special Collections.

Connections among Ottomans in the Pacific Northwest extended further. As Bension Maimon recalled, an Armenian from Tekirdağ, Kirkor Marderos, immigrated to Seattle and retained such close relations with Ottoman Jews that he spoke fluent Ladino.[61] Marderos was recorded in *La Amerika* in 1918 as making a financial contribution to support a *Turkino* fundraising effort in Seattle in conjunction with the celebration of the Jewish holiday, *Frutikas* (Tu Bishvat).[62] A decade later, in 1928, he took out an ad for his "Independent Grocery" in the brochure for a theater production organized by the Ladies Auxiliary of the Sephardic Bikur Holim Congregation.[63] Marderos remained so interconnected with Seattle's Ottoman Jewish population that a photo of him at his grocery store from the 1920s is even included in the collection of the Washington State Jewish Historical Society.[64]

---

61 Maimon, *The Beauty of Sephardic Life*, 50. On complex attitudes expressed by Ottoman-born Jews in Seattle regarding their Armenian neighbors and their fate during the 1890s massacres, see Adatto, "Sephardim and the Seattle Sephardic Community," 257–262; Cohen; *Becoming Ottomans*, 74–78.

62 Shabetai Naon, "Una selebrasyon de las frutas (Tu Bishvat) al benefisio de la Aliansa," *La Amerika*, February 22, 1918, 6.

63 See theater brochure for "The Massacres of the Jews in Russia," hosted by the Ladies Auxiliary of the Sephardic Bikur Holim, Seattle, December 16, 1928, Leon Behar Papers, University of Washington Special Collections, Acc. No. 2416–0004.

64 Photo of Madras Kirkor, proprietor of Kirkor's Grocery, 1621 Yesler Way, Seattle, c. 1925–1929, Washington State Jewish Archives, University of Washington Libraries

Whether Ottoman Jews in Seattle crossed paths with the two Ottoman-born Armenian founders of Aplets and Cotlets, a popular Washington state version of Turkish delights established in 1920, requires further research.

Not only did the first Jews from Marmara and Rhodes to come to Seattle learn about the city—and meet each other—thanks to connections to their Ottoman Greek friends, but they also made sense of their new residence in the distant context of the American Pacific Northwest by analogizing it to the geography of their empire of origin. Various testimonies emphasize that upon their arrival in the Puget Sound, some of these "pioneers" reportedly took a deep breath and expressed satisfaction that the climate was sufficiently similar to that of the eastern Mediterranean and that Mercer Island, in Lake Washington, resembled the island of Marmara.[65] Drawing the analogy further, Seattle, the regional metropolis, was to be understood as a new Istanbul, and Mercer Island as the new island of Marmara. That the "pioneers" settled not on Mercer Island (which had racial restrictive covenants in place beginning in the 1920s) but rather the city of Seattle itself suggests that, like for many other entrepreneurial Ottoman-born men of their generation from more provincial locales, the big city proved enchanting: the move from small islands and the countryside to big cities like Istanbul at the turn of the twentieth century coincided with, and sometimes preceded, waves of emigration that brought hopeful young men to America's burgeoning metropolises. It should be noted, however, that those from bigger cities in the Ottoman Empire like Istanbul were much less impressed with Seattle and characterized it as a "village" with "shabby homes" and "uncouth and uncultured" residents.[66]

The tale of Ottoman Jewish "pioneers" taking a deep breath of Seattle's fresh air and conceptualizing the region in terms of familiar Ottoman geography not only served as a vehicle to domesticate the foreign but also resonated with images of Seattle circulating in the press since World War I, if not earlier. In an article published in 1916 in New York's Ladino newspaper, *El Progresso*, Aron Benezra, a native of Gallipoli who served as a spiritual leader in Seattle for a short time (and as the newspaper's correspondent in that city), reflected on the draw of the Pacific Northwest. He emphasized the agreeable climate, the ample water sources, the cleanliness, and the rich natural environment. He recommended that all those with health concerns visit—or permanently move—to Seattle, due to the conditions in the region that he saw as conducive to restoring health. Perhaps Benezra had in mind figures like

---

Special Collections, PH Coll 650.BenezraH3.

65   Adatto, "Sephardim and the Seattle Sephardic Community," 192.

66   Ibid., 197.

Moise Alhadeff, from Rhodes, whose photo appeared in *The Seattle Times* in 1909 with a caption claiming that he had been cured of his rheumatism through one of the treatments available in the city.[67] Benezra went so far as to claim that those *Turkinos* in Seattle, poor and rich alike, lived with calm and rest, beside beds of roses, just as their ancestors once did in Palestine, the Holy Land.[68] In less grandiose terms, Albert Adatto referred multiple times to the "salt water atmosphere" and "fresh water lakes" of Seattle as an attractive feature for Jews from the eastern Mediterranean region.[69]

But the utopian imagery contrasted with the more ambivalent realities that had sent the city's *Turkino* pioneers, Calvo and Policar, back and forth to Marmara on several occasions. They, as well as other early Ottoman Jews in Seattle, returned home to find brides. By 1906, the number of Ottoman Jews had increased to eighteen—seventeen bachelors, but only one woman, Dora Cohen from Istanbul—necessitating return migration.[70] Labor disputes in the region—including a violently repressed sawmill strike in 1912 organized by Greeks at Grays Harbor, a hundred miles from Seattle where, in the town of Aberdeen, a cluster of Ottoman-born Jews also settled—may have sparked return.[71] The apparent absence of Calvo and Policar from Seattle in 1912 may explain, in part, why *La Amerika* claimed that year that the *Turkino* experience in the city started with someone else: "The first *Turkino* who arrived in Seattle is Mr. David Levy, president of the Ahavat Ahim society, twelve years ago [c. 1900]."[72]

Regardless of who the first really was, *La Amerika* identified all of the pioneers as *Turkinos*, regardless of their specific place of origin, whether Istanbul and its environs (like eastern Thrace or the island of Marmara), the island of Rhodes, or elsewhere in the eastern Mediterranean, regardless of political boundaries. The title of the article referred to "our brothers from Turkey in Seattle" and indicated that the city's *Turkinos* were initially employed delivering fish to train companies, restaurants, and hotels; selling fruit, operating postcard stands, working as shoe shiners, and as construction workers for ship companies. Young men would work two years and accumulate $400–500, enough to bring over brides from the Ottoman

---

67   "Bake Oven Cured Him," *The Seattle Times*, April 9, 1909, 8.

68   Aron Benezra, "Impresiones de Siatel," *El Progresso*, August 18, 1916, 2

69   Adatto, "Sephardim and the Seattle Sephardic Community," 33, 60, 186.

70   Ibid., 196–198.

71   Philip Dreyfus, "The IWW and the Limits of Inter-Ethnic Organizing: Reds, Whites, and Greeks in Grays Harbor, Washington, 1912," *Labor History* 38:4 (1997): 450–491.

72   The other reason *La Amerika* may have characterized Levy as "the first" was that indeed he may have arrived earlier than Calvo and Policar. "Raporto por la situasion de nuestros ermanos de Turkia en Siatli," *La Amerika*, May 10, 1912, 2.

Empire.[73] By 1916, of the 800 members of the Seattle "colony," *El Progresso* reported that nearly a third of the 300 men were independently employed: fifty fruit vendors, twenty-five fish vendors, fifteen shoe repairmen, ten tailors, six barbers, two dress sellers, and a smattering of others. Eight already owned their own homes—a sign of economic status.[74] Ottoman Jewish bootblacks also took on leadership roles in establishing the first union for their trade in Seattle.[75]

Like many immigrant groups, local place of origin served as the principal building block of social organization and communal institutions among *Turkinos* in Seattle, for whom the principle of *hemşehrilik* (regional compatriotism in Ottoman Turkish) reigned.[76] Two groups of *Turkinos* initially coalesced around certain residential blocks in Seattle, in "Jerusalem Town," a neighborhood in the central area of the city inhabited by Ashkenazi and Sephardic Jews alike, as well as other communities, including Japanese immigrants and later African Americans.[77] Jews from Marmara and Tekirdağ, *La Amerika* indicated, resided along Jackson, Main, and King Streets, between 10th and 14th avenues. In contrast, a second group comprised not only of those from Rhodes but also a smattering of Jews from Istanbul, Salonica, and Izmir congregated a few blocks away at 16th Avenue and Washington Street.[78] *Turkinos* established two mutual aid organizations according to local affiliation—Kupat Ezra Bessaroth de Rodes and the Sosiedad Bikur Holim Oriental de Rodosto—from which sprung the first two synagogues among the Seattle "colony." Groups from Marmara, Gallipoli, and Istanbul each initially established their own funds.[79] Of the smaller groups, only the Marmara contingent—including the pioneers Calvo and Policar—established their own congregation, Ahavat Ahim in 1922, which merged with the Tekirdağ group in 1940.

Formed around extended kin networks and in recognition of the divergent religious customs of each group, and perhaps dialectical differences in Ladino,[80]

73 Ibid.

74 Benezra, "Impresiones de Siatel," *El Progresso*, August 18, 1916, 2.

75 "Bootblacks succeed in organizing union," *The Seattle Times*, August 7, 1913, 7.

76 On the concept of *hemşehrilik,* see Lisa DiCarlo, *Migrating to America: Transnational Social Networks and Regional Identity among Turkish Migrants* (London, 2008).

77 Quintard Taylor, *The Forging of a Black Community: Seattle's Central District from 1870 through the Civil Rights Era* (Seattle: University of Washington Press, 1994).

78 "Raporto por la situasion de nuestros ermanos de Turkia en Siatli," *La Amerika*, May 10, 1912, 2.

79 Angel, *La America*, 159.

80 On the perpetuation of dialectical differences between varieties of Ladino spoken by Jews from Rhodes and those from eastern Thrace in Seattle, see Mary K. FitzMorris, "The Last

the perpetuation of local differences did not prevent unified action among all *Turkinos* in the name of the Ottoman homeland. Amidst the Balkan Wars, which resulted in the Ottoman loss of key locales such as Salonica and Rhodes, the Ladino newspaper *El Tiempo* in Istanbul reported in the spring of 1913 that Solomon (Sam) Alhadeff, a fish merchant who soon became the first president of Seattle's Congregation Ezra Bessaroth, initiated a fundraising campaign not to support Italy, the new sovereign of his native island of Rhodes, but rather the Ottoman Empire! Alhadeff informed Haim Nahoum, the chief rabbi in Istanbul, that his campaign had raised $1,000 (today approximately $25,000) to support Jewish war refugees who had sought shelter in Istanbul. Such an act of philanthropy led *El Tiempo* to declare: "Seattle is where many Jews who originate from Turkey are found and who are always attached to their motherland from which they came."[81] Alhadeff, from Italian-occupied Rhodes, was deemed just as connected to his Ottoman homeland as any of the other *Turkinos* in Seattle.

Alhadeff's initiative in Seattle to support the Ottoman Empire during the Balkan Wars found parallels elsewhere in the country. In a dramatic incident in Los Angeles in the summer of 1912, a "Turkino youth" named Moise Fresco, confined to a hospital bed with an undisclosed sickness, got into a fistfight with the Italian patient in the cot adjacent to his over the war between the Ottoman Empire and Italy. The nurses fled in fear, and six police officers rushed the scene to break up the fight. *La Amerika* praised the "Ottoman Jew's patriotism."[82] Following the Ottoman victory at the Battle of Gallipoli in 1916 during the Great War, Shimon Nessim, from Salonica (already part of Greece by that time), celebrated the Ottoman war effort and expressed his firm belief that rather than face its demise, the Ottoman Empire "still exists and will exist for a long time to come."[83]

Not only did Nessim's prediction not come to fruition as the Ottoman Empire collapsed with the conclusion of the war, but *Turkinos* across the United States, Seattle included, recognized that continued identification with the Ottoman

Generation of Native Ladino Speakers? Judeo-Spanish and the Sephardic Community in Seattle," MA Thesis, University of Washington, 2014.

81 "En ayuda de los refujiados de gerra djidios en Konstantinopla," *El Tiempo*, April 2, 1913, as quoted in Eyal Ginio, "Jewish Philanthropy and Mutual Assistance: Between Ottomanism and Communal Identities," in Katrin Boeckh and Sabine Rutar, eds., *The Wars of Yesterday: The Balkan Wars and the Emergence of Modern Military Conflict, 1912–1913* (New York: Berghahn Books, 2018), 344–372, esp. 357.

82 "El patriotizmo de nuestros turkinos por la Turkia," *La Amerika*, August 30, 1912, 1.

83 Shimon S. Nessim, "La Turkia de oy," *La Bos del Pueblo*, July 28, 1916, 3. See Naar, *Turkinos*, 199.

Empire—even calling themselves *Turkinos* or Turkish Jews—posed increasing obstacles, especially as the Great War progressed and Ottoman or Turkish citizens in the United States feared being classed as "enemy aliens." In 1912, *The Seattle Star*, known as the "working man's paper," highlighted the curious news of a "cosmopolitan" bootblack Reuben Alcana, "a Turkish Jew, born at Rhodes, Turkey," who could shine shoes in seven different "jostling jargons" at his Third Avenue stand.[84] *The Seattle Star* referred in a neutral manner to the city's "Turkish Jews" and their celebration of the Jewish New Year still in 1915.[85]

But Seattle's *Turkinos* soon needed to clarify their position—and identity—with regard to the ongoing wars involving their home country. In 1917, once the United States had declared war against Germany and diplomatic relations were severed with the Ottoman Empire, an article in *The Seattle Star* emphasized that "Turkish Jews in Seattle are backing Uncle Sam": 44 of them had purchased liberty bonds, totaling $2,750 ($55,000 today), to support the American war effort.[86] *The Seattle Times* even reported that Seattle's Jacob Capeluto, "a Turk by birth" who spoke "Spanish, French, Italian, Turkish, and Arabian [sic] fluently," was serving as an interpreter for Uncle Sam's infantry in Europe; and, that Sam Alhadeff, from "Rodi, Egeo, Turkey," was also serving in the U.S. infantry, having come to America several years before, reportedly to escape Ottoman military service. These announcements sought to demonstrate that although "Turks by birth," these men were a far cry from "enemy aliens" but, rather, willing to risk their lives for their adopted country—even to go to war against their kin. The newspaper did not fail to mention that Alhadeff's brother was serving in the Ottoman army.[87]

Two decades later, Albert Adatto elaborated on the kinds of clues present in the contemporary newspaper reports by emphasizing that mixed attitudes regarding the war had emerged among Seattle's Ottoman-born Jews: some caught a "patriotic fever" in support of the American war effort, even "excessively" so; some suffered from "endless heartaches" considering the fate of their loved ones back in the Ottoman Empire; and, others expressed sadness recognizing that Jews would be on both sides of the war. Over a dozen Ottoman-born Jewish men from Seattle served in the U.S. armed forces during the war. But Adatto did not recall that any

---

84   "Get your shoes shined in 7 different languages," *The Seattle Star*, May 13, 1912, 7.

85   "Jewish New Year's Day celebrated," *The Seattle Star*, September 8, 1915, 7.

86   "Seattle makes strong finish in purchasing liberty bonds," *The Seattle Star*, October 27, 1917, 1.

87   "Draft men urged to bring extra clothing," *The Seattle Times*, October 2, 1917, 3.

expressed concern over the fate of the Ottoman Empire itself.[88] The zeal and the accompanying expressions of American jingoism appear to have completely displaced any sense of political allegiance to the Ottoman state, at least in retrospect.

The most radical illustration of this new posture, tantamount to relinquishing any public claim of loyalty to the Ottoman Empire, emerged in a report in *The Seattle Star* in April, 1918: "With the hope that the war may overthrow Mohammedan rule in Turkey, Turkish Jews in Seattle have subscribed $4,000 [$68,000 today] to the Third Liberty Loan. Their wives are actively engaged in Red Cross work."[89] Such revolutionary rhetoric and aspirations for overthrowing Ottoman and Muslim rule were unprecedented in the annals of Ottoman Jewish history. By June 1918, the designation of "Turkish Jews" largely disappeared from the pages of the English-language newspapers in Seattle, and instead a new moniker emerged to designate the group: "Spanish Jews."[90] This would be the same designation used in another newspaper reporting on Seattle Jewish life in 1920 and would become the new norm moving forward.[91]

Perhaps ironically, the high profile visit to Seattle of the former chief rabbi of the Ottoman Empire, Haim Nahoum, as part of his tour of the United States in 1921, solidified the processes by which Ottoman-born Jews strategically distanced themselves from their empire of birth and reconceptualized themselves as "Spanish" or "Sephardic" Jews.[92] Born in Manisa and educated in Tiberias, Izmir, Istanbul, and Paris, Nahoum served in the coveted role of *hahambaşi* (chief rabbi) of the Ottoman Empire from 1908 until 1920. A confidant of Young Turk leaders and supported by the Alliance Israélite Universelle in Paris (a Jewish educational and philanthropic organization that promoted the transformation of Jews into good and productive citizens in whichever country they lived), Nahoum made noteworthy inroads into the Ottoman political establishment, serving as a representative of the Ottoman state in Washington D.C. at certain junctures during and after World War I (even referred to as the "Kemalist envoy to Washington"[93]) and at the Paris Peace Conference in 1919. Opposition mounted by Zionists within the Jewish community in Istanbul led Nahoum to resign from the post of chief rabbi in 1920, at

---

88   Adatto, "Sephardim and the Seattle Sephardic Community," 85.

89   "Liberty spirit to flame this week," *The Seattle Star*, April 22, 1918, 10.

90   "Dedicate synagogue," *The Seattle Star*, June 8, 1918, 10.

91   "From the Central Conference of American Rabbis," *The Jewish Voice* [St. Louis], July 9, 1920, 3.

92   See Naar, *Turkinos*, 200–201.

93   "Rabbi as Kemalist envoy to Washington," *American Jewish World*, August 11, 1922, 2.

which point he embarked upon a fundraising campaign in the United States on behalf of the Alliance Israélite Universelle.[94]

The Alliance had already captured the attention of Ottoman-born Jews across the United States, including in Seattle, and stirred intense interest among the various "colonies" from coast to coast. They viewed Nahoum's visit not only as an opportunity to connect with the man who had served as the spiritual and political leader of their mother community, but also to come together in support of an educational organization that so many Ottoman-born Jews had attended prior to their migration to the United States. In the process, they sought to demonstrate their fidelity to the allegedly Western and European—indeed American—values of liberalism and patriotism they saw as embodied by the Alliance. Already in 1918, La Amerika's agent in Seattle, Shabetai Naon, an alumnus of the Alliance school in his hometown of Tekirdağ (est. 1901), coordinated a fundraiser that netted $350.50 for the Alliance in conjunction with the first major public celebration of Frutikas (the Jewish holiday of Tu-Bishvat) among Turkinos in the United States.[95] The next year, in 1919, La Amerika published a report from Seattle about a "Sephardic Jew, a nationalist, and a splendid American patriot" named Albert Uziel, from Tekirdağ, who was then serving in the U.S. military and stationed in the "glorious country" of France. Inspired by his time in the land of the headquarters of his alma mater, the Alliance, Uziel made a contribution to support the institution and called on all those who also benefitted from it to follow his example.[96] The collection of funds in Seattle for the Alliance continued apace, even as the Spanish Flu swept across the country in 1919.[97]

By contributing to the Alliance, Ottoman-born Jews in the United States, including in Seattle, sought to express their commitments to liberalism and patriotism, to show to themselves and to the broader society that they belonged in the United

94 Esther Benbassa, *Haim Nahum: a Sephardic Chief Rabbi in Politics, 1892–1923* (Tuscaloosa, Ala., 1995). On the Alliance and its ideology, see Aron Rodrigue, *French Jews, Turkish Jews: The Alliance Israélite Universelle and the Politics of Jewish Schooling in Turkey, 1860–1925* (Bloomington, Ind., 1990).

95 Shabetai Naon, "Una selebrasyon de las frutas (Tu Bishvat) al benefisio de la Aliansa," *La Amerika*, February 22, 1918, 6.

96 "Un buen egzempio en favor de la Aliansa Israelita," *La Amerika*, March 28, 1919, 2. Uziel numbered among more than a dozen Ottoman-born Jews in Seattle who served in the U.S. armed forces during the Great War, according to Adatto, "Sephardim and the Seattle Sephardic Community," 84.

97 Nessim Behar, New York, to Jacques Bigart, Paris, February 11, 1919, Archive of the Alliance Israélite Universelle, États-Unis I A 05.

States, and that, despite their origins, they had become part of the civilized West rather than the backwards Orient. These kinds of goals may help explain why none of the coverage of Nahoum's visit in *La Amerika* involved the designation "Turkinos" to describe the newspaper's constituencies, but instead insisted on referring to them as "Spanish Jews" or "Sephardic Jews."

In the case of Seattle, that strategic reframing was most clearly articulated in the organizing committee's name: "The Jewish Sephardic Committee for the Reception of Rabbi Haim Nahoum."[98] The committee coalesced around members of the Tifereth Israel Club, established in Seattle in 1916 by a group of young men in their twenties drawn from both Ezra Bessaroth and Sephardic Bikur Holim who shared a set of aims: to enhance the intellectual, moral, and social conditions impacting the "colony"; to "defend the honor of all Sephardic Jews in our city"; and, to represent Sephardic Jews to the local Ashkenazi Jewish establishment.[99] Members of the organization had also been involved in the previously-mentioned campaigns in 1918 and 1919 to support the Alliance. Furthermore, the reception committee viewed Nahoum's visit as an opportunity to advance Tifereth Israel's principal goals: to "build solidarity among Sepharadim" across local affiliations and to work toward "union and progress."[100]

Arriving in time for the celebration of Passover, Nahoum drew unprecedented crowds to his sermons. The four hundred people who attended Passover evening services, *La Amerika* reported, represented the first time "all the different societies harmoniously celebrated the holiday under a single roof." The eight hundred people who attended his final speech at Congregation Ezra Bessaroth constituted the largest crowd ever to gather together at the same place in the history of the Seattle "colony" until that time. Nahoum gave long lectures that inspired deep emotions and even brought attendees to tears; others took the opportunity to celebrate and imbibe raki (despite the legal restrictions imposed by Prohibition).[101] The coordina-

---

98　Shabetai Naon, "El grandiozo resivo a Ribbi Haim Nahoum en Siatli," *La Amerika*, June 3, 1921, 1, 4.

99　"Korespondensia de Siatel," *El Progresso*, September 8, 1916, 2

100　Naon, "El grandiozo resivo a Ribbi Haim Nahoum en Siatli," *La Amerika*, June 3, 1921, 1, 4.

101　Eugene Normand and Albert S. Maimon, "The Sephardic Drinking Song, 'I give my life for a taste of raki,'" *Sephardic Horizons* 5, no. 1–2 (Fall 2015). For reportage on Ottoman-born Jews picked up by Seattle police for violating Prohibition laws, see: "3 raids made by dry squad," *The Seattle Star*, December 15, 1921, 19; "All set for Yuletide; police take it all," *The Seattle Times*, December 16, 1921, 2; "Names of Seattle customers found in moonshiner's home," *The Seattle Times*, March 26, 1922, 12.

FIGURE 1.3. Rabbi Haim Nahum (center) attending Passover dinner hosted by the Barokas family, Seattle, 1921. University of Washington Libraries, Special Collections.

tors of the visiting committee encouraged attendees to support the Alliance to their fullest capacity: "every Sepharadi, man or woman, should come to the aid of this institution, which works for the progress of our unfortunate brothers and sisters in the Orient." The committee promptly received pledges of $3,798 ($50,300 today) from more than 150 households in Seattle, whose names were published in *La Amerika*.[102] The final meeting during Nahoum's visit concluded with the singing of the American national anthem and the Jewish nationalist anthem, Hatikvah, symbolically capturing how the organizers sought to position themselves: as patriotic Americans and as Jews.

The Seattle Times also dedicated several columns to Nahoum's visit—and even published a photo of him—all of which presented Nahoum as a European figure catering to the local community of Jews of "Spanish and Portuguese ancestry." Perhaps most remarkably of all, not one of the articles mentioned that Nahoum had served as the chief rabbi of the Ottoman Empire. The articles did not even mention that he was from the Ottoman Empire or Turkey, but instead indicated that he was "of Paris," that he merely "sojourned" in Istanbul during the Great War, and that his main contributions involved valiantly, although unsuccessfully, lobbying for "Turkey" to join the Entente. *The Seattle Times* associated Nahoum with other political figures tied to the Entente: Eleftherius Venizelos, the Greek Prime Minister; Boghos Nubar, the chairman of the Armenian National Convention; and, Henry Morgenthau, the U.S. Ambassador to the Ottoman Empire. *The Seattle Times* did mention Nahoum's work representing an unnamed organization (i.e., the Alliance) dedicated to educating "Hebrew youth of the Balkans, the Near East and Africa" and its impressive reach

---

102 "Ribbi Haim Nahoum parte a Pariz," *La Amerika*, July 1, 1921, 2–3.

(50,000 students) and annual budget ($6 million). But the paper did not hint at the fact that Nahoum's hosts themselves were from that part of the world, but rather referred to them as "Sephardic Jews of Portuguese and Spanish ancestry."[103]

Reflecting on Nahum's visit nearly two decades later, in 1939, Albert Adatto confirmed the significance of the former Ottoman chief rabbi's visit for Seattle's "Sephardic Jews." For Adatto, the most important facet of Nahum's visit was his ability to impress the Ashkenazim, who "looked down upon" the Sepharadim, in part, because they allegedly did not have a "first rate rabbi" among them. Adatto further emphasized that from the perspective of Sephardic Jews, Nahoum was considered "far superior to any Ashkenazi rabbi." For Adatto, therefore, Nahoum's greatest achievement was speaking at the Ashkenazi Reform congregation, Temple de Hirsch, Seattle's flagship synagogue established by German Jews in 1899. Nahoum's visit, Adatto concluded, represented a "spiritual bath for the community" as Nahoum was "the most distinguished Sephardic [person] ever to visit Seattle and his stay will be remembered for many years to come."[104]

La Amerika hoped that Nahoum's visit to Seattle would galvanize support for the unification of the various local societies and consolidate them into an integrated communal structure. To the contrary, however, the power of *hemşehrilik* reigned supreme: Nahoum's visit inspired those from Marmara—the first *Turkinos* in Seattle— to create their own congregation, Ahavat Ahim (est. 1922), which became the third locally-based Ottoman Jewish institution to erect a synagogue in the city, following Ezra Bessaroth, established by Jews from Rhodes, and Bikur Holim, by Jews from Tekirdağ. Perhaps ironically, Nahoum's visit contributed to the fortification of local identities, while erasing Ottoman imperial affinities. In the wake of Nahoum's visit, all discussion of "unity" among the institutions transpired in the language of "community," rather than "colony," and in the name of "Sephardic" or "Spanish" Jews, rather than "Ottoman," "Turkish," or "Oriental" Jews.

Seattle's Sephardic Jews and the Challenge of Race and Nationality

Only three years after Nahoum's visit to the United States, the newly refashioned "Sephardic community" institutions in Seattle awaited the arrival of Rabbi Abraham Maimon, whom they hoped would serve as a unifying force. But all of the efforts that Seattle's communal leadership had expended to represent themselves to the American public as being of "Spanish and Portuguese ancestry" could not alter how

103 "Jewish leader here," *The Seattle Times*, April 22, 1921, 5.
104 Adatto, "Sephardim and the Seattle Sephardic Community," 88–90.

United States government officials—and society at large—viewed them. As a citizen of the new Republic of Turkey, one of the many non-Western European countries targeted by the new immigration restriction legislation in 1924, Rabbi Abraham Maimon only gained authorization to land at New York harbor for himself, his wife Vida, and six of their eight children (only those under the age of eighteen) as a result of a special exemption that enabled "ministers" of any religion to bypass the strict quotas imposed on those from Turkey—limited to one hundred slots per year (the two eldest daughters, excluded due to the quotas, resorted to additional methods to navigate the new laws).[105] Yet, upon the family's arrival at Ellis Island in September 1924, immigration officials designated the Maimons as "Turkish" not only in terms of their nationality but also their "race"—and they were promptly detained and slated for exclusion. This was just the beginning of a new phase in their treacherous immigration ordeal that reveals how connections between Ottoman-born Jews and the Ottoman Empire or Turkey could not be shirked, often, although not always, to their detriment with regard to the processes of immigration and naturalization.

Regardless of Rabbi Maimon and his family's perspectives at the time of their arrival—did they identify with post-Ottoman Turkey or consider themselves to be "Turks" in terms of their "racial" essence?—U.S. immigration officials imposed on them a nominal, yet legally binding, connection to the Ottoman Empire and Turkey, replicating the dynamics that shaped the Ottoman Jewish immigration experience since the first decade of the twentieth century. Immigration officials did identify other Jews as Jews—in fact, the person registered right before the Maimons on the ship manifest recorded at Ellis Island was classified as "Hebrew" by "race" and Romanian by nationality.[106] Indeed, Jews were registered as "Hebrews" by "race" for immigration purposes in the United States well into the 1940s. But the particular constellation of names, languages, places of origin, and other characteristics may have rendered the Maimons unrecognizable as "Hebrews" by the immigration authorities. The first

---

105 See Jonathan Sarna and Zev Eleff, "The Immigration Clause that Transformed Orthodox Judaism in the United States," *American Jewish History* 101, no. 3 (July 2017): 357–376. See letter from Henry Benezra of Sephardic Bikur Holim Congregation, Seattle, to Rabbi David Markus, Istanbul, January 31, 1925, UW-SSDC, ST-1198, requesting that Markus assist Rabbi Maimon's two daughters gain entry into the U.S. under the quota system.

106 Avraam Maimon and family, List or Manifest for Alien Passengers for the United States Officer at Port of Arrival, S.S. La Layette, September 22, 1924 in "New York, Passenger and Crew Lists (including Castle Garden and Ellis Island), 1820–1957," via Ancestry. com. For an overview of race and migration, see Mae Ngai, *Impossible Subjects: Illegal Aliens and the Making of Modern America* (Princeton University Press, 2014).

Turkinos in Seattle, Calvo and Policar, were not even initially recognized as Jews by Jews of Eastern European origin, given the primacy of Yiddish as the key marker of Jewish identity in the United States. The Maimons may have also found themselves as particular targets of United States immigration officials due to their status as "Turks" in an era, from 1917 to 1927, in which the Ottoman Empire, and subsequently the Republic of Turkey, and the United States did not have diplomatic relations.

The stated reason for the Maimons being detained at Ellis Island and threatened with deportation was the claim that Vida Maimon, the matriarch, was suffering from an unspecified illness: the Ellis Island manifest recorded the family unit as a whole as suffering from a "ph[syical] def[ect]" and classed as LPCs ("likely public charges").[107] *La Vara* published a front-page story expressing suspicion that the claim about Vida Maimon's health was trumped-up, but one that nonetheless instilled great anxiety: "It is still not known if they will be liberated or deported."[108] A subsequent front-page story in *La Vara* described the family's plight over the ten days in detention, during which they were forced to observe the Jewish New Year, Rosh Ashana , in Ellis Island's detention facility. One of the members of the editorial staff of *La Vara*, Moise Soulam, from Salonica, visited Ellis Island on a daily basis seeking to "liberate" the family and received the help of the Sephardic Brotherhood of America, the largest of the mutual aid societies catering to Ottoman-born Jews in New York, as well as Anshe Rodosto, comprised of Jews from Tekirdağ. Soulam finally succeeded in having Mrs. Maimon examined by another doctor, who declared she was in "prefect health," confirming *La Vara*'s suspicions that prejudice, not medical concerns, were at play.

The Maimon's ordeal resonates less with the mythic narratives of welcome associated in the popular American imagination with Ellis Island and more with a case of *pidyon shevuyim* (the rabbinic obligation for the "ransoming of captives"), except in this case the perpetrators were not pirates or enslavers but rather the United States government. According to *La Vara*, Ellis Island officials demanded payment for the family's train tickets to Seattle. Soulam and his colleague furnished a check for $930, but it was rejected on the grounds that only cash would be accepted. The Maimons were thus forced to remain in detention at Ellis Island for the duration of the holiday. Only once it concluded did Shabetai Naon, *La Vara*'s agent in Seattle, wire the requisite sum to secure the "liberation" of the Maimons, who swiftly boarded a train to the west coast. Upon arrival in Seattle, Maimon, as well as the leaders of Congregation Bikur

---

107 Avraam Maimon and family, Record of Aliens Held for Special Inquiry, S. S. La Layette, September 22, 1924 in "New York, Passenger and Crew Lists (including Castle Garden and Ellis Island), 1820–1957," via Ancestry.com.

108 "Ribi Avram Maimon detenido en Elis Ayland," *La Vara*, September 26, 1924, 1.

Holim, expressed their profound gratitude to Soulam, *La Vara*, and the Sephardic Brotherhood for "liberating" the family from the "clutches of deportation."[109]

Officials at Ellis Island detained and excluded individuals whom they classified as "Turks of the Hebrew Race," who did not always successfully negotiate the treacherous immigration system and American racial hierarchy, both of which favored neither Jews (in general) nor those from the Ottoman Empire or successor states. From 1790 until 1952, American law permitted only "free white persons" (and Blacks, after the Civil War) to become naturalized citizens. Whiteness was not about skin color, or not only, but contingent on culture, language, religion, mores, and behavior as determined both by "race science" thinking at the time, as well as the perceptions of the common person. The U.S. courts adjudicated many cases over those whose racial status was ambiguous—especially people born in the Ottoman Empire, including Syrians and Armenians—to determine whether they were white and thus eligible for citizenship. A major article published in *The New York Times* in 1909, "Is the Turk A White Man," equivocated on the question, suggesting that although Turks should be conceptualized as a mixed race with some European roots, the Turkish "mind" remained decidedly barbaric and not European; the article provoked extensive debate among the American public.[110] While it is unclear whether any cases of Ottoman Jews came before the court to adjudicate their "whiteness," a lower district judge did indicate in a case from 1913–1914 that he theoretically would exclude from the privilege of naturalization all "Syrians"—including Syrian Jews—on the grounds that they were not white.[111] Eventually that decision was overturned, and people from the Middle East came to be identified as "white" for purposes of the U.S. census—another reminder of the constructed nature of race and its persistence into the contemporary moment.

While Ottoman-born Jews were sometimes recognized as "Hebrews" by officials at Ellis Island, often they were recorded instead as "Turks," as in the case of the Maimons, or Greeks, Syrians, Spaniards, Mexicans, Italians, and Frenchmen—both due to error, as well as the intentions of migrants who sought to bypass immigration restrictions or position themselves more favorably in the American racial hierarchy, i.e., as more European, more white. At Ellis Island, other hopeful *Turkinos* were not as fortunate as the Maimons and faced exclusion due to illness (often trachoma)

---

109 "Ribbi Avram Maimon liberado de Elis Ayland," *La Vara*, October 3, 1924, 1.

110 "Is the Turk a White Man?" *The New York Times*, September 30, 1909, 8.

111 Ian Haney López, *White By Law: The Legal Construction of Race* (New York: New York University Press, 2006); Sarah M. A. Gualtieri, *Between Arab and White: Race and Ethnicity in the Early Syrian American Diaspora* (Berkeley: University of California Press, 2009), 64–68.

and claims that they were destined to become "public charges"—both claims the Maimons were able to overcome. Additional grounds for exclusion included claims that, as Ottoman subjects, they could be construed as enemy aliens in the context of World War I; following the implementation of the literacy test in 1917, an inability to pass—especially among women; or, faulty, illegitimate, or fabricated documentation. Mutual aid organizations based in New York, including the Sephardic Brotherhood of America and the Federation of Oriental Jews, and occasionally the much larger Hebrew Immigrant & Aid Society, appealed decisions on the grounds that the migrants could not return to their native cities due to war and antisemitic violence in their place of birth.[112]

While an unknown number of Ottoman-born Jews were nonetheless excluded, others were "liberated" from the "prison" of Ellis Island and entered New York. Their celebrated stories often made the front pages of the New York Ladino newspapers, not only the Maimon case, but also that of Seattle's first *Turkino* rabbi, Shelomo Azouz, who was slated for exclusion upon arrival at Ellis Island in 1911 until *La Amerika* intervened.[113] Moreover, the immigration restriction law enacted in 1924 severely reduced the number of Jews from the former Ottoman Empire entering the United States. Rabbi Maimon's eldest daughter, for example, eventually entered the U.S. via Canada on a visitor visa that she subsequently overstayed.[114]

Within a framework of exclusions and differentiated privileges and rights based on race, nationality, and class, it is not surprising that due to the precarious nature of their claims to whiteness, Seattle's first *Turkinos* did not, or could not, readily acquire American citizenship. The seemingly slow rate at which Ottoman-born Jews in Seattle, as across the country, became naturalized citizens has often been attributed to "procrastination" or "hesitation" on the grounds that they preferred to live in their own enclaves.[115] But not all "pioneers" among Seattle's *Turkinos* fully embraced the prospect of tying their permanent fate to that of their new country of residence, and many appear to have experienced obstacles as they embarked upon the naturalization process. According to *La Amerika*, only in 1912, when their numbers had increased to 600, did the first *Turkino* in Seattle advance toward achieving

---

112 On HIAS' reluctance to take on cases of Levantine Jews, see Ben-Ur, *Sephardic Jews in America*, 117–120.

113 "La imigrasyon," *La Amerika*, August 11, 1911, 1.

114 Kadon (sic) Maimon, "Manifest," September 21, 1927, "U. S. Border Crossings from Canada to U. S., 1895–1960," via Ancestry.com.

115 Papo, *Sephardim in Twentieth Century America*, 71; Bali, *From Anatolia to the New World*, 112.

American citizenship.[116] A shoe salesman from Gallipoli, Moise (Morris) Varon arrived in the United States in 1907 and initiated his naturalization process in 1909.

The Seattle pioneers, Solomon Calvo and Jacob Policar, in contrast, did not become American citizens for decades. The owner of a general store on the island of Marmara that sold equipment to fisherman and grain and other foodstuffs to local clientele, Calvo became a fish merchant in Seattle. He soon returned to Marmara to wed his spouse, Luna. But Luna was completely uninterested in leaving her island and venturing to the unknown terrain of North America. According to their daughter, Fortuna, Luna's mother packed her bags and forced her onto the ship to follow her husband back to the United States: "If he is going to China, you are going to China because you married him."[117] Given the resistance to coming to the United States, perhaps it becomes less surprising that Solomon Calvo did not declare his intention to become an American citizen until 1938—thirty five years after his initial arrival in the country.[118]

First selling fish and meat and later working as a plumber before finding employment as a sheet metal worker in Seattle, Policar initially stayed in the United States for about three years before returning to Marmara where he married his spouse, Esther, who gave birth to their first three children there. Policar returned to Seattle in 1912, and his family joined him there in 1920; but only in 1940 did he file his first papers and in 1943 his petition for naturalization—forty years after he first set foot in the United States.[119] Like Calvo, Policar remained connected to the Ottoman Empire—and subsequently the Republic of Turkey—through travels, family, and legal status, having retained Ottoman—and subsequently Turkish—citizenship for many decades.

Yuda ("Gordon") DeLeon, who came from Rhodes to Seattle as a child in 1912, recalled that prejudice in the American judicial system, and no other reason, accounted for the delayed acquisition of citizenship among many Ottoman-born Jews in the city: "Everybody wanted to become citizens. My dad went to school to take naturalization classes . . ." But DeLeon then described how, as one of the

116 "El primer sudito Amerikano Turkino en Siatli," *La Amerika*, December 20, 1912, 1.

117 Fannie Roberts, interview with Fortuna Calvo, February 9, 1976, Washington State Jewish Historical Society Oral History Collection, University of Washington.

118 Marco Solomon Calvo known as Sam Calvo, Declaration of Intention no. 39626, December 10, 1938, U. S. Naturalization Records, 1840–1957, via Ancestry.com.

119 Jake Policar, Declaration of Intention no. 45225, June 4, 1940, Washington, Petitions for Naturalization, 1860–1991, via Ancestry.com; Jacques Policar also known as Jake Policar, Petition for Naturalization no. 34939, December 8, 1942 (Oath of Allegiance signed March 8, 1943), Washington, Petitions for Naturalization, 1860–1991, via Ancestry.com.

first Sephardic students at the University of Washington, he went before the federal naturalization judge to take his citizenship exam in the 1920s. He claimed that the judge—whom he characterized as an "S. O. B."—was notorious for stymieing the naturalization process for Sephardic Jews. Emboldened by his education and class status, DeLeon confronted the judge. "'But I want to tell you one thing,'" DeLeon recalled telling the "very mean" judge during his exam: "'You've been the cause for a lot of our Sephardic Jews in the city of Seattle from becoming citizens of America.' I said, 'Many of those men are good citizens, raise nice families, they have never committed any crimes, they've lived as law abiding citizens.' I said, 'Every time they come here you scare them. You do everything to keep them from citizenship.'"[120] The English-language teacher at a "foreigner's class" in Seattle that many Sephardic Jews attended in preparation for their naturalization exams even encouraged DeLeon to petition the federal government in Washington D.C. to intervene with regard to the judge's antipathy toward Sephardic Jews.

Given that the judge in question, John Speed Smith, as the District Director of Naturalization in Seattle, favored the exclusion of Armenians and others from "Asia Minor"—including Turks—from the right to naturalize on the grounds that they did not meet the white racial prerequisite, perhaps Smith drew on the same justifications to exclude Ottoman-born Jews from citizenship.[121] A pro-Americanization magazine published in Portland and dedicated to "group elimination" credited Smith with rendering the naturalization process more rigorous throughout the Pacific Northwest.[122] Furthermore, in a private letter to his sister, Smith, born in Kentucky and descended from English settlers in the colony of Virginia, emphasized that "real Americans" needed to interest themselves more in the work of "Americanizing" foreigners in order to "preserve our institutions." He even characterized a popular missionary book of the era, *Christian Americanization*, which defined American and Christian identity as synonymous, as too open-minded and "international" in its willingness to engage with immigrants from all over.[123] The influence of a figure like Smith overseeing the naturalization process in Seattle may help explain

120 Howard Droker, interview with Gordon DeLeon, February 17, 1982, Washington State Jewish Historical Society Oral History Collection, University of Washington.

121 Earlene Craver, "On the Boundary of White: The Cartozian Naturalization Case and the Armenians, 1923–1925," *Journal of American Ethnic History* 28, no. 2 (Winter 2009): 30–56, esp. 38.

122 "Safeguarding our naturalization laws: Easy roads to citizenship must be closed," *The Western American: A Magazine of Good Citizenship* 1, no. 4 (January 1923): 3–6.

123 Letter from John Speed Smith, Seattle, to Alma Smith Rogers, February 1, 1920, Rogers Family Papers, MSS 14, Hanover College, Indiana. For a biography of Smith, see Clar-

why individuals such as Policar and Calvo, as well as other Ottoman-born Jews, did not become citizens for so long after their initial arrival in the country.

For Jews from Rhodes, like DeLeon, the dynamic was even more complicated, as their island, along with the Dodecanese archipelago, ceased being part of the Ottoman Empire as a result of the Italo-Ottoman War (1911–1912). The transformation of Rhodes into an Italian colonial holding began with the Treaty of Ouchy on October 18, 1912. While the Treaty stipulated that the island would be returned to Ottoman control, it never materialized, and instead the Treaty of Lausanne in 1923 formalized Italian possession of Rhodes. DeLeon's father, Haim, a notable figure in the *Turkino* colony, who had arrived in Seattle in 1907, had retained his Ottoman citizenship and had to renounce his allegiance to "Mehmed V, Emperor of the Ottomans" when he submitted his first papers for citizenship in 1917.[124] By the time his son, Gordon, submitted his first papers in 1925, he had to renounce his allegiance to Victor Emmanuel III, King of Italy.[125]

For others from Rhodes, the transition from Ottoman to Italian rule rendered their citizenship status ambiguous and created major stumbling blocks toward the acquisition of American citizenship, as they ran the risk of being classified as "enemy aliens" during both World Wars. The case of the aforementioned Solomon ("Sam") Alhadeff, who organized the pro-Ottoman fundraising campaign among *Turkinos* in Seattle during the Balkan Wars in 1913 and became a leader of Congregation Ezra Bessaroth, is a case in point. During World War I, when the U.S. government compelled all residents to register, Alhadeff indicated his status as a citizen of "Turkey."[126] While the United States and the Ottoman Empire never declared war on each other, and Ottoman nationals residing in the United States were never technically classified as "enemy aliens," their status as representatives of the Central Powers rendered their position in the United States tenuous. Discussions of transferring Ottoman nationals out of the United States to Europe took place, but never materialized. The insecurities that Ottoman affiliation posed for figures like Alhadeff may also explain why he wound up filing his first papers with the intention of becoming a citizen of the

ence Bagley, *History of Seattle from the Earliest Settlement to the Present Time* (Chicago: Clarke Publishing Co, 1916), III: 65–67.

124 Haim Leon, Declaration of Intention no. 8476, February 15, 1917, U. S. Naturalization Records, 1840–1957, via Ancestry.com.

125 Yuda Leon known as Gordon Leon, Declaration of Intention no. 23353, July 11, 1925, U. S. Naturalization Records, 1840–1957, via Ancestry.com.

126 Sam Alhadeff, Registration Card no. 444, September 12, 1918, U. S. World War I Draft Registration Cards, 1917–1918, via Ancestry.com.

United States on multiple occasions—first in 1905, while an Ottoman citizen, and then again in 1928, when he claimed "Italian" as his nationality.[127]

For reasons that remain unclear, but perhaps due to the onset of the Depression or the biases of Seattle's naturalization judges identified by Gordon DeLeon, Alhadeff did not move forward with the naturalization process in 1928. A dozen years later, he submitted his first papers again, for at least the third time, on June 21, 1940, notably claiming once more to be "Italian."[128] But a week later, on June 28, 1940, with heightened xenophobia and fears of espionage and sedition in the context of the war, Congress passed the Alien Registration Act (aka the Smith Act), which compelled 5.6 million non-citizens resident in the United States to register with the Immigration and Naturalization Service.[129] As a result of the new federal statute, Alhadeff cleverly registered as "stateless" and as previously having been a citizen of Turkey.[130] Alhadeff recognized that claiming Italian nationality at the time would have rendered him liable to be classified as an "enemy alien" in the context of World War II. This may also explain why, on his military draft registration card filed in 1942, he claimed to be from "Rhodes, Turkey," recognizing that unlike during the Great War, during World War II, it was perhaps unexpectedly more advantageous in the American context to be a Turkish rather than an Italian national.[131] The claim did not pass unnoticed by the Immigration and Naturalization Service, which investigated Alhadeff's status, determined he was in fact an Italian national and thus an "enemy alien." He was not interned, as were nearly two thousand Italian nationals resident in the United States (or, more infamously, like 120,000 Japanese Americans).[132] But Alhadeff was denied the right to become a citizen until he filed a special "certificate of loyalty," pledging his allegiance to the

---

127 Chelomo Alhadef (sic), Declaration of Intention, November 6, 1905, U. S. Naturalization Records, 1840–1957, via Ancestry.com; Chelomo Alhadeff known as Solomon Alhadeff, Declaration of Intention no. 30304, February 15, 1928, U. S. Naturalization Records, 1840–1957, via Ancestry.com.

128 Solomon D. Alhadeff, Declaration of Intention no. 45283, June 20, 1940, Washington, Petitions for Naturalization, 1860–1991, via Ancestry.com

129 See Scott Martele, *The Fear Within: Spies, Commies and American Democracy on Trial* (New Brunswick: Rutgers University Press, 2011).

130 Solomon David Alhadeff, Alien Registration Form no 3832866, Registry File 80830, U. S. Citizenship and Immigration Services, Washington, D. C.

131 Solomon D. Alhadeff, Registration Card serial number 2884, April 25, 1942, U. S. World War II Draft Registration Cards, 1942, via Ancestry.com.

132 Chelomo Alhadeff, Alien Enemies ref. no. 3604-P-35566, July 13, 1943, U.S. Subject Index to Correspondence and Case Files of the Immigration and Naturalization Service, 1903–1959, via Ancestry.com.

United States and disavowing any affiliation with Italy (Turkey was not relevant to these deliberations).[133] When Alhadeff became a U.S. citizen on December 14, 1943, the nearly forty-year ordeal relating to his citizenship status finally came to a conclusion.[134] Notably, at least for instrumental reasons, Alhadeff continued to claim affiliation with Turkey as late as 1942 in a continuing echo of post-Ottoman affinities at work among Seattle's Sephardic Jews.

While Alhadeff tried to claim Turkish nationality during World War II as a clever way to advance toward becoming an American citizen, associations with the Ottoman Empire or Turkey tended to be a disadvantage not only for immigration and naturalization purposes, but also in terms of socialization. This was especially the case while diplomatic relations between the United States and the Ottoman Empire, and subsequently the Republic of Turkey, remained severed, from 1917 to 1927. In the mid-1920s, virulent anti-Turkish and anti-Muslim campaigns shaped Congressional debate, most infamously as the result of the publication of a provocative pamphlet by the Committee Opposed to the Lausanne Treaty entitled "Kemal's Slave Market and the Lausanne Treaty." The pamphlet claimed that Mustafa Kemal had enslaved hundreds of thousands of Christians and that "white, Christian women, girls, and children" needed to be protected against the "foul indignity and bestial brutality" of the Turks.[135]

Even as formal U.S. relations with the new Republic of Turkey moved toward being formally re-established, anti-Turkish sentiment remained prevalent across the United States, including in Seattle. In 1926, *The Seattle Times* ran a disparaging two-page, illustrated spread under the headline, "Waking Old Turkey from its Centuries-Long Sleep," which emphasized that with the new hat reforms in the county, Turkey was finally beginning on the path of "progress" that rendered "the Terrible Turk no longer terrible": "he looks, except for his swarthy complexion, quite like the typical American businessman."[136] But the negative associations persisted, with material and social ramifications. The Blue Ridge Club, in the vicinity of

---

133 Chelomo Alhadeff known as Solomon D. Alhadeff, Certificate of Loyalty, November 25, 1943, A Number File: 3832866, U. S. Citizenship and Immigration Services, Washington, D. C.

134 Solomon D. Alhadeff, Certificate of Naturalization, December 13, 1943, A Number File: 3832866, U. S. Citizenship and Immigration Services, Washington, D. C.

135 John M. Vander Lippe, "The 'Other' Treaty of Lausanne: The American Public and Official Debate on Turkish-American Relations," *The Turkish Yearbook* XXIII (1993): 31–63.

136 "Waking Old Turkey from its Centuries-Long Sleep," *The Seattle Times*, April 11, 1926, 84–85.

Seattle's Ballard neighborhood, indicated in its official articles of incorporation in 1941 that certain populations would be expressly forbidden from membership: "No Asiatic, Negro or any person born in the Turkish Empire, nor any lineal descendant of such person, shall be eligible for membership in the Club."[137] While the exclusion of Blacks and Asians was typical in many areas of Seattle at the time, the specific reference to those from the "Turkish Empire" was not. Remarkably, approximately twenty years after the demise of the Ottoman Empire, an organization nearly halfway across the world retained a population category for people "born in the Turkish Empire" *and their descendants*. In this context, being Ottoman—born in the Turkish Empire—became an unalterable genealogical stain transmitted to one's progeny across the generations. As Sephardic Jews were the largest Ottoman-born contingency in Seattle (larger than the Armenian population and likely larger than the Ottoman-born Greek population), it seems likely that *Turkinos* were the principal target of the restriction.

Seattle's Ottoman Jewish Afterlife

Among his major accomplishments in Seattle, Rabbi Abraham Maimon presided over the opening of the new building of Congregation Sephardic Bikur Holim in 1929—a day that *La Vara* described as the "happiest day of his life."[138] An elaborate procession involved the transfer of the Torah scrolls to the new building, with men and women representing all of the city's Sephardic organizations parading through the streets of the Central District while waving American and Jewish flags and following the lead of a boys choir, with "Reverend" Maimon at the head. The patriotic display of flags reveal that the congregation's leaders sought to demonstrate publicly not only their status as Jews, but also their belonging as Americans. Indeed, as part of the processional, Rabbi Shabetai Israel of Congregation Ahavat Ahim chanted the *noten teshua,* the Hebrew-language prayer for the sustenance of the government—in this case, that of the United States.[139] The process of transforming *Turkinos* into *Siatelinos*, Ottoman Jews into American Jews, was on display.[140]

---

137 "Articles of Incorporation of the Blue Ridge Club, Inc," April 21, 1941. I thank attorney Douglas Dunham for sharing the document with me. See also "New Blue Ridge Clubhouse Open," *The Seattle Times*, April 27, 1941, 10. More research is required to determine with certainty the targeted populations in the club's restrictions.

138 "Nekrolojia," *La Vara*, February 6, 1931, 1, 4.

139 "Grandioza fiesta en Siatli," *La Vara*, November 22, 1929, 7.

140 "Cornerstone of new synagogue is laid," *Seattle Times*, July 8, 1929, 12.

גראנדיאוזה פייסטה אין סיאטלי

אריביית: דה סירעמאני דייערי דה נאאירעה קהלה.
אבאשי: איל רבינו שלמו ריטסמאנוי דה בנגרישגין די שהויגז.

FIGURE 1.4. Albert Levy, scrap book entitled, "Suvenires de mis aktivdades en Nuyork dezde el 1920 asta el 1931," clipping from *La Vara*, November 22, 1929, photos of the opening of the new building of Sephardic Bikur Holim, Seattle. Sephardic Studies Digital Collection, University of Washington. Courtesy of Sephardic Bikur Holim.

Continuing the transformative process into the next generation, Rabbi Maimon's youngest son, Solomon, a small boy when the family came to the United States in 1924 and ten years old at the time of the synagogue's opening in 1929, continued in his father's footsteps as a rabbi but diverged with regard to the specific path that he followed. A graduate of Seattle's Garfield public high school, Solomon Maimon became the last Ottoman-born Jew to serve as a rabbi in the United States and the first Ottoman-born Jew to be educated at an Ashkenazi, Orthodox, American rabbinical school: Yeshiva University in New York.[141] As the only Ottoman-born Jew among his classmates in the late 1930s and early 1940s, the younger Maimon had to learn Yiddish to keep up with the lessons and, in yet another example, could not escape being designated—mocked—as a "Turk" by the most famous rabbinical

141 Ben-Ur, *Sephardic Jews in America*, 103.

scholar at the school, Rabbi Joseph Soloveitchik.[142] Maimon returned to Seattle, where, among many roles, he served as the rabbi of Congregation Bikur Holim and dedicated special attention to youth as the founder of the Sephardic Adventure Camp, the only summer youth recreation enterprise in the United States where children learn to pray in the Ottoman Jewish style and sing songs in Ladino. After many decades of service, the symbolic irony of the timing of his death cannot be escaped. At age 100, exactly 95 years to the week after he arrived in the United States, on September 26, 2019, Maimon passed away in Seattle on the same day as a massive 5.8 earthquake struck his hometown of Tekirdağ.

Over the course of the twentieth century, the worlds that the Maimons inhabited over the course of multiple generations, as for so many other families, were irrevocably transformed. Jews' affinities for the Ottoman Empire in the late nineteenth and early twentieth centuries contributed to their self-designation as *Turkinos*, led them to cultivate relationships with other Ottomans abroad (whether Armenians or Greeks), and even inspired some to defend their empire of origin from afar with words and funds. For those *Turkinos* in Seattle, as across the United States, the Great War not only upended their sense of connectivity to the Ottoman Empire—an enemy empire on the brink of dissolution—but also solidified the need to distance themselves from their region of birth in the Orient, a geography associated in American culture and politics with backwardness, despotism, and ambiguous racial status.

In the process, they developed strategies to re-root themselves in their new political, cultural, and physical environment in the Pacific Northwest: by analogizing its terrain and climate to that of their places of birth; by establishing new religious and civic institutions, such as synagogues and clubs and participating in a countrywide Ladino cultural sphere; and, most poignantly, by reframing their sense of identity—as "Spanish" or "Sephardic" Jews—these new names evidenced their desire to reposition themselves within a European, Western, and thus white, framework. The earlier expressions of allegiance to the Ottoman Empire gave way to public statements calling for their native empire's fall as they invested in the principles

---

142 Solomon Maimon's pronunciation of Yiddish apparently led Soloveitchik to tell him, in Yiddish, that he spoke "like a Turk"—in other words, he spoke Yiddish poorly, in an incomprehensible manner. See Eugene Normand, "The True Secret of How Crown Royal Whisky was Developed," available online: https://www.academia.edu/34834405/ The_True_Secret_of_Crown_Royal_Whiskey. Rabbi Aaron Rakeffet recalled that Soloveitchik told Solomon Maimon, in Yiddish, that he spoke like a "drunk Turk," in audio recording at Yeshiva University, October 6, 2019, transmitted to author by Albert S. Maimon, November 1, 2019.

and practices of American patriotism in seeking to prove their worth and their belonging—especially as their position in their new society, even their eligibility to enter the country and to become citizens, continued to be called into question.

Just as Ottoman Jews' embrace of the Ottoman state had emerged both out of a genuine sense of loyalty and of vulnerability, so, too, did Sephardic Jews embrace their new self-designation and their new displays of allegiance to the United States due to a sense of sincerity, as well as the recognition of their tenuous position. The American legal system, reinforced by broader political and cultural dynamics, offered privileges, protections, and opportunities for those who could demonstrate their Europeanness and their whiteness, and thus their suitability for participation in (white Christian) American society. These dynamics compelled Ottoman-born Jews, both in conscious and more insidious ways, to chart a path for themselves that involved the erasure of their "Ottoman" affiliation. That erasure was required for them to leave a "Sephardic" imprint, as "Americans," on their new city and country.

For a variety of reasons that require further investigation, Seattle's Sephardic Jews appear to have largely succeeded in navigating the treacherous American political, cultural, and economic terrain, perhaps more than fellow Ottoman Jews in other parts of the country, whether due to their larger numbers and greater visibility in the Jewish community, the greater extent to which they seem to have engaged in civic enterprises in the city, or the disproportionately prominent role that they played in Pike Place Market, Seattle's iconic business center. Rabbi Samuel Koch, the spiritual leader of Temple de Hirsch, Seattle's flagship (Ashkenazi Reform) synagogue, observed already in 1919 with the regard to "Levantine Jews" that the "conditions in Seattle are different." He emphasized that "a fine feeling" existed between "the Levantine Jew and the Russian Jew, and especially between the Levantine Jew and the American Jew" (by which he meant those Jews of German background affiliated with his congregation and resident in the city already for a few generations). He also noted that only the "Sephardic group" agreed to cooperate with his synagogue for an annual "Jewish union Thanksgiving service"—a fundamentally American holiday—whereas the other congregations comprised of Orthodox Ashkenazi Jews with roots in the Russian Empire declined to do so. The Levantine Jewish group, he concluded, perhaps aspiringly, "is purely American in spirit and an integral part of the community."[143]

---

143 Rabbi Samuel Koch, "The Levantine Jewish Community of Seattle," *Central Conference of American Rabbis* XXIX (1919): 64–66. It would come as no surprise that many Ottoman-born Jews and their descendants would join Koch's prominent synagogue over the years.

The concept and category of the Ottoman Empire, which initially framed Sephardic Jewish life in Seattle, faded with the empire itself, as Ottoman-born Jews and their kin sought to enter—however tentatively and at great cost in terms of language, culture, and communal cohesion—into the white American mainstream. In the wake of World War II, the whiteness of Ottoman-born Jews, and Jews more broadly, can literally be observed while being constructed in official government documents, as in the case of the Abraham and Mathilde Barkey family of Rhodes (Abraham, from Aydin, retained Ottoman/Turkish nationality, whereas the rest of the family had become Italian nationals). Repeatedly denied visas beginning in 1938 due to the strict immigration quotas imposed on those from Southern and Eastern Europe, as well as Turkey, the family fled to Tangier, in North Africa, where they survived the war years in a refugee settlement. When they finally gained legal permission to enter the United States in 1947 following great efforts on the part of their eldest daughter, Claire, and the advocacy of relatives in Seattle, who secured the intervention of a Washington state congressman, the Barkeys were initially listed on their arrival manifest as "Hebrews" according to "race." But "Hebrew" was crossed out, and above it was written "white."[144] This subversion, enacted by the stroke of a pen, transformed the racial classification system operative in the country, revealing precisely how contrived it is.

The recognition of their status as more secure on the white side of the American racial divide in the wake of World War II provided an opportunity for Ottoman-born Jews and their descendants to more readily reclaim an association not with their empire of birth—for that no longer existed—but rather with its successor states, such as Turkey. The emergent Cold War and American support for Turkey (and Greece) against communism with the Truman Doctrine and the Marshall Plan provided the context for such reclamation. In Seattle's famed Pike Place Market, Morris Tacher, a native of Istanbul, together with his wife, Zelda, opened a "Turkish restaurant," which *The Seattle Times* profiled in 1949 for its delectable yet "exotic" "old world dishes" from "far-away Eastern Mediterranean countries": fava beans, lamb, garbanzo beans, baklava, halvah, yogurt, and "cash cabal" cheese.[145] A photo of the restaurant reveals

---

144 Mathilde Capolluto Barki [sic] and children, List or Manifest of Alien Passengers for the United States Immigrant Inspector at Port of Arrival, SS Magallanes, June 8, 1946, "New York, Passenger and Crew Lists (including Castle Garden and Ellis Island), 1820–1957," via Ancestry.com; Cynthia Flash Hemphill, ed., *A Hug from Afar: One family's dramatic journey through three continents to escape the Holocaust* (Seattle: Flash Media Services, 2016).

145 Nancy Davis, "Old World Dishes in Pike Place Café," *The Seattle Times*, December 4, 1949, 11.

FIGURE 1.5. Clipping from newspaper or magazine of interior of Cozy Corner restaurant, Seattle. University of Washington Libraries, Special Collections.

the Turkish flag with the star and crescent hanging on the wall behind the counter beside images of Turkey, the American flag, signs for "Turkish shish kebab," and even a photo of the owner as a young man dressed in his Ottoman military uniform.[146] Like the Maimon's grocery store, the Tacher's restaurant in Pike Place Market served as a communal gathering space, yet one that was also open to everyone.

The reigning collective memory in Seattle, echoed in the contemporary media, has readily integrated the geopolitical realities emerging from the collapse of the Ottoman Empire and the consolidation of new nation-states into Sephardic Jewish self-understandings. Today, Seattle's Sephardic Jews are perceived as divided into two distinct subgroups, according to present-day national boundaries: founded by Jews from the Island of Rhodes, Congregation Ezra Bessaroth is often described as a "Greek" synagogue whose members are called *Rodeslis* (even though Rhodes only became part of Greece in 1947, and no members of the congregation lived on the island since it became Greek; the founders, like the Alhadeffs, came as Ottomans; many came after 1912 as Italian nationals). Similarly, Congregation Sephardic Bikur Holim, established by Jews from Marmara and Tekirdağ, is designated as a "Turkish" synagogue, whose members sometimes refer to themselves as *Turkinos*. The reality, however, is that the founders of both institutions were born and raised in the Ottoman Empire and, as this chapter has sought to demonstrate, initially

---

146 Ashley Bobman, "A Seattle Sephardic Restaurant," in *A Sephardic Lighthouse: Albert Levy & the Sephardic Jewish Journey*, available online: https://jewishstudies.washington.edu/albert-levy-sephardic-lighthouse-salonica-seattle/12-seattle-sephardic-restaurant/.

viewed themselves together as *Turkinos* and saw their fate intimately connected to that of fellow Ottoman Jews and their empire of origin. Just as, by recasting themselves as "Spanish," they sought to render their identities more legible to the outside world, so, too, did identifying their institutions with reference to the geopolitical borders of the contemporary map. Those categories, once intended for an outside audience, have since been internalized through a process that erases the shared Ottoman origins of Seattle's Sephardic Jews.

The future of the Ottoman Jewish afterlife of Seattle remains unclear. This chapter has sought to provide some tentative suggestions as to how to evaluate and contextualize the past. The more than 140,000 pages of source materials—from published books to unpublished manuscripts, private correspondence, photographs, and more— are only a tiny portion of that which has been referenced in these pages, as well as that which has been centralized and digitized through the University of Washington's Sephardic Studies Program in collaboration with Seattle's Sephardic institutions and with nearly one hundred families. These fresh materials will undoubtedly provide additional access points for continued research for students, scholars, and community members alike. Although with Rabbi Solomon Maimon's passing in 2019, the last Ottoman Jew in Seattle has departed, and although the shift from *Turkinos* to *Siatelinos* may appear complete in today's generation, the dynamic processes of identity and communal transformation and their significance today are primed for further investigation.

Bibliography

"3 raids made by dry squad." *The Seattle Star*, December 15, 1921.

"A los abonados de Siatli." *La Vara*, July 31, 1936.

Adatto, Albert. "Sephardim and the Seattle Sephardic Community." M.A. Thesis, University of Washington, 1939.

Alhadef, Chelomo (sic). Declaration of Intention, November 6, 1905, U. S. Naturalization Records, 1840–1957, via Ancestry.com.

Alhadeff, Chelomo, known as Solomon Alhadeff, Declaration of Intention no. 30304, February 15, 1928. U. S. Naturalization Records, 1840–1957, via Ancestry.com.

Alhadeff, Chelomo, known as Solomon D. Alhadeff. Certificate of Loyalty, November 25, 1943. A Number File: 3832866, U. S. Citizenship and Immigration Services, Washington, D. C.

Alhadeff, Chelomo. Alien Enemies ref. no. 3604-P-35566, July 13, 1943. U.S. Subject Index to Correspondence and Case Files of the Immigration and Naturalization Service, 1903–1959, via Ancestry.com.

Alhadeff, Sam, Registration Card no. 444, September 12, 1918. U. S. World War I Draft Registration Cards, 1917–1918, via Ancestry.com.

Alhadeff, Solomon D. Certificate of Naturalization, December 13, 1943, A Number File: 3832866, U. S. Citizenship and Immigration Services, Washington, D. C.

Alhadeff, Solomon D. Declaration of Intention no. 45283, June 20, 1940 Washington, Petitions for Naturalization, 1860–1991, via Ancestry.com.

Alhadeff, Solomon D. Registration Card serial number 2884, April 25, 1942. U. S. World War II Draft Registration Cards, 1942, via Ancestry.com.

Alhadeff, Solomon David. Alien Registration Form no 3832866, Registry File 80830, U. S. Citizenship and Immigration Services, Washington, D. C.

"All set for Yuletide; police take it all." *The Seattle Times*, December 16, 1921, 2.

Angel, Marc. "Notes on the Early History of Seattle's Sephardic Community," *Western States Jewish Historical Quarterly* 7, no. 1 (October 1974): 22–30.

——— "The Sephardim of the United States: An Exploratory Study," American Jewish Yearbook 74 (1973): 85.

——— *La America: The Sephardic Experience in the United States*. Philadelphia: Jewish Publication Society, 1982.

"Articles of Incorporation of the Blue Ridge Club, Inc." April 21, 1941.

"Asiguradvos la vida." *La Amerika*, September 7, 1917, 2.

Bagley, Clarence. *History of Seattle from the Earliest Settlement to the Present Time*. Chicago: Clarke Publishing Co, 1916.

"Bake Oven Cured Him." *The Seattle Times*, April 9, 1909, 8.

Bali, Rifat. *From Anatolia to the New World: Life Stories of the First Turkish Immigrants to America*. Istanbul: Libra Kitap, 2013.

Barki [sic], Mathilde Capolluto and children. List or Manifest of Alien Passengers for the United States Immigrant Inspector at Port of Arrival, SS Magallanes, June 8, 1946. "New York, Passenger and Crew Lists (including Castle Garden and Ellis Island), 1820–1957," via Ancestry.com.

Behar, Nessim, New York, to Jacques Bigart, Paris, February 11, 1919. Archive of the Alliance Israélite Universelle, États-Unis I A 05.

Benbassa, Esther. *Haim Nahum: a Sephardic Chief Rabbi in Politics, 1892–1923*. Tuscaloosa, Ala., 1995.

Benmayor, Rina. "A Greek Tragoúdi in the Repertoire of a Judeo-Spanish Ballad Singer," *Hispanic Review* 46.4 (1978): 475–479.

Benezra, Aron. "Impresiones de Siatel." *El Progresso*, August 18, 1916, 2.

Benezra, Henry of Sephardic Bikur Holim Congregation, Seattle, to Rabbi David Markus. Letter. Istanbul, January 31, 1925, UW-SSDC, ST-1198.

Ben-Ur, Aviva. *Sephardic Jews in America: A Diasporic History*. New York: NYU Press, 2009.

——— "In Search of the American Ladino Press: A Bibliographic Survey, 1910–1948." *Studies Bibliography and Booklore* 21 (Fall 2001): 11–51.

Bobman, Ashley. "A Seattle Sephardic Restaurant." In *A Sephardic Lighthouse: Albert Levy & the Sephardic Jewish Journey*, available online: https://jewishstudies.washington.edu/albert-levy-sephardic-lighthouse-salonica-seattle/12-seattle-sephardic-restaurant/.

"Bootblacks succeed in organizing union." *The Seattle Times*, August 7, 1913, 7.

Bornstein, Roz, oral history with Rebecca Benaroya. "Weaving Women's Words." Nicki Newman Tanner Oral History Archive, Jewish Women's Archive, July 17, 2001.

Boyden, Eddie. "Negro Patriot Routes Greeks, Saving Flag." *The Seattle Times*, September 2, 1913, 4.

Calvo, Marco Solomon, known as Sam Calvo, Declaration of Intention no. 39626, December 10, 1938. U. S. Naturalization Records, 1840–1957, via Ancestry.com.

Craver, Earlene. "On the Boundary of White: The Cartozian Naturalization Case and the Armenians, 1923–1925." *Journal of American Ethnic History* 28, no. 2 (Winter 2009): 30–56.

Cohen, Julia Phillips. *Becoming Ottomans: Sephardi Jews and Imperial Citizenship in the Modern Era*. New York: Oxford University Press, 2014.

——— "Oriental by Design: Ottoman Jews, Imperial Style, and the Performance of Heritage." *American Historical Review* 119, no. 2 (April 2014): 364–398.

"Cornerstone of New Synagogue Is Laid." *Seattle Times*, July 8, 1929, 12.

Davis, Nancy. "Old World Dishes in Pike Place Café." *The Seattle Times*, December 4, 1949, 11.

"Dedicate synagogue." *The Seattle Star*, June 8, 1918, 10.

DiCarlo, Lisa. *Migrating to America: Transnational Social Networks and Regional Identity among Turkish Migrants*. London: I.B. Tauris, 2008.

"Draft Men Urged to Bring Extra Clothing." *The Seattle Times*, October 2, 1917, 3.

Dreyfus, Philip. "The IWW and the Limits of Inter-Ethnic Organizing: Reds, Whites, and Greeks in Grays Harbor, Washington, 1912." *Labor History* 38, no. 4 (1997): 450–491.

Droker, Howard and Jacqueline B. Williams. *Family of Strangers: Building a Jewish Community in Washington State*. Seattle: University of Washington Press, 2003.

Droker, Howard interview with Gordon DeLeon, February 17, 1982. Washington State Jewish Historical Society Oral History Collection, University of Washington.

Eisenberg, Ellen and Ava Fran Kahn. *Jews of the Pacific Coast: Reinventing Community on America's Edge*. Seattle: University of Washington Press, 2009.

"El mijor berber turkino." *La Amerika*, June 30, 1922, 3.

"El patriotizmo de nuestros turkinos por la Turkia." *La Amerika*, August 30, 1912, 1.

"El primer sudito Amerikano Turkino en Siatli." *La Amerika*, December 20, 1912, 1.

"Eldrige Street sentro turkino." *La Bos del Pueblo*, August 4, 1916, 2.

Evans, William A. "Daily Health Talk: Types of Mankind." *The Seattle Times*, June 23, 1925, 6.

Farenthold, Stacey. *Between the Ottomans and the Entente: The First World War in the Syrian and Lebanese Diaspora, 1908–1925*. New York: Oxford University Press, 2019.

FitzMorris, Mary K. "The Last Generation of Native Ladino Speakers? Judeo-Spanish and the Sephardic Community in Seattle." M.A. Thesis, University of Washington, 2014.

"From the Central Conference of American Rabbis." *The Jewish Voice* [St. Louis], July 9, 1920, 3.

Gadol, Moise. List or Manifest of Alien Passengers for the United States Immigration Officer at Port of Arrival, S. S. La Lorraine, July 16, 1910. In "New York, Passenger and Crew Lists (including Castle Garden and Ellis Island), 1820–1957," via Ancestry.com.

Gadol, Moses Solomon. Declaration of Intention no. 18260, July 25, 1913. In "New York, State, and Federal Naturalization Records, 1794–1943," via Ancestry.com.

"Get your shoes shined in 7 different languages." *The Seattle Star,* May 13, 1912, 7.

Ginio, Eyal. "Jewish Philanthropy and Mutual Assistance: Between Ottomanism and Communal Identities." In *The Wars of Yesterday: The Balkan Wars and the Emergence of Modern Military Conflict, 1912–1913*, edited by Katrin Boeckh and Sabine Rutar, 344–372. New York: Berghahn Books, 2018.

Grandin, Greg. *The End of the Myth: From the Frontier to the Border Wall in the Mind of America*. New York: Metropolitan Books, 2019.

"Grandioza fiesta en Siatli." *La Vara*, November 22, 1929, 7.

Grigoriadis, Ioannis. "Türk or Türkiyeli? The Reform of Turkey's Minority Legislation and the Rediscovery of Ottomanism." *Middle Eastern Studies* 43, no. 3 (May 2007): 432–438.

Gualtieri, Sarah M. A. *Between Arab and White: Race and Ethnicity in the Early Syrian American Diaspora*. Berkeley: University of California Press, 2009.

Harris, Tracy. *Death of a Language: The History of Judeo-Spanish.* University of Delaware Press, 1994.

Harris, Taryn. "Sephardic Jews in Washington," *History Link* (2014). https://www.historylink.org/File/10778.

Heinzelmann, Tobias. "The Ruler's Monologue: The Rhetoric of the Ottoman Penal Code of 1858." *Die Welt des Islams* 54 (2014): 292–321.

Hemphill, Cynthia Flash, ed. *A Hug from Afar: One family's dramatic journey through three continents to escape the Holocaust.* Seattle: Flash Media Services, 2016.

"Is the Turk a White Man?" *The New York Times*, September 30, 1909, 8.

Jerusalmi, Isaac, ed. *Kanun Name de Penas.* Cincinnati, Ohio: 1975.

"Jewish Leader Here." *The Seattle Times*, April 22, 1921, 5.

"Jewish New Year's Day Celebrated." *The Seattle Star*, September 8, 1915, 7.

Kasaba, Reşat. *A Moveable Empire: Ottoman Nomads, Migrants, and Refugees*. Seattle: University of Washington Press, 2009.

Khater, Akram. *Inventing Home: Emigration, Gender and the Making of a Lebanese Middle Class, 1861–1921*. Berkeley: University of California, 2001.

Kirkor, Madras (Photo) proprietor of Kirkor's Grocery, 1621 Yesler Way, Seattle, c. 1925–1929, Washington State Jewish Archives, University of Washington Libraries Special Collections, PH Coll 650.BenezraH3.

Koch, Samuel (Rabbi). "The Levantine Jewish Community of Seattle." *Central Conference of American Rabbis* XXIX (1919): 64–66.

"Korespondensia de Siatel." *El Progresso*, September 8, 1916, 2.

"La imigrasyon." *La Amerika*, August 11, 1911, 1.

Leon, Haim. Declaration of Intention no. 8476, February 15, 1917. U. S. Naturalization Records, 1840–1957, via Ancestry.com.

Leon, Yuda known as Gordon Leon, Declaration of Intention no. 23353, July 11, 1925, U. S. Naturalization Records, 1840–1957, via Ancestry.com.

Levy, Albert, New York, to Bension Maimon, Seattle, 1935–1937. Letters. Sephardic Studies Digital Collection (SSDC), University of Washington, ST-1835–1842.

Lewis, Annie. "Precarious Whiteness: Reimagining the Seattle Sephardic Origin Story." University of Washington, 2018. https://digital.lib.washington.edu/researchworks/handle/1773/41904.

"Liberty spirit to flame this week." *The Seattle Star*, April 22, 1918.

Lippe, John M. Vander. "The 'Other' Treaty of Lausanne: The American Public and Official Debate on Turkish-American Relations." *The Turkish Yearbook* XXIII (1993): 31–63.

——"The 'Terrible Turk': The Formulation and Perpetuation of a Stereotype in American Foreign Policy." New Perspectives on Turkey 17 (1997): 39–57.

López, Ian Haney. *White By Law: The Legal Construction of Race*. New York: New York University Press, 2006.

"Los mas nuevos sortes de chapeos." *La Amerika*, June 14, 1912, 4.

"Los mijores i mas baratos vino i raki turkino." *El Progresso*, September 1, 1916, 3.

Maimon, Avraam and family, List or Manifest for Alien Passengers for the United States Officer at Port of Arrival, S. S. La Layette, September 22, 1924. In "New York, Passenger and Crew Lists (including Castle Garden and Ellis Island), 1820–1957," via Ancestry.com.

Maimon, Avraam and family, Record of Aliens Held for Special Inquiry, S. S. La Layette, September 22, 1924 in "New York, Passenger and Crew Lists (including Castle Garden and Ellis Island), 1820–1957," via Ancestry.com.

Maimon, Kadon (sic). "Manifest," September 21, 1927, "U. S. Border Crossings from Canada to U. S., 1895–1960," via Ancestry.com.

Maimon, Sam B. *The Beauty of Sephardic Life*. Seattle: MAIMON IDEaS, 1993.

Martele, Scott. *The Fear Within: Spies, Commies and American Democracy on Trial*. New Brunswick: Rutgers University Press, 2011.

Mays, Devi. "'I Killed Her Because I Loved her Too Much': Gender and Violence in the 20th Century Sephardi Diaspora," *Mashriq & Mahjar* 3 (2014): 4–28.

Mootafes, Dorothea, et al. *A History of Saint Demetrios Greek Orthodox Church and Her People*. Seattle, 2007.

Moreno, Aitor García. "Salomon Israel Cherezli's Nuevo chico diccionario judeo-español–francés (Jerusalem 1898–1899) as a Judeo-Spanish Monolingual Dictionary." In *Sepharad as Imagined Community. Language, History and Religion from the Early Modern Period to the 21st Century*, edited by Saul Mahir Saul and José Ignacio Hualde, 192–211. New York: Peter Lang, 2017.

Naar, Devin E. "'Sephardim Since Birth': Reconfiguring Jewish Identity in America." In *The Sephardi and Mizrahi Jews in America*, edited by Saba Soomekh, 75–104. Purdue University Press, 2016.

———— "From the 'Jerusalem of the Balkans' to the 'Goldene Medina': Jewish Immigration from Salonika to the United States," *American Jewish History* 93.4 (2007): 435–473.

———— "Turkinos beyond the Empire: Ottoman Jews in America, 1893–1924," *Jewish Quarterly Review* 105, no. 2 (Spring 2015): 174–205.

———— *Jewish Salonica: Between the Ottoman Empire and Modern Greece*. Palo Alto: Stanford University Press, 2016.

"Names of Seattle customers found in moonshiner's home." *The Seattle Times*, March 26, 1922, 12.

Naon, Shabetai. "Una selebrasyon de las frutas (Tu Bishvat) al benefisio de la Aliansa." *La Amerika*, February 22, 1918, 6.

———— "El grandiozo resivo a Ribbi Haim Nahoum en Siatli." *La Amerika*, June 3, 1921, 1, 4.

Naon, Shabetai. "Korespondensia de Siatli. Rabi Avraam Maimon ala ovra." *La Vara*, November 7, 1924, 4.

"Nekrolojia." *La Vara*, February 6, 1931, 1, 4.

Nessim, Shimon S. "La Turkia de oy." *La Bos del Pueblo*, July 28, 1916, 3.

"New Blue Ridge Clubhouse Open." *The Seattle Times*, April 27, 1941, 10.

Ngai, Mae. *Impossible Subjects: Illegal Aliens and the Making of Modern America*. Princeton University Press, 2014.

"No vos olvidesh." *La Amerika*, December 29, 1911, 1.

Normand, Eugene and Albert S. Maimon. "The Sephardic Drinking Song, 'I give my life for a taste of raki'." *Sephardic Horizons* 5, no. 1–2 (Fall 2015).

Normand, Eugene. "The True Secret of How Crown Royal Whisky Was Developed." Available at https://www.academia.edu/34834405/The_True_Secret_of_Crown_Royal_Whiskey.

"Nota de la redaksion." *La Vara*, October 31, 1924, 7.

"Nuevo kafe i kabaret turkino." *La Amerika*, November 3, 1916, 1.

"Nuevo kafe i restaurante turkino." *La Amerika*, April 2, 1915, 2.

"Panaderia Palestina." *La Amerika*, July 12, 1912, 4.

Papo, Joseph M. *Sephardim in Twentieth Century America: In Search of Unity.* San Jose, California, 1987.

"Por la emigrasion de Turkia en Amerika." *La America*, November 11, 1910, 1.

"Protejad vuestros kompatriotes." *La Amerika*, September 20, 1912, 3.

Policar, Jacques, also known as Jake Policar, Petition for Naturalization no. 34939, December 8, 1942 (Oath of Allegiance signed March 8, 1943). Washington, Petitions for Naturalization, 1860–1991, via Ancestry.com.

Policar, Jake, Declaration of Intention no. 45225, June 4, 1940. Washington, Petitions for Naturalization, 1860–1991, via Ancestry.com.

"Rabbi as Kemalist envoy to Washington." *American Jewish World*, August 11, 1922, 2.

"Rabbi Maimon to give address on Sunday, April 12." *The Jewish Transcript*, April 10, 1925, 1.

"Raporto por la situasion de nuestros ermanos de Turkia en Siatli." *La Amerika*, May 10, 1912, 2.

"Ribbi Avram Maimon liberado de Elis Ayland." *La Vara*, October 3, 1924, 1.

"Ribbi Haim Nahoum parte a Pariz." *La Amerika*, July 1, 1921, 2–3.

"Ribi Avram Maimon detenido en Elis Ayland." *La Vara*, September 26, 1924, 1.

Roberts, Fannie interview with Fortuna Calvo, February 9, 1976. Washington State Jewish Historical Society Oral History Collection, University of Washington.

Rodrigue, Aron. *French Jews, Turkish Jews: The Alliance Israélite Universelle and the Politics of Jewish Schooling in Turkey, 1860–1925.* Bloomington, Ind., 1990.

Rodrigue, Aron and Sarah Abrevaya Stein, eds. *A Jewish Voice from Ottoman Salonica.* Palo Alto: Stanford University Press, 2012.

Romero, Elena. *Entre dos (o más) fuegos: Fuentes poéticas para la historia de los sefardíes de los Balcanes.* Madrid, 2008.

Romero, Elena. "La polémica sobre el judeoespañol en la prensa sefardí del imperio otomano: más materiales para su estudio." *Sefarad* 70, no. 2 (July-Dec. 2010): 435–473.

Sarna, Jonathan and Zev Eleff, "The Immigration Clause that Transformed Orthodox Judaism in the United States." *American Jewish History* 101, no. 3 (July 2017): 357–376.

"S. Aguado i Abrevaya ermanos." *La Amerika*, November 11, 1910, 4.

"Safeguarding our naturalization laws: Easy roads to citizenship must be closed." *The Western American: A Magazine of Good Citizenship* 1, no. 4 (January 1923): 3–6.

"Se bushka." *La Amerika*, May 22, 1914, 1.

"Se bushka." *La Amerika*, September 1, 1916, 1.

"Seattle makes strong finish in purchasing liberty bonds." *The Seattle Star*, October 27, 1917, 1.

"Si keresh transportar." *La Amerika*, July 22, 1918, 1.

Smith, John Speed, Seattle, to Alma Smith Rogers. Letter, February 1, 1920. Rogers Family Papers, MSS 14, Hanover College, Indiana.

Stein, Sarah Abrevaya. *Making Jews Modern: The Yiddish and Ladino Press in the Russian and Ottoman Empires*. Indiana University Press, 2006.

Soulam, Moise. "Nuestro Ahi." La America, July 31, 1914, 3.

Taylor, Quintard. *The Forging of a Black Community: Seattle's Central District from 1870 through the Civil Rights Era*. Seattle: University of Washington Press, 1994.

"The Massacres of the Jews in Russia" (Theater brochure). Hosted by the Ladies Auxiliary of the Sephardic Bikur Holim, Seattle, December 16, 1928, Leon Behar Papers, University of Washington Special Collections, Acc. No. 2416–0004.

Thrush, Coll-Peter. *Native Seattle: Histories of the Crossing-Over Place*. Seattle: University of Washington, 2007.

"Un banketo en Siatel [sic]." *La Bos del Pueblo*, July 14, 1916, 2.

"Un buen egzempio en favor de la Aliansa Israelita." *La Amerika*, March 28, 1919, 2.

Varol, Marie-Christine. "Du bon usage des langues dans une communauté plurilingue: les histoires drôles des judéo-espagnols d'Istanbul." *Langage et societé* 61 (1992): 31–54.

"Venid todos este alhad al pik-nik turkino." *La Amerika*, July 19, 1912, 1.

"Waking Old Turkey from Its Centuries-Long Sleep." *The Seattle Times*, April 11, 1926, 84–85.

Young, George, ed. *Corps de droit ottoman; recueil des codes, réglements, ordonnances et lois*. Oxford: Clarendon Press, 1906.

"Yayin gefen kasher le-Pesah." *La Amerika*, April 18, 1913, 1.

CHAPTER TWO

"The Seeds for a New Judaeo-Spanish Culture on the Shores of Puget Sound"?: Building the Sephardic Studies Collection at the University of Washington

TY ALHADEFF

In his groundbreaking study on the history of the Sephardic Jews in Seattle, undertaken as his master's thesis at the University of Washington in 1939, Istanbul-born Albert Adatto lamented the present state of his community and its members' attenuating connection to the culture they had brought with them from the Ottoman Empire. He writes:

> Sephardic culture is gradually disappearing in Seattle . . . the seeds for a new Judaeo-Spanish culture on the shores of Puget Sound were simply too weak and impotent to blossom forth into a fresh growth . . . With the gradual replacement of English for Ladino and American customs for those of the Old World, it seems very unlikely that Sephardic culture will be maintained even for the next fifty years.[1]

Adatto was, in some ways, correct. English did replace Judeo-Spanish (aka Ladino) as the daily language, and very few native speakers remain. With some important exceptions, the present generations of Sephardic Jews in Seattle generally cannot read texts in Ladino, especially not those written in the traditional Hebrew alphabets, including the now-obscure Sephardic cursive, *soletreo*.

At the same time, contrary to Adatto's dire prediction, Seattle does maintain Sephardic culture: it hosts two synagogues, Sephardic Bikur Holim and Congregation Ezra Bessaroth; the Sephardic Brotherhood burial society; Sephardic Adventure Camp, a summer camp dedicated to perpetuating Sephardic pride and culture in children and teens; and the Ladineros, a group of Ladino aficionados

---

1   Albert Adatto, "Sephardim and the Seattle Sephardic Community" (M.A. thesis University of Washington Department of History, 1939), 164–166.

that meet weekly to read stories in Ladino and reminisce. Sephardic Jews in Seattle tend to retain a fondness for their ancestral culture and have held on to their family books and letters as talismans and as material connections to the world from which their forbearers came and which continue to serve as symbols of their sense of identity and community.

Interestingly, Adatto drives the nail into the coffin of his dire prediction with an observation of almost breathtaking irony: "The dynamic forces of twentieth century technological civilization has literally suffocated the growth of this anachronistic Sephardic culture." In fact, it is entirely possible that without the efforts of the University of Washington Sephardic Studies Program to preserve materials online, many significant books and records may have been lost, or at the very least, never seriously evaluated and properly preserved—proving Adatto's conclusion true.

Crowdsourcing the Past: Collecting and Assessing Seattle's Ladino Materials

The arrival of Professor Devin Naar to the University of Washington in 2011 provided the opportunity for local community members to rally to reclaim textual and material vestiges of their Sephardic culture that their parents, grandparents, or great-grandparents brought to the Pacific Northwest from the lands of the former Ottoman Empire. When Seattle residents realized that Naar was proficient in reading and translating Judeo-Spanish in all of its varieties and involved in his own process of reclaiming the language and history of his family, they began to bring him their texts and artifacts, seeking a deeper knowledge of their contents, the meanings of the inscriptions and marginalia, and the broader context in which they were created and used. One of the first, Menache Israel, already in his 90s and the child of Jews from Rhodes, brought Naar a document whose inscrutable swirling script had gone unread for seventy years. Naar began to decipher the *soletreo* text and read it aloud. The two quickly realized the profundity of the document: it was Israel's grandfather's emotional last will and testament penned in Seattle in 1942.[2]

This discovery launched an unexpected exploration into the bookshelves, attics, and basements of Sephardic families in Seattle. In partnership with the local Sephardic communal institutions, Naar advertised in newsletters and set up booths at seasonal bazaars to collect Sephardic materials. Relying on "crowdsourcing," calls and emails came in from around the region and beyond. Recognizing that

---

2   Nissim Israel's Ethical Will, May 20, 1942 (Sephardic Studies Collection, University of Washington, ST001179), Courtesy of Menache Israel. (Hereafter, books or manuscripts found in the Sephardic Studies collection will be indicated with the corresponding inventory number in brackets, ex. [ST001179]).

some families did not want to part with their heirlooms, Naar initiated a massive digitization effort in order to preserve the intellectual content digitally for the sake of posterity and scholarship, while ensuring that families retain ownership.

To be sure, dedicated individuals in the Seattle community made contributions to the preservation of Sephardic culture through the years. The Washington State Jewish Historical Society maintains an invaluable collection of oral histories, and families like the Adattos, Azoses, Behars, Maimons, and Scharhons have saved books and documents dating back centuries. But a digital solution addressed another major issue: the absence and inaccessibility of original source materials in Judeo-Spanish and pertaining to the Sephardic experience, more generally. While various archives and libraries around the world have increasingly turned to the internet to render their collections accessible to anyone with online access, no enterprise had yet focused on Ladino print culture. The dearth of digitally accessible Ladino literature—not to mention the lack of awareness of Ladino and Sephardic culture generally—stands in contrast to Yiddish, which is supported by institutions like the Yiddish Book Center and generous donors, like Steven Spielberg. This is not to say that important Ladino collections of books, archives, and audio recordings do not exist; indeed, they do. In the 1930s, for example, Judeo-Spanish–speaking activists in British Palestine coordinated an effort to create a Ladino section at the newly established Hebrew University of Jerusalem's library. That collection now includes more than a thousand volumes. The Central Archives for the History of the Jewish People in Jerusalem now house sections of the vast archives of the Jewish communities of Salonica, Istanbul, and Izmir. The Ben Zvi Institute for the Study of the Jewish Communities of the East, in Jerusalem, contains a vast collection of Ladino newspapers, books, and archives. In the United States, the American Sephardi Federation in New York, as well as the Library of Congress, Yeshiva University, the Jewish Theological Seminary, and Harvard University, also house their own Ladino collections. But virtually none of those resources are available online and certainly not in any systematic way.[3]

Under the direction of Aron Rodrigue, the Sephardi Studies Project at Stanford University has begun an important online publishing initiative to make available a selection of Ladino texts with a focus on transcriptions into Latin characters and translations in English.[4] Those texts serve as invaluable teaching resources in the

---

3   Devin E. Naar, "Sephardic Archives from Analog to Digital: Three Tales of Memory and Visibility" (Lecture, University of California, Santa Cruz, May 3, 2018).

4   The Sephardi Studies Project at Stanford University, Taube Center for Jewish Studies, https://jewishstudies.stanford.edu/sephardi-studies-project.

classroom and have been further complemented by the publication of Sarah Abrevaya Stein's and Julia Phillips Cohen's unprecedented source reader on the Judeo-Spanish experience, which includes 150 primary sources translated into English from more than a dozen languages, including Ladino.[5] Whereas Stein and Cohen did not include literary sources, or provide access to the originals, Rodrigue's project focuses on selected literary texts, rather than archival materials.

The absence of literary texts emerged as an issue of particular interest. Part of the lack of attention stems from varying disciplinary interests, goals, and limitations, but also from a longstanding orientalist assumption that Jews in the Ottoman Empire did not engage in cultural creativity in Judeo-Spanish, and certainly not what might be called "secular" literature, like novels. The notion of Ottoman Jews as "uncivilized" residents of the purportedly backwards and declining Muslim Orient surely shaped such a conception. Replicating the preconceptions of nineteenth century orientalists, Bernard Lewis argued that even if Ottoman Jews had produced any literature after the "golden age" of the sixteenth century, it remained of "limited appeal":

> Evidence about the religious and cultural life among the Ottoman Jews after the sixteenth century is meager, and it is difficult to resist the conclusion that the paucity of evidence reflects the poverty of life. At the beginning of the period rabbinical learning was of great importance, and there is a large, rich, and valuable literature of responsa [rabbinical decisions]. There was also an active mystical movement, and a considerable cabalistic literature. But none of this lasted much beyond the sixteenth century, after which Jewish literature, whether in Hebrew or in the Judaeo-Spanish vernacular, is of limited appeal.[6]

Much more sympathetic to the fate of Ladino culture, a more recent scholar, Ilan Stavans, nonetheless arrived at a similar conclusion: "For a variety of historical and linguistic reasons, Ladino failed to metamorphose itself into a literary language. For one thing, it was never used for intellectual discussion." He acknowledged that modern genres of Ladino print emerged in the nineteenth century, including newspapers, plays, novellas, and the like, but concludes: "the success of the Ladino press never gave birth to a full-blown aesthetic movement, complete with a cadre of internationally renowned authors."[7]

---

5   Julia Philips Cohen and Sarah Abrevaya Stein, *Sephardi Lives: A Documentary History, 1700–1950* (Stanford: Stanford University Press, 2014).

6   Bernard Lewis, *The Jews of Islam* (New Jersey: Princeton University Press, 1984), 128–129.

7   Ilan Stavans, ed., *The Schocken Book of Modern Sephardic Literature* (New York: Schocken Books, 2005), xxii.

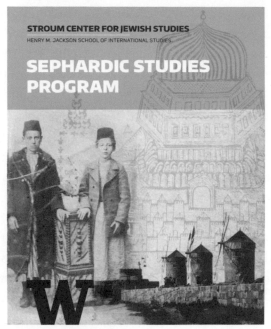

FIGURE 2.1. Brochure cover of the Sephardic Studies Program at the Stroum Center for Jewish Studies, University of Washington.

Could the "crowdsourced" texts gathered from community members in Seattle and beyond begin to shed light on these issues? Perhaps even challenge the assumptions?

With seed money contributed by local Sephardic families and with the support of the Stroum Center for Jewish Studies and the Jackson School of International Studies, Naar hired Ty Alhadeff to help coordinate the accession, cataloging, metadata notation, and digitization of the source materials that began coming in by the dozens and then by the hundreds. More than eighty individuals, families, and institutions have contributed to date. Some shared a single family letter, postcard, Ladino novel, or prayer book; others shared hundreds of pages of correspondences, institutional records, or vast libraries consisting of dozens or even hundreds of volumes.[8]

Now the Sephardic Studies Collection at the University of Washington has more than two thousand catalogued items and constitutes one of the world's largest and fastest growing repositories of original source materials pertaining to the Sephardic experience. Over one thousand items, totaling more than 150,000 pages (plus more

---

8   Ty Alhadeff, "By The Numbers: Building the Sephardic Studies Digital Collection," Stroum Center for Jewish Studies, University of Washington, May 14, 2015, https://jewishstudies.washington.edu/sephardic-studies/building-sephardic-studies-digital-library/.

than 200 audio and video recordings), have been digitized and account for more than 12 gigabytes of data. With 403 discrete Ladino book titles from the seventeenth to the twentieth century—representing more than ten percent of the known published books in Ladino—the Sephardic Studies Collection now boasts more Ladino books than the Library of Congress, Harvard University, or New York Public Library.

While the language of these sources is largely Ladino, they also include Hebrew, Aramaic, Turkish, Arabic, Yiddish, French, English, Greek, and Italian. Most of the artifacts originated in the former Ottoman Empire, broadly defined, including present-day Turkey (Istanbul and Izmir), Greece (Salonica and Rhodes), Bulgaria (Sofia), Serbia (Belgrade), and Romania (Craiova), as well as Israel (Jerusalem), Egypt (Cairo), and Iraq (Baghdad). Notably, many books were printed in Vienna or Livorno, as was the case for the publications of other non-Muslim populations from the Ottoman Empire who could more easily bypass the sultan's censors by publishing abroad.[9] Other materials originated in Brussels, Khorramshahr, Tangiers, Havana, Buenos Aires, Amsterdam, and in the United States in New York, Los Angeles, and Seattle.

The Collection showcases a wide array of published and unpublished materials. The unpublished items in the Collection include manuscripts, family correspondence, wedding contracts, theater scripts, recipes, photographs, postcards, visas, travel documents, and communal records. The published materials include adapted and original novels, prayer books, bibles, religious commentaries, newspapers, magazines, songbooks, calendars, hagiographies, memoirs, historical narratives, grammar books, language primers, political tracts, and more.

The Collection also comprises a sound archive of Ladino songs (especially ballads, known as *romansas*) and folklore recorded among Sephardic Jews in Los Angeles and Seattle by scholar Rina Benmayor in the 1970s. These recordings served as the source material for Benmayor's dissertation and subsequent book on Judeo-Spanish ballads.[10] Today, all 145 recordings from Seattle are available online at The Benmayor Collection of Eastern Sephardic Ballads and Other Lore hosted by the Sephardic Studies Collection at the University of Washington.

The bulk of the Collection, however, remains dedicated to the written word. The books, for example, reflect the spiritual realm of Ottoman Jews; other items from the nineteenth and twentieth centuries reveal vibrant cultural creativity through

9   Johann Strauss, "Who Read What in the Ottoman Empire (19th-20th Centuries)?," *Middle Eastern Literatures* 6, no. 4 (January 2003): 39–76.

10   Rina Benmayor, *Romances Judeo-Españoles de Oriente: Nueva recolección* (Madrid: Cátedra Seminario Menéndez Pidal-Gredos, 1979).

FIGURE 2.2. The cover of Eliya Karmona's *Komo Nasyo Eliya Karmona* (Istanbul, El Djugeton, 1926). ST00493, Sephardic Studies Digital Collection, University of Washington. Courtesy of Richard Adatto.

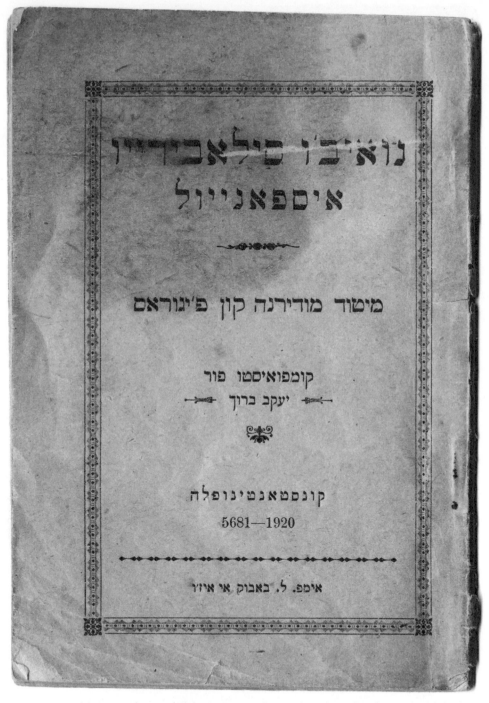

FIGURE 2.3. The cover of *Nuevo Silaberio Espanyol metod moderna kon figuras*, published in Istanbul, in 1920. ST00136, Sephardic Studies Digital Collection, University of Washington. Courtesy of Sephardic Bikkur Holim.

adaptations of Shakespeare, the *Count of Monte Cristo*, and *Robinson Crusoe. Komo Nasyo Eliya Karmona,* published in Istanbul in 1926, Elia Carmona's picturesque memoir—one of his forty works of mostly fiction in Ladino—charts his unlikely rise to fame as a Judeo-Spanish journalist. As testament to the text's popularity, three copies have come to us (from the libraries of Albert Adatto, Albert Maimon, and Reverend Morris Scharhon).[11]

Some of the books in the Collection are extremely rare, whether from the eighteenth or twentieth centuries. Included among the many items shared by Isaac Azose, the hazzan emeritus of Congregation Ezra Bessaroth, is the only known complete copy of a 1916 guidebook for Sephardic immigrants coming to America.[12] Printed in New York by the publisher of *La Amerika,* the first Ladino newspaper in the United States, the guidebook introduces readers to the skyscrapers, public parks, an elevated train in New York City, and the American immigration laws and provides glossaries of common (and some seemingly obscure) phrases in English, transliterated in Hebrew letters (*rashi* script), in Judeo-Spanish, and, remarkably, in Yiddish—the languages the publisher believed the new Sephardic immigrant would need in order to succeed as an American and as an American Jew.[13] Once word spread that this item had been accessioned into our Collection, a scholar based in Spain traveled all the way to Seattle to see it in person: she had been searching for the complete text for many years and was amazed to discover that it had been preserved in the Pacific Northwest.[14]

Another very rare book that soon surfaced was a first Ladino edition of *Shevet Musar* ("Rod of Instruction"), a famous ethical treatise by Rabbi Eliyahu ha-Kohen of Izmir translated from Hebrew by Abraham Asa and published in Istanbul in 1741/1742.[15] So famous was this work—it includes a well-known allegorical debate between Man and Earth over the source of the world's problems—that it made a major impact beyond the realm of the Ottoman Empire. In fact, it was translated

---

11   Eliya Karmona, *Komo Nasyo Eliya Karmona* (Istanbul, El Djugeton, 1926), [ST00493, ST00751, ST001552].

12   Moise S. Gadol, *Livro de embezar las linguas Ingleza i Yudish* (New York, La Amerika), [ST0007].

13   Devin Naar, "A Guidebook for Sephardic Immigrants," Stroum Center for Jewish Studies, University of Washington, November 6, 2012, https://jewishstudies.washington.edu/sephardic-studies/a-guide-for-sephardic-immigrants/.

14   Julie Scolnik, "Libro de embeźar las linguas ingleśa y yudiš: La América's Guidebook to Learning English and Yiddish and Becoming an American Citizen," *Miscelánea de Estudios Árabes y Hebraicos. Sección Hebreo* 63 (2014): 285–297.

15   Rabbi Eliyahu ha-Kohen, *Sefer Shevet Musar* (Istanbul, Benyamin Behor Moshe Rusi, 1741/1742), [ST0091].

into Yiddish even before the Ladino edition appeared. The existence of the Ladino edition in our Collection compels us to revise the chronology, as scholars previously surmised that the first edition did not appear until 1748.[16] Part of the library of the Sephardic Bikur Holim and in fragile condition, the volume in our collection was, at some point, rebound using paper bags from a Seattle grocery store; it also includes a stamp, "Made in Turkey," on the title page.

Interpretation and Interaction: Bringing Ladino Culture to the Present Day

We began with reference to Albert Adatto's pessimistic predictions back in 1939 about the future of Sephardic culture in Seattle. It is ironic that his library now constitutes a backbone of our Collection and has staved off what he anticipated to be the inevitable dissolution of Ladino culture. Born in Istanbul and raised in Seattle, Adatto later became a colonel in the U.S. military. He and his sister Emma pioneered the field of Sephardic Studies in the United States, with each of them writing a master's thesis at the University of Washington in the 1930s. A Sephardic historian and Ladino bibliophile, Albert Adatto spent much time abroad seeking to promote peace and in search of Ladino books. Adatto also created his own Sephardic amulets, called *ojas*, that provided greetings and blessings for their recipients. Adatto sent his *ojas*, written in Judeo-Spanish and an occult script known in Latin as *transitus fluvii*, to world leaders and celebrities, including Anwar Sadat and Johnny Carson.[17]

Adatto amassed more than three hundred items in his personal collection. Not only is this the largest private collection of Ladino materials in Seattle, graciously shared with us by his son, Richard Adatto, but it is also unique in that Adatto actively pursued Ladino books through contacts with international libraries, book dealers, and on his travels abroad. He also inherited items from his mother Anna Adatto (née Perahia), his friends, and fellow community members. His collection includes novels such as Alexander Benghiat's *La brigante* (*The Woman Brigand*), published in Jerusalem in 1911, which deals with the adventures of a band of robbers in the state of Missouri,[18] and a much older and more technical text of a religious nature, the anonymously authored *Sefer Heshek Shelomo*, a glossary of all the non-Hebrew

16 Mathias B. Lehman, *Ladino Rabbinic Literature and Ottoman Sephardic Culture* (Bloomington: Indiana University Press, 2005), 6.

17 Emily Thomson, "Finding Sephardic Blessings and Johnny Carson in the WSJHS Archives," Stroum Center for Jewish Studies, University of Washington, January 26, 2016, https://jewishstudies.washington.edu/sephardic-studies/sephardic-blessings-wsjhs-archives/.

18 Alexander Benghiat, *La brigante* (Jerusalem: Shelomo Yiśrael Sherezli, 1911), [ST00606 and ST00607].

FIGURE 2.4. *Sefer Heshek Shelomo* by Rabbi Gedalia Cordovero (editor), published in Venice in 1624. ST00419, Sephardic Studies Digital Collection, University of Washington, Courtesy of Richard Adatto.

words appearing in the Bible with their equivalents in Ladino. Rabbi Gedalia Cordovero edited the volume and printed it in Venice in 1624.[19] That date makes this Ladino book one of the very oldest in our Collection.

Although Adatto dedicated his life to collecting and studying these rare texts, historically, there has been a lack of scholarly and public attention dedicated to the literature produced by Sepharadim from the Ottoman Empire. In 2019, Professor Devin Naar discussed how the Sephardic Studies Collection will help to change current ambivalent attitudes towards printed Ladino texts, during his lecture at the "Seattle Sephardic Legacies"[20] event, held at the University of Washington. Naar

---

19   Rabbi Gedalia Cordovero, ed., *Sefer Heshek Shelomo* (Venice: Bragadini printing family, 1624), [ST00419].

20   Makena Mezistrano, "'Hidden manuscripts, come out!': Seattle Sephardic Legacies Highlights Ladino Literature," Stroum Center for Jewish Studies, University of Washington, August 14, 2019, https://jewishstudies.washington.edu/sephardic-studies/hidden-manuscripts-come-out-seattle-sephardic-legacies-recap/.

pointed to the forty Ladino novels produced by Elia Carmona and the wealth of Ladino literature preserved in the over 400 Ladino books collected from Seattle to dispute the claims of historians such as Heinrich Graetz, who wrote that the Sephardim from the Ottoman Empire "did not produce a single great genius who originated ideas to stimulate future ages, nor mark out a new thought for men of average intelligence." With support from a National Endowment for the Humanities Common Heritage Grant, many of these previously neglected Ladino books were displayed for the first time, in a multimedia presentation that challenged past and current assumptions about Sephardic culture and literature. The program included an onsite digitization project, where attendees brought dozens of new artifacts to be preserved for posterity and included in the Collection. Following the event, the nearly 250 guests were invited to visit display panels that highlighted some of the largest and most diverse family libraries provided to the Sephardic Studies Collection.

The materials in the Collection have already been put to use by undergraduate and graduate students at the University of Washington. As a student in the Near and Middle East Interdisciplinary PhD program at the University of Washington, Oscar Aguirre-Mandujano developed a research project on notebooks containing Ottoman and Ladino ballads: "A Song of War and Friendship: The Ottoman Poetry of Leon Behar,"[21] which explores the notebook of a Jewish writer from Istanbul, who signs the notebook as an officer of the Ottoman army and adapted patriotic songs in Ottoman Turkish (in Arabic script) and Ladino (in Hebrew script) in support of his homeland. In 2015, Aguirre-Mandujano's research on Behar's poetry reached the attention of the creators of a PBS television special, *The Jewish Journey: America*, which featured images of one of Behar's handwritten notebooks.

Receiving her PhD in the Linguistics Department at the University of Washington, Molly FitzMorris focused on the particular features of the Rhodes dialect of Ladino as preserved—remarkably—in Seattle. Relying on historical evidence for her study that complements her ethnographic work, FitzMorris has drawn from texts related to families from Rhodes, and, notably, primarily written by women. One such text is a *boreka* recipe written in Ladino by a Jewish woman from Rhodes who wrote down the recipe in the hope that her American-born children would continue to prepare the cuisine she first encountered on her native island.[22] FitzMorris also fo-

---

21 Hannah Pressman, "A Soldier's Ladino Poems of Ottoman-Jewish Pride," Stroum Center for Jewish Studies, University of Washington, November 10, 2014, https://jewishstudies. washington.edu/sephardic-studies/soldier-ladino-poems-ottoman-jewish-pride/.

22 Ty Alhadeff, "The Flavor of Rhodes: Paradise Lost, Recipe Saved," Stroum Center for Jewish Studies, University of Washington, December 2, 2016, https://jewishstudies.

cused on the corpus of letters written by a young woman, Claire Barkey, from her native Rhodes to her aunt and uncle in Seattle. Begun in 1930, when Barkey was only nine years old, and continuing for more than fifteen years, the correspondence details the status of Jews on the island and their frantic efforts to flee with the onset of World War II. The letters reveal that with her aunt and uncle's assistance, Barkey successfully orchestrated their family's escape to a refugee camp in Tangiers prior to their settlement in Seattle after the war.[23]

As a graduate student in the History department, Sarah Zaides completed her dissertation on the interactions of Russian and Ottoman Jews in Istanbul during the late nineteenth and early twentieth centuries. With a title that alludes to Sholem Aleichem's famous tale that became the basis of *Fiddler on the Roof*, Zaides' dissertation, "Tevye's Ottoman Daughters: The Making of Ashkenazi and Sephardi Jews in the Shatterzones of Empire, 1882–1923,"[24] drew on resources from the Sephardic Studies Collection, including a letter from Henry Benezra, president of Seattle's Sephardic Bikur Holim, to Rabbi David Markus, the leader of the Ashkenazi community in Istanbul and noted political activist at the time, to assist the daughters of Rabbi Abraham Maimon, who remained alone in Istanbul because they were not able to emigrate with the rest of their family due to immigration restrictions placed on immigrants from Turkey. As the focus of an online essay, "Learning Ladino— Then and Now,"[25] Zaides also analyzed a Ladino school primer from Istanbul and the varying moral and political messages it conveyed—including with regard to the Balfour Declaration of 1917. Discovering the existence of the primer through Zaides' post, the directors of the National Museum of American Jewish History in Philadelphia decided to include it in its traveling exhibition: "1917—How One Year Changed the World."[26]

---

washington.edu/sephardic-studies/rhodes-boreka-recipe-saved/.

23 Claire Barkey Flash, *A Hug From Afar: One family's dramatic journey through three continents to escape the Holocaust* (Bellevue: Flash Media Services, 2016).

24 Sarah Michelle Zaides, "Tevye's Ottoman Daughters: The Making of Ashkenazi and Sephardi Jews in the Shatterzones of Empire, 1882–1923" (PhD diss., University of Washington, 2017).

25 Sarah Michelle Zaides, "Learning Ladino–Then and Now," Stroum Center for Jewish Studies, University of Washington, April 10, 2016, https://jewishstudies.washington.edu/sephardic-studies/learning-ladino-ottoman-empire/.

26 Makena Mezistrano, "The circuitous travels of a Ladino schoolbook through Istanbul, Seattle, the East Coast and Missouri," Stroum Center for Jewish Studies, University of Washington, April 8, 2019, https://jewishstudies.washington.edu/sephardic-studies/the-circuitous-travels-of-a-ladino-schoolbook/.

As a final example, as an undergraduate nursing student, Ashley Bobman, discovered that her great-grandfather, Albert Levy (1896–1963), had been a prominent Ladino journalist, writer, and educator in his native Salonica and subsequently in New York and Seattle. His notebooks were located early in the creation of the Sephardic Studies Collection—in grocery bags at the Sephardic Bikur Holim. Drawing on her basic knowledge of Spanish and Hebrew, she worked for several years with Professor Naar to read and translate a selection of Levy's poems dealing with Sephardic history, communal institutions, the importance of women's education, and other themes, and developed a digital exhibition on the Stroum Center for Jewish Studies' website that narrates the life and times of her great-grandfather: "A Sephardic Lighthouse: Albert Levy and the Sephardic Jewish Journey."[27] For her efforts, the University of Washington awarded Bobman the President's Medal, a prestigious honor bestowed upon the most outstanding student in each undergraduate class. Bobman's work on her great-grandfather's poems even inspired her to pen her own, which she presented at International Ladino Day at the University of Washington—a program dedicated to promoting awareness of and engagement with the Sephardic heritage.

We have published some of our own research on selected artifacts through "Sephardic Treasures" articles in which we have discovered rare books, songs, and customs while attracting readers from across the globe to the Collection. These "highlight" posts focus on specific Sephardic documents, publications, themes, or figures that provide the general public with concise introductions to select artifacts, while also addressing important cultural, historical, literary, or linguistic issues.[28] These articles include select images and links to the original artifacts, which are hosted online at the University of Washington Digital Library. The articles also feature translations and transliterations, audio recordings, and links to other resources. With these curated posts, we are able to share Jewish history through the prism of Sephardic Jews in a more global context: Spain and Spanish, Turkey and Greece, the Middle East, Islam, endangered languages, and contemporary events.

In order to publicize the Collection and the various research projects that draw on our resources, we have leveraged our online presence and social media accounts to increase our reach and pursue readers. Today we have over 9,600 combined followers in 45 countries on Facebook, Twitter, and Instagram. As we spread the word

---

27 Ashley Bobman, "A Sephardic Lighthouse: Albert Levy and the Sephardic Jewish Journey," Stroum Center for Jewish Studies, University of Washington, July 14, 2015, https://jewishstudies.washington.edu/sephardic-digital-museum.

28 Sephardic Treasures Archive, Stroum Center for Jewish Studies, University of Washington, https://jewishstudies.washington.edu/category/digital-sephardic-treasures/.

about our Collection via social media, we have inspired individuals in far-flung locations to reach out to us and share their own materials with us. In one instance, after reading about our project online, a woman from South Africa sent us what appears to be the only known copy of a book of poems for the High Holidays in Ladino, composed and published in Craiova, Romania, by the last Chief Rabbi of Rhodes; rather than appearing in Ladino in the traditional Hebrew script, it was printed in Latin transliteration with footnotes in Romanian![29]

Additions like the High Holidays poems in Ladino sent to us from South Africa continually increase and diversify the holdings of the Sephardic Studies Collection. Our catalog includes over 2,000 items, each with over 40 searchable categories of metadata that identify artifacts by title, edition, author, translator, editor, publisher, languages, scripts, city, and date of publication. Additional metadata is also recorded, including the number of pages, size, subjects, genres, and physical descriptions identifying missing and damaged pages, the quality of paper and binding, the inclusion of printer marks, stamps, dedications, inscriptions and other marginalia, notes on the content, donor information, links to relevant scholarly articles, and references to other known copies in world libraries.[30] We are one step closer to the creation of what Aviva Ben-Ur called "a comprehensive, annotated and nuanced bibliography of this literature and its authors."[31]

A few generations ago, educators like Albert Adatto and other leaders in Seattle recognized the precise intellectual value of their family heirlooms that have helped to preserve Ladino literature for future generations. They saw themselves as lone activists among general disinterest and apathy. With a new corpus of Ladino source materials now accessible online, may Adatto's pessimistic assessment that Ladino culture is doomed be revised? Could a digital afterlife for Ladino culture be made possible by online technologies, including the University of Washington's Sephardic Studies Collection, that would enable orderly access to a wide corpus of Ladino books to anyone in the world with an Internet connection? Such a Collection, we hope, will help

---

29   Ty Alhadeff, "Old Media, New Media," *AJS Perspectives* (Spring 2018): 60.

30   WorldCat, the most comprehensive library catalog, Abraham Yaari's *Reshimat Sifre Ladino*, Meyer Kayserling's *Biblioteca Espnaola-Portuguesa-Judaic*, Moshe D. Gaon's *Ha-Itonut be-Ladino*, Aron Rodrigue's *The Guide to Ladino Materials in the Harvard Library Collection*, Henry V. Besso's *Ladino Book in the Library of Congress*, Ben-Ur's *A Ladino Legacy: The Judeo-Spanish Collection of Louis N. Levy*, David Bunis' *Judezmo (Ladino/Judeo-Spanish) printed books in the YIVO Institute Library*, and the catalog of the National Library of Israel.

31   Aviva Ben-Ur, "Ladino in Print: Toward a Comprehensive Bibliography," *Jewish History* 16, no. 3 (2002): 309–326.

to preserve Ladino culture, perhaps for "the next fifty years." It could also plant "the seeds for a new Judaeo-Spanish culture on the shores of Puget Sound"—and beyond.

Bibliography

Adatto, Albert. "Sephardim and the Seattle Sephardic Community." M.A. thesis, University of Washington Department of History, 1939.

Alhadeff, Ty. "By The Numbers: Building the Sephardic Studies Digital Collection." Stroum Center for Jewish Studies, University of Washington, May 14, 2015, https://jewish-studies.washington.edu/sephardic-studies/building-sephardic-studies-digital-library/.

————— "The Flavor of Rhodes: Paradise Lost, Recipe Saved." Stroum Center for Jewish Studies, University of Washington, December 2, 2016, https://jewishstudies.wash-ington.edu/sephardic-studies/rhodes-boreka-recipe-saved/.

————— "Old Media, New Media." *AJS Perspectives* (Spring 2018): 60.

Barkey Flash, Claire. *A Hug From Afar: One family's Dramatic Journey through Three Continents to Escape the Holocaust.* Bellevue: Flash Media Services, 2016.

Benghiat, Alexander. *La brigante.* Jerusalem: Shelomo Yiśrael Sherezli, 1911 (Sephardic Studies Collection, University of Washington, ST00606 and ST00607).

Benmayor, Rina. *Romances Judeo-Españoles de Oriente: Nueva recolección.* Madrid: Cátedra Seminario Menéndez Pidal-Gredos, 1979.

Ben-Ur, Aviva. "Ladino in Print: Toward a Comprehensive Bibliography." *Jewish History* 16, no. 3 (2002): 309–326.

Bobman, Ashley. "A Sephardic Lighthouse: Albert Levy and the Sephardic Jewish Journey." Stroum Center for Jewish Studies, University of Washington, July 14, 2015, https://jewishstudies.washington.edu/sephardic-digital-museum.

Cohen, Julia Philips and Sarah Abrevaya Stein. *Sephardi Lives: A Documentary History, 1700–1950.* Stanford: Stanford University Press, 2014.

Cordovero, Gedalia, ed. *Sefer Heshek Shelomo.* Venice: Bragadini printing family, 1624 (ST00419).

Gadol, Moise S. *Livro de embezar las linguas Ingleza i Yudish.* New York, La Amerika (ST0007).

ha-Kohen, Eliyahu. *Sefer Shevet Musar.* Istanbul, Benyamin Behor Moshe Rusi, 1741/1742 (ST0091).

Karmona, Eliya. *Komo Nasyo Eliya Karmona.* Istanbul, El Djugeton, 1926 (ST00493, ST00751, ST001552).

Lehman, Mathias B. *Ladino Rabbinic Literature and Ottoman Sephardic Culture.* Bloomington: Indiana University Press, 2005.

Lewis, Bernard. *The Jews of Islam.* New Jersey: Princeton University Press, 1984.

Mezistrano, Makena. "The circuitous travels of a Ladino schoolbook through Istanbul, Seattle, the East Coast and Missouri." Stroum Center for Jewish Studies, University of Washington, April 8, 2019, https://jewishstudies.washington.edu/sephardic-studies/the-circuitous-travels-of-a-ladino-schoolbook/.

———"'Hidden manuscripts, come out!': Seattle Sephardic Legacies Highlights Ladino Literature." Stroum Center for Jewish Studies, University of Washington, August 14, 2019, https://jewishstudies.washington.edu/sephardic-studies/hidden-manuscripts-come-out-seattle-sephardic-legacies-recap/.

Naar, Devin. "A Guidbook for Sephardic Immigrants." Stroum Center for Jewish Studies, University of Washington,November 6, 2012, https://jewishstudies.washington.edu/sephardic-studies/a-guide-for-sephardic-immigrants/.

———"Sephardic Archives from Analog to Digital: Three Tales of Memory and Visibility." Lecture, University of California, Santa Cruz, May 3, 2018.

Nissim Israel's Ethical Will, May 20, 1942. Sephardic Studies Collection, University of Washington (ST001179).

Pressman, Hannah. "A Soldier's Ladino Poems of Ottoman-Jewish Pride." Stroum Center for Jewish Studies, University of Washington, November 10, 2014, https://jewishstudies.washington.edu/sephardic-studies/soldier-ladino-poems-ottoman-jewish-pride/.

Scolnik, Julie. "Libro de embeźar las linguas ingleśa y yudiš: La América's Guidebook to Learning English and Yiddish and Becoming an American Citizen." *Miscelánea de Estudios Árabes y Hebraicos. Sección Hebreo* 63 (2014): 285–297.

Stavans, Ilan, ed. *The Schocken Book of Modern Sephardic Literature*. New York: Schocken Books, 2005.

Strauss, Johann. "Who Read What in the Ottoman Empire (19th-20th Centuries)?" *Middle Eastern Literatures* 6, no. 4 (January 2003): 39–76.

Thomson, Emily. "Finding Sephardic Blessings and Johnny Carson in the WSJHS Archives." Stroum Center for Jewish Studies, University of Washington, January 26, 2016, https://jewishstudies.washington.edu/sephardic-studies/sephardic-blessings-wsjhs-archives/.

Zaides, Sarah Michelle. "Learning Ladino–Then and Now." Stroum Center for Jewish Studies, University of Washington, April 10, 2016, https://jewishstudies.washington.edu/sephardic-studies/learning-ladino-ottoman-empire/.

———"Tevye's Ottoman Daughters: The Making of Ashkenazi and Sephardi Jews in the Shatterzones of Empire, 1882–1923." PhD dissertation, University of Washington, 2017.

PART TWO

Studies: Reading the Past through the Seattle Sephardic
Studies Collection

CHAPTER THREE

From the Aegean to the Pacific:
Ottoman Legacies in Seattle Sephardi Synagogues

MAUREEN JACKSON

The male voice is strong, resonant, nasal. The singer ascends and descends melodiously, expressing a sense of lamentation or supplication reminiscent of a Muslim call to prayer. A cluster of Hebrew words gives way to a single long tone, embellished very slowly and subtly in microtones. His voice suddenly leaps upward in crescendo, then draws a single vowel through a dense line of melody.[1] As he sings, his solitary voice, rich melodic embellishment, and seemingly free-form meter give the impression, too, of an Ottoman *gazel* or vocal improvisation.[2] This is the 1951 recording of Samuel Benaroya (1908–2003), hazzan (cantor) of the Sephardi Jewish congregation in Geneva, Switzerland, mailed to the Sephardic Bikur Holim congregation in Seattle, Washington.[3] The Seattle community sought a new hazzan after the retirement of Morris Scharhon and had come together as a group to listen to their prospective employee. In lieu of an interview, the record showcased two popular liturgical songs for Yom Kippur, "Avinu Malkeinu" and "L'Ma-ancha Elokai." Hearing only these two songs and never meeting him in person, the congregation raised their hands in unanimous agreement to hire Benaroya immediately.

The popularity of Benaroya's vocal performance among Seattle's Turkish Jewish community confirms their ongoing embrace of Ottoman-style liturgical music and prayer texts since their first reported immigration to the United States at the turn of the twentieth century. In fact, Benaroya represented the height of Ottoman-Hebrew musical knowledge and training, growing up as he did in a historical center for

---

1   A changing line of music sung on a single vowel is called melisma.

2   In this context, a gazel is a vocal improvisation utilizing a text and meter-free music.

3   Samuel Benaroya, interview by Eric Offenbacher, 17 Jan 1988; Samuel Benaroya, Recording, Geneva, Switzerland, 1951. As a cantor or prayer leader, the hazzan performs religious liturgy in a Jewish congregation. Ottoman and Turkish hazzanim often fulfilled other religious duties, especially for smaller congregations.

FIGURE 3.1. Samuel Benaroya's Turkish Passport. ST00274, Sephardic Studies Digital Collection, University of Washington. Courtesy of Judy Amiel.

Jewish religious music, Edirne, a city in Thrace where he was born into a lineage of hazzanim in 1908. He was brought to the attention of the Seattle congregation by David de Sola Pool, rabbi of the Spanish-Portuguese congregation, Shearith Israel, in New York City. Although de Sola Pool represented an older Sephardi community with historical ties to Northern Europe rather than the eastern Mediterranean, he nonetheless extended himself through his religious networks to facilitate the hiring of Benaroya. Benaroya had emigrated from his hometown of Edirne to Geneva in 1934, serving, with some frustration, a congregation that was often too small for a *minyan,* in a country where *shechitah* (ritual slaughter) was forbidden.[4] With the assistance of two Washington state congressmen in an era of immigration quotas for

---

4 Benaroya and his family left Edirne for Geneva (through Istanbul) to escape violence against Jewish residents during the "Thrace Incidents" in 1934. Minyan refers to the minimum number of ten men for worship. The person who performs *shechitah* (ritual slaughter) according to religious law is referred to as a *shochet.*

Turkish nationals, de Sola Pool orchestrated Benaroya's entry to the United States under the title of a credentialed "Reverend," thus easing his immediate employment by Seattle Bikur Holim.[5]

The Spanish-Portuguese congregation in New York did not always play such a supportive role of cultural advocacy among their more recent Sephardi brethren in the Pacific Northwest. A centuries-old immigrant community, the congregation claimed ancestry from *converso* Jews who had migrated a century after the Spanish Inquisition to Northern Europe, settling primarily in what is now the Netherlands, Germany, and Britain. By the twentieth century, the community boasted well-established institutions on the east coast, including a religious press and the Union of Sephardic Congregations. Established in 1929, the latter sought to unite non-Ashkenazi Jewish congregations as a distinctive sub-minority among the more populous Ashkenazi religious minority by training Sephardi religious leaders, establishing Sephardi religious schools, and standardizing a national religious rite. Indeed, a hierarchical relationship, born of a Eurocentric concept of "Sephardim" tied to a superior cache of socio-economic resources, developed between the older centralizing New York institutions and newer relatively decentralized post-Ottoman communities across the country. These more recent immigrants hailed from what had been Ottoman imperial lands in North Africa and the Middle East, where the vast majority of Jews migrated from Spain in the immediate aftermath of the Inquisition. The tension among the disparate diaspora communities is nowhere more obvious than in the publication and national dissemination of a Sabbath siddur in the Spanish-Portuguese custom in the mid-1930s. The prayerbook aimed to unify, empower, and culturally shape a Sephardi-American minority in the US based on a particular Northern European strand of liturgical practice and fueled by viewpoints about who and what counted as "Sephardi," thus promulgating European Sephardi practices and practitioners while effectively demoting those immigrating from beyond the conceptually accepted edges of Europe.[6]

---

5   Congressmen Henry "Scoop" Jackson and Warren Magnuson reportedly facilitated the immigration process.

6   For a comprehensive history of the diversity of Sephardim in the United States, see Aviva Ben-Ur, *Sephardic Jews in America: a Diasporic History* (New York: New York University Press, 2009). Scholars have debated the changing complexity of terms to identify diverse Jews from Northern Europe, the Middle East, North Africa, and West Asia. For example, see Ibid., 18–22; Matthias B. Lehmann, "Introduction: Sephardi Identities," *Jewish Social Studies: History, Culture, Society* 15, no. 1 (2008): 1–9. This article will generally refer to Northern European-origin Jews with ancestries in Spain as Spanish-Portuguese and their counterparts from Ottoman territories as Ottoman or Turkish. The contested and

Such homogenizing efforts on the part of the New York congregation and Union of Sephardic congregations, as we shall see, were not entirely successful: Sephardi communities, such as Seattle's, upset unifying missions simply through ongoing daily and local worshipping based on Ottoman-era prayerbooks, orally transmitted music, and a modified use of the nationally disseminated prayerbook within cohesive immigrant neighborhoods. Even so, the tensions around nationalizing and localizing liturgical practices can be illuminated by the theoretical framework of cultural genealogies – concepts of heritage that organized competing social categories of "Sephardim" in North America.[7] On the one hand, the ethno-religious genealogy historicizing Spanish-Portuguese immigrants rooted itself in post-Inquisition migration patterns beginning in the seventeenth century, beginning with *converso* Jews from Portugal to Northern Europe, where they progressively established urban centers in Amsterdam, Hamburg, and London, with Amsterdam becoming a primary source of authority in a variety of administrative and scholarly areas. De Sola Pool's discourse about Sephardim in the U.S. reflects this cultural genealogy composed of branches extending as far as a Western European heartland—Northern Europe and Spain—while "pruned" of the branches of previous generations circling the Mediterranean. The Seattle community, on the other hand, similarly drew a distant European ancestry from Spain, but its subsequent branches extended eastward around the Mediterranean coastal region, especially Ottoman territories, where the largest numbers of Spanish Jews migrated after the Inquisition. Following World War II and the Holocaust, when many post-Ottoman Jewish communities in the Balkans and Near East had been destroyed, these separate and unequal genealogies were called into question, becoming entangled through the recognition that Middle Eastern Sephardi communities in the U.S. represented the main surviving Ottoman-origin Jewry outside the State of Israel, yet only to be lost, again, through cultural homogenization. De Sola Pool's cultural advocacy for Seattle through mediating the employment of Benaroya reflects these conceptual shifts. Embracing a measure of Sephardi-American diversity, he figuratively grafted his eastern Mediterranean co-religionists onto the national Sephardi family tree and began to destabilize the prevailing liturgical and cultural hierarchies of previous decades.

---

changing use of 'Sephardi' in the United States among the communities under study exemplifies the fluid nature of this term.

7   See Eviatar Zerubavel's creative research into socially constructed genealogies, in which he draws on Darwin's theory of evolution and biological taxonomies to illuminate cultural categories of thought. Eviatar Zerubavel, *Anncestors and Relatives: Genealogy, Identity, and Community* (Oxford: Oxford University Press, 2012).

This paper focuses on the emergence of Seattle as a local liturgical and cultural center apart from New York and in response to changing Sephardi-American genealogical constructions, rising community capital, and newer immigration of Middle Eastern and North African Jews across the twentieth century.[8] Indeed, Seattle's ongoing cultivation of Ottoman-era liturgies is reflected not only in the employment of Samuel Benaroya in the early 1950s and his assiduous training of junior hazzanim, but also in the publication of a series of prayerbooks, based in Seattle's historical practices, by Isaac Azose between 2002 and 2014. These in turn began to fill the practical religious needs of post-Ottoman congregations contemporaneous with Seattle's immigrant history, as well as even more recent Jewish immigrants around the United States from Mediterranean and Middle Eastern regions. By probing the historical settlements of Jews from Spain to Northern Europe and the Ottoman Empire, respectively, the study elucidates cultural divergences underpinning intra-religious tensions in twentieth century North America. At the same time, by extending its reach into the early modern period, the research uncovers Inquisition-era connections that competing "Sephardi" genealogies on North American soil have trimmed from view. Both communities, in fact, share a post-Inquisition Mediterranean past rife with interactive movement of peoples and publications. It is later that the regional contexts of Northern Europe and the Ottoman Empire progressively shaped distinctive musical liturgies, religious practices, and institutional structures, brought into an uneasy hierarchical relationship in the United States both conceptually through competing cultural genealogies and practically through the contested nationalization of religious practices. Institutional imbalances, however, failed to claim liturgical winners and losers. Whether pressured to assimilate into Spanish-Portuguese practices or recognized as a valuable sub-minority in a post-Holocaust world, the Seattle community maintained local distinctiveness through oral transmission of music and oral modification of national prayerbooks, eventually textualizing those practices in their own publications. Responding to commercial demand from other congregations, moreover, they began to align themselves with more recent immigrants in a post-Ottoman and Mediterranean ancestral and liturgical line. Simultaneously entangled in an expanded post-war definition of "Sephardim," the Seattle community generated its own orbit of diverse liturgical kith and kin over time in a changing North American immigrant landscape.

---

8   Some material in this study was discussed in Maureen Jackson, "Reaching Beyond the Local: The Itineraries of an Ottoman-Sephardic-American Minhag," *Contemporary Jewry* 35, no. 1 (2015): 89–105. Adapted/Translated by permission from Springer Customer Service Centre GmbH: Springer (Copyright 2015).

Art Music: Distinctive Liturgical Trajectories

From the time of their settlements in the Ottoman empire and Northern Europe, Jewish émigrés from Spain were integrally involved in the ambient art music of their respective regions. As music linked to court culture and high musical learning, art music held a cross-regional cultural status considered appropriate to diverse houses of worships, including synagogues. It is this music, its theoretical system, performance practice, and transmission patterns, cultivated in the course of several centuries, that would later represent in part the particular "ancestral" liturgical music for immigrant congregations in the United States and distinguish the cultural lineages of the Spanish-Portuguese and Ottoman-origin congregations. In the Ottoman Empire, it was cross-communal interactions with court culture that gave rise to the *Maftirim* repertoire, a Hebrew language suite of music paralleling the forms, melodies, and rhythms of the Ottoman court suite or *fasıl*. Beginning in the sixteenth century in Edirne, an early Ottoman capital with an established court culture, the music created a sacred fasıl by adapting to Jewish religious space and law—through Hebrew texts and vocal-only arrangements—court music genres by Jewish and non-Jewish composers alike. Performed para-liturgically before Sabbath services, Maftirim singing spread to other major Ottoman Jewish communities, including Istanbul, Salonika, and Izmir, where early morning gatherings before Sabbath services continued well into the twentieth century.[9]

Significantly, a long history of relations between Jewish and Mevlevi (*whirling dervish*) musicians informed music-making in the synagogue.[10] The Mevlevi represented the Sufi brotherhood of the aristocracy and imperial government, ever-present at court and in urban lodges known for religious and musical learning, as well as for some of the most complex of imperial court musical forms, the suite accompanying their religious ritual (*ayin*). Samuel Benaroya's life story in Edirne testifies to the long term nature of these inter-religious relationships and their impact on Jewish religious music. As he remembered years later, his maternal uncle accompanied him to the Mevlevi lodge in Edirne every Friday evening:

---

9   For an extended socio-historical study of the Maftirim repertoire that focuses on nineteenth through twenty-first century textual and ethnographic sources, see Maureen Jackson, *Mixing Musics: Turkish Jewry and the Urban Landscape of a Sacred Song* (Stanford: Stanford University Press, 2013). For a historical overview, see Edwin Seroussi, "Introduction" in *Maftirim*, ed. Karen Gerson Şarhon (Istanbul: Gözlem, 2009), 43–77.

10   For a comprehensive collection of historical examples and their sources, see Jackson, *Mixing Musics*, 181n15.

FIGURE 3.2. Benaroya Family in Edirne, c. 1913. University of Washington Libraries, Special Collections.

In this period of twelve, thirteen, fourteen years we get acquainted with the people who used to sing in the Mevlane [sic]. Mevlane was the gathering in the mosque every Friday that the dervish people used to have their services by turning and performing and dancing and playing some instruments, which were very appreciated by us because we wanted to learn also from them.

Now with the time we got well-acquainted with some of these people. We invited them in our synagogue to listen what we are singing and also vice versa they invited us to listen or to take advantage of their knowledge of what they were singing. . . . [We] used to sing in Hebrew from Shire Yisrael and they sang their own liturgical [song]. . . . Their melody we interpreted with our Hebrew words and we were singing [it] in our synagogue. . . . They didn't need to [learn our songs] because they were much more up-to-date, much more learned than we were.[11]

Through Benaroya's recollections we also gain a window onto broader Jewish integration into Ottoman musical culture. Even though he came from a family of modest means, Benaroya rose through the musical and religious ranks because of his fine ear and memory, a prized gift in an Ottoman musical culture of oral

---

11 Samuel Benaroya, interview with Edwin Seroussi, October 24, 1992. Video recording by Judith Amiel.

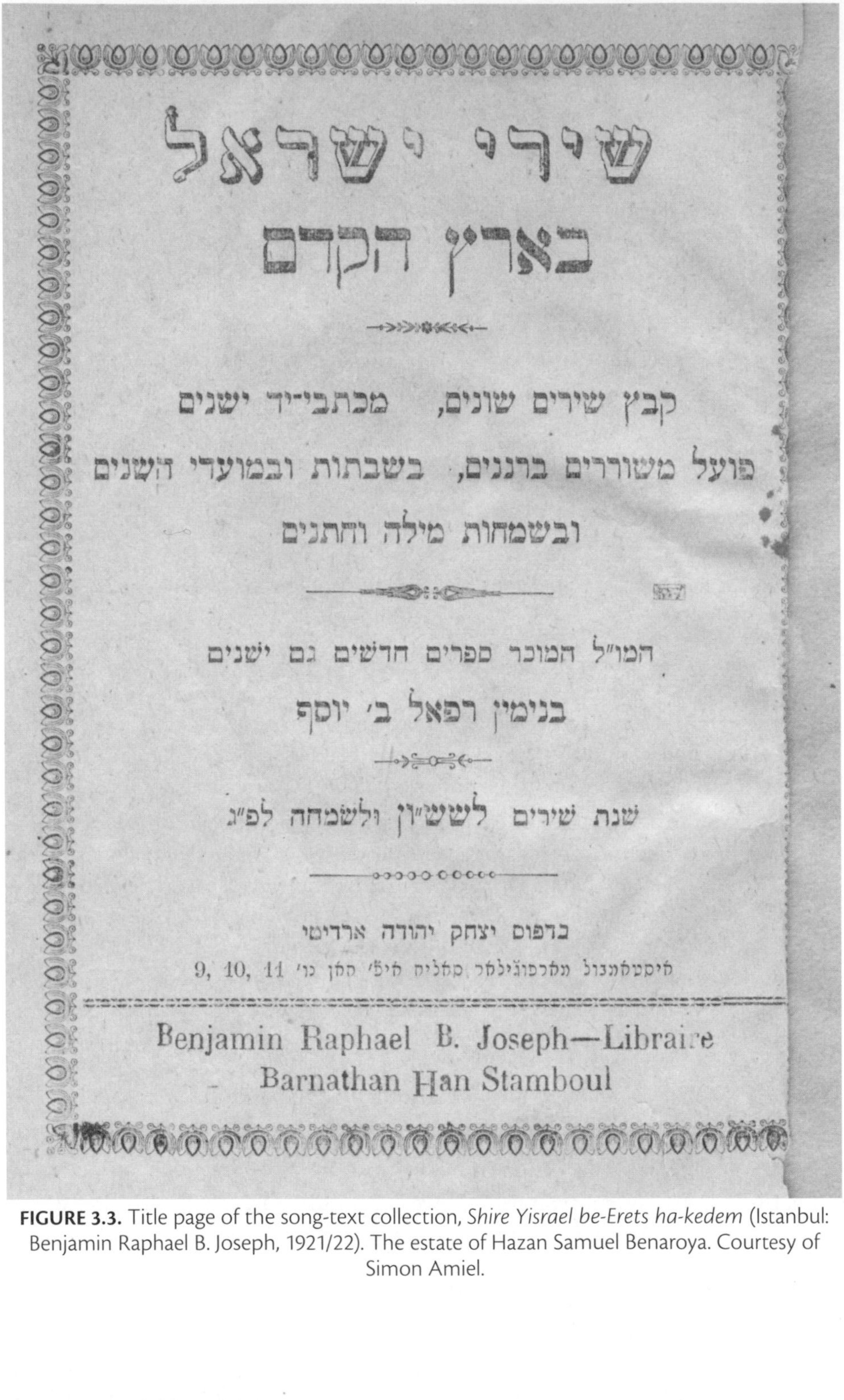

שירי ישראל

באֶרֶץ הקדם

קבץ שירים שונים, מכתבי־יד ישנים

פועל משוררים ברנים, בשבתות ובמועדי השנים

ובשמחות מילה וחתנים

המו"ל המוכר ספרים חדשים גם ישנים

בנימין רפאל ב' יוסף

שנת שירים לששׂון ולשׂמחה לפ"ג

בדפוס יצחק יהודה ארדיטי

מיסטאמנול מאכיפוג'ילאר קאלוֹיה חיל׳ האן נו' 9, 10, 11

Benjamin Raphael B. Joseph—Libraire

Barnathan Han Stamboul

FIGURE 3.3. Title page of the song-text collection, *Shire Yisrael be-Erets ha-kedem* (Istanbul: Benjamin Raphael B. Joseph, 1921/22). The estate of Hazan Samuel Benaroya. Courtesy of Simon Amiel.

learning through non-monetary master-pupil relationships. And even though he exclusively performed in the synagogue, Benaroya interacted with Jewish composers of non-religious music, thus acquiring broad art music knowledge at a high level. To be sure, Jewish and non-Jewish, religious and non-religious musicians historically participated together in art music worlds of which synagogues were a part, thus contributing to the development of Ottoman musical norms in liturgical music. From at least the eighteenth century on, composers of Jewish and other ethnicities performed and taught music at the court, co-developing Ottoman art music styles; participating in Ottoman musical practices for teaching, learning, and scoring music; and, often working as hazzanim or composers in their communities as well. In non-notated *güfte mecmuaları* (song-text collections), moreover, Jewish musicians documented music through Ottoman methods, with collections increasingly aligning with empire-wide counterparts from the seventeenth century onward by providing lyrics with musical cues.[12] In the early 1920s, the Chief Rabbinate in Istanbul sponsored the publication of *Shire Yisrael be-Erets ha-Kedem*, a song-text collection of Maftirim compositions aiming to document a feared-to-be-lost historical repertoire, providing lyrics for subsequent generations, and traveling abroad with émigré hazzanim, like Samuel Benaroya to the Seattle Sephardic Congregation.[13]

In a related but contrasting development, European art music between the seventeenth and nineteenth centuries, scored in 5-staff notation, provided the Spanish-Portuguese congregations in the eastern United States with their core musical endowment. Constituting a large corpus of music for the congregations in both Amsterdam and London, these pieces were composed by Jewish and non-Jewish composers and reflected changing forms of European art music after the seventeenth century in diverse arrangements for soloist or choir, with or without instruments.[14] Some of these compositions were commissioned for Jewish holidays, with certain numbers becoming traditionalized by hazzanim as cantorial solos, and others performed on para-liturgical occasions, such as to commemorate the founding

---

12 Song-text collections generally organized pieces by *makam* with indication of *usul* (rhythm pattern), genre, and composer, all of which represented memory aids in an orally transmitted musical practice.

13 *Shire Yisrael be-Erets ha-Kedem* (Istanbul: Benjamin Raphael B. Joseph, c. 1921).

14 Some non-Jewish composers were connected directly with synagogues, for example the Christian composer C.F. Hurlebusch (1696–1765) was associated with the Sephardi congregation in Amsterdam. A number of Jewish composers were conservatory-trained hazzanim. Edwin Seroussi, *Spanish-Portuguese Synagogue Music in the 19th Century Reform Sources from Hamburg: Ancient Tradition in the Dawn of Modernity* (Jerusalem: Magnes Press-Hebrew University, 1996), 56.

of a synagogue.[15] European notation appears to have gone hand in hand with the development of polyphonic arrangements of Sephardi melodies by the nineteenth century—developments that in turn constituted part of a "traditional" repertoire of New York City immigrant congregations.[16]

Significantly, nineteenth century Ashkenazi reform synagogues placed high aesthetic value on traditional Sephardi *piyyutim* and thus had impact on liturgical music and transmission in Northern European Spanish-Portuguese congregations themselves.[17] In an era of national citizenship in Europe, Spanish-Portuguese congregations were viewed as a model of socio-economic and religious integration in Christian Europe, as were pre-Inquisition Sephardi Jewry in a multi-religious *convivencia* in Spain.[18] Ashkenazi reform synagogues in Northern and Central Europe embraced "older" Sephardi *piyyutim* for their neo-classical aesthetic of "ancient" beauty and simplicity, as well as a more participatory style of music than the elaborate solos of Ashkenazi hazzanim.[19] Importantly for Sephardi liturgies on both sides of the Atlantic, after the Ashkenazi Hamburg Reform Temple hired a number of Spanish-Portuguese hazzanim, including David Meldova (1780–1861), musical personnel at the synagogue began to transcribe the "older" Sephardi melodies, apparently for future performance by hazzanim, as well as for

---

15 Ibid., 23.

16 It goes without saying that notated scores would not halt oral learning among Spanish-Portuguese Jewry in Northern Europe, but rather would co-exist in a context of mixed transmission patterns.

17 Generally referred to as the *Haskalah*, or "Jewish Enlightenment," these reform trends represent, in the broadest terms, a concern with framing Judaism and Jewish religious practice within European nation-states presenting values of national citizenship, a scientific worldview, and Protestant forms of religious administration and liturgy, including a particular "aestheticization" of services emphasizing decorum and formality, restricting the roles of "wandering hazzanim," and minimizing the spontaneous and emotive. "Protestant norms" were not necessarily unchanging or uniform.

18 Convivencia is a contested historiographical term referring to the harmonious co-existence of Jews, Muslims, and Christians in Spanish history from the eighth century to the Spanish Inquisition.

19 Some early nineteenth century reform leaders also compared the Sephardi melodies with their own German chorales: simple, rhythmic, easy-to-learn melodies that could either replace or accompany these familiar forms. Ibid., 49. Within this context of religious reform, Jewish and non-Jewish composers alike continued to write music for the synagogue, among them the influential composer/hazzanim Salomon Sulzer (1804–1890) in Vienna, Louis Lewandowsky (1821–1894) in Berlin, and Samuel Naumbourg (1815–1880) in Paris, who adapted "older" Ashkenazi and Sephardi melodies to a contemporary aesthetic, among other varieties of liturgical art music compositions.

inclusion in printed songbooks.[20] Such documentation offered a format conducive to polyphonic choral, rather than normative solo voice, or to the monophonic arrangement of Spanish-Portuguese song.[21] A subsequent publication by Sephardi hazzan David de Sola and arranger Emanuel Aguilar (*The Ancient Melodies of the Liturgy of the Spanish and Portuguese Jews*, London 1857) includes melodies arranged in four parts with keyboard accompaniment, possibly representing an initiative by the Spanish and Portuguese themselves to preserve and canonize an orally-transmitted tradition in the face of increasingly dramatic liturgical changes among Reform congregations.[22] Indeed, by the first half of the nineteenth century, some reform synagogues included choirs in services, in addition to organs, employed Christian musicians to play them, and linked them with the reform values—associated with Protestant worship—of harmony and decorum during services.[23] In this way, a Sephardi "tradition," retrieved by reformist Ashkenazim, contributed to the liturgical corpus of the immigrant New York congregation through an aesthetic of choral arrangements and scoring norms grounded in the techniques of their European predecessors.

Mediterranean Confluences

On North American soil, the New York and Seattle Sephardi congregations identified most closely with their pre-immigration "homelands"—an identification heard particularly clearly in the distinctive aristocratic art music worlds that infused their liturgies. In fact, the communities share Spain in their ancient historiographies, as well as the Mediterranean as a whole, in the cultural flows from Sephardic settlements bordering the Mediterranean to those established in Northern Europe after the Inquisition. Indeed, through the theoretical lens of ethno-cultural ancestries,

---

20 Ibid., 40.

21 For example, in one songbook by Eduard Kley (1827), the Sephardi melodies are arranged in multiple parts, presumably for solo voice, choir, and organ. Ibid., 45.

22 While a musicological analysis would be necessary, it is possible that such transcription altered older, modal material by fitting it into European scales and rhythms, thus removing it further from a shared Ottoman repertoire. Judith K. Eisenstein, "Medieval Elements in the Liturgical Music of the Jews of Southern France and Northern Spain," *Musica Judaica* XIV (1999), 15.

23 Seroussi, *Spanish-Portuguese Synagogue Music*, 35. Reform synagogues challenged the prohibition against instruments (in this case organs) by claiming their relationship with the original Temple instrument, the *magrefah*. Unlike Central European reform synagogues, the Spanish-Portuguese congregations of Amsterdam and London established choirs later, in the final decades of the century—a development in which musical transcription and notated polyphonic arrangements were useful for choral direction and performance.

inclusiveness emerges when communities, including Sephardi-Americans, are historicized in a more distant geographical past, whereas subsequent regional trajectories define divergences, as reflected in the underlying political tensions between east and west coast Sephardi-American congregations in the twentieth century.[24] A common Mediterranean geographical history evolved through migration routes from Spain to the Ottoman Empire and Northern Europe, as well as the circulation of religious music and musicians in the century following the Inquisition. Important numbers of Jewish exiles, as we have seen, had migrated to North Africa and southern Europe, with the vast majority settling in the Ottoman Empire and expanding, or creating, Jewish communities in a number of Ottoman urban centers. Because of their critical mass of scholarly, musical, and religious expertise, eastern Mediterranean Sephardim played important roles in intellectual commerce with early Spanish-Portuguese communities in Northern Europe.

Initially, the community in Amsterdam looked toward the more well-established congregations in the Ottoman Empire, North Africa, and Italy for institutional models, publications, and religious personnel, through whom common musical liturgies traveled. In addition to their superior numbers of practitioners, the closer temporal proximity to Spanish "roots" and geographic proximity to Palestine presumably credentialed these southern *"non-converso"* brethren with a measure of religious authority. In the area of clerical posts, a number of hazzanim were hired from the Salonika/Venice region in the early seventeenth century: Joseph Pardo and his son David in 1608, as well as R. Saul Levi Mortera in 1611 and Joseph Shalom Gallego in 1614. Isaac ben Abraham Uziel from Fez, a hazzan and poet with ties to Ottoman poets, was employed in the same period, becoming a religious leader, as well as a teacher to younger poets in Amsterdam.[25] Additionally, the compositions of poet-musician Israel Najara (1550–1620) journeyed south to north during or shortly after his lifetime. Associated with the mystic studies of Kabbalah in Safed in Palestine, Najara composed Hebrew songs intertwining mystical themes from the Biblical Song of Songs with imagery related to Ottoman poetry, adapting his poetry primarily to popular Turkish, and secondarily to Greek, Arabic, and Spanish, melodies.[26] His Hebrew poems, or *piyyutim*, were published not only in

---

24 For a discussion of temporality as a factor in genealogical inclusivity or exclusivity, see Zerubavel, *Ancestors and Relatives*, 87.

25 Seroussi, *Spanish-Portuguese Synagogue Music*, 135.

26 For a full discussion of Najara's songs, see Andreas Tietze and Joseph Yahalom, *Ottoman Melodies Hebrew Hymns: A 16th Century Cross-Cultural Adventure* (Budapest: Akademiai Klado, 1995).

Safed (1587), but also in Salonika (1599) and Venice (1600)—print sources that, in addition to oral transmission, account for Najara's *piyyutim* in later European sources.[27] Up until the present day, moreover, the prevalent inclusion of *Lechah Dodi*, a piyyut by sixteenth century Salonikan poet Shlomo Halevi Alkabetz included in the Sabbath worship services of diverse Jewish congregations, attests to the prior widespread circulation and transformation, westward and northward, of Ottoman Jewish mystical compositions.

In the modern era, there also exist verifiable musical links between Ottoman and Northern European congregations that co-existed with the influx of distinctive regional art music styles. In the nineteenth century, for example, Spanish-Portuguese synagogue music in Northern Europe reflects a core liturgy (primarily the music of High Holy Days and Festivals) shared with Ottoman and Moroccan Jewry. Individual prayer leaders sustained this shared repertoire within congregations pressing for personnel qualified through a lineage of master hazzanim, thus attesting to oral transmission from the Ottoman Empire and Fez northward beginning in the seventeenth century.[28] Such south to north lines of communication, in fact, reached across the Atlantic at the same time: the very first recorded hazzan of the fledgling Spanish-Portuguese congregation in New York was Saul Pardo (d. 1702/3), the grandson of Joseph Pardo of Salonika/Venice. Official twentieth century historiography of the congregation, however, does not detail Pardo's religious background or tenureship with the congregation, although at the time he was undoubtedly valued for his Ottoman or Mediterranean familial pedigree. Indicative of recent aversion to identifying with "eastern" heritage in favor of locating the ancestral "homeland" in Europe, Saul Pardo is historicized as an early example of the congregation's gaze toward Northern European Sephardi settlements, specifically Amsterdam and secondarily London, as a source of religious personnel (hazzanim and later rabbis) from the late seventeenth to twentieth century.[29]

---

27 A particular melody by Najara, for example, was in vogue in Amsterdam and London in the mid-eighteenth century, while another was adopted as the hymn of the Sabbateans and followers of Jacob Frank. Seroussi, *Spanish-Portuguese Synagogue Music*, 54n51.

28 In seeking musical sources and cross-regional commonalities, Seroussi correlates notated nineteenth century European sources with current practitioners in both Europe and former Ottoman territories, thereby placing certain melodies within an identifiable "class of equivalence." "Class of equivalence" refers to ". . . the 'melody' from an emic point of view . . . (retaining) enough formal characteristics (sequences of intervals, rhythmic patterns, duration and order of melodic units such as motifs and phrases) that once decoded by a performer in a latter period an authorized informant can associate it with its 'class'." Ibid., 62.

29 David de Sola Pool, *An Old Faith in a New World: Portrait of Shearith Israel 1654–1945* (New York: Columbia University Press, 1955), 159–60.

On North American Soil, Together and Apart

By the time of Ottoman and Turkish Jewish immigration to the United States in
the early twentieth century, the Spanish-Portuguese Jewish institutions in New
York City had developed a sense of Sephardi identity rooted in their European
regional "homeland" and in Jewish intellectual and religious currents more broadly
on both sides of the Atlantic. They had historically looked to the Amsterdam community—sometimes via the London congregation—for synagogue architecture,
institutional structure, clerical personnel, music, and prayerbooks, with statutes
privileging lay leadership and the city's "mother synagogue," encouraging a measure
of institutional and liturgical standardization.[30] By the mid-nineteenth century,
moreover, New York's Spanish-Portuguese had been eclipsed by Central European
Jewish immigrants to the city:[31] its synagogue Shearith Israel progressively instituted
not only liturgical practices conforming to European religious reform and echoing developments across the Atlantic (polyphony, 5-staff notation, organ); it also
instituted the position of rabbi/preacher above that of hazzan, based on agitations
among prominent Jewish-American religious reformers to privilege the position of
Protestant-style rabbi-preachers in synagogues.[32] The demotion of the position of
solo hazzan was further complicated by the institution of a regular choir of men

30   From the 1700s to the present day, Shearith Israel has employed the majority of its haz-
     zanim, and later rabbis as well, from Holland, secondarily from England, and lastly from
     the United States, North Africa, and the Caribbean. Ibid., 158–210. Other *conversos*
     congregations in Hamburg, London, Brazil, and the Caribbean also viewed Amsterdam
     as a model. For example, the Sephardi congregations in London, Curacao, and New York
     adopted statutes from the Amsterdam congregation; they also modeled their synagogue's
     architecture on the main synagogue (1675) in Amsterdam. Miriam Bodian, "Amsterdam,
     Venice, and the Marrano diaspora in the 17th century" in *Dutch Jewish History*, ed.
     Jozeph Michman (Jerusalem: Institute for Research on Dutch Jewry-Hebrew University,
     1989), 64; Yoss Turisky, Director, *The Story of Two Synagogues*. VHS (Tel Aviv: Museum
     of the Jewish Diaspora/ Beth Hatefutsoth, 1992).

31   Ben-Ur, *Sephardic Jews in America*, 82–83.

32   Before this decision in the second half of the nineteenth century, the synagogue partici-
     pated in heated controversy over the prospect of the popular hazzan Jacques Judah Lyons
     (1839–1877) sharing the stage with a rabbi. Eventually, at Shearith Israel the hazzan was
     referred to as "assistant hazzan," with the rabbi implicitly serving as primary hazzan by
     performing not the daily Sabbath liturgy, but rather special High Holy Day pieces such
     as the "Kol Nidre." de Sola Pool, *An Old Faith*, 188–190; Mark Slobin, *Chosen Voices: The
     Story of the American Cantorate* (Urbana & Chicago: University of Illinois Press, 1989),
     207. As former assistant hazzan Abraham Lopes Cardozo notes, "A Sephardic hazzan is
     not a cantor in the Ashkenazi sense, but rather a reader and a leader of services," reciting
     scripture in biblical cantillation and performing solo-breaks with the choir. Ibid.

and boys during services in the synagogue, led by a series of choirmasters trained in European conservatories who transcribed liturgical melodies in notated, polyphonic arrangements for the purpose of conducting and reproducing harmonized song.[33] David de Sola Pool had high praise for the male choir that sang during every Sabbath, as well as festivals, High Holy Days, special occasions, and weddings during the mid-century: ". . . [it is] one more element of beauty and dignity in the synagogue service. Its leadership of congregational singing, its finely rendered choral music, and its expert direction, give a high musical character to the service."[34] The hazzan, on the other hand, who "remains the leader in prayer, and . . . chants the Torah, is not called on to sing the involved note groupings of the Oriental Sephardi tradition, or the coloratura cadences often heard in Ashkenazi synagogues."[35] Indeed, congregational recordings from the early 1960s present a series of choral hymns—polyphonic arrangements with solo-breaks by the hazzan—while High Holy Day services feature more complex vocal solos by a number of religious staff in addition to the hazzan.[36]

In the same period, by contrast, during the lengthy Sabbath services of the early twentieth century immigrants to Seattle, the hazzan played a prominent role, as in his Ottoman community, through the cantillation of Torah readings, vocal solos, and leading the congregation in recitation or song. During High Holy Days, the compositions sung by the hazzan became increasingly complex and demanding. The newly hired Samuel Benaroya exemplified this late Ottoman aesthetic through his virtuosic solos and lengthy holiday services, an Ottoman liturgical norm that by the 1950s actually became a thorn in the side of some congregants.[37] In contrast

---

33   de Sola Pool, *An Old Faith*, 154–56. Previously, Shearith Israel used choirs for not infrequent paraliturgical occasions, such as synagogue commemorations and American national holidays, where the audience would include Christian colleagues and friends. Like Northern European Spanish-Portuguese congregations, Shearith Israel began to transcribe its liturgical music in the mid-nineteenth century, when hazzan Lyons was asked by the lay board to document his melodies, presumably for a kind of canonization and recreation by subsequent hazzanim. The synagogue's organ was reportedly donated by George Gershwin in the mid-1880s. Ibid., 144. According to a staff member, it is used infrequently today (personal communication, 2002).

34   Ibid., 155.

35   Ibid., 157.

36   Shearith Israel. *Music of the Congregation Shearith Israel: Songs of the Sabbath.* New York, NY. Cassette of master tape-recorded in 1963; Shearith Israel. *Music of the Congregation Shearith Israel: The High Holy Days and the Festivals.* New York, NY. Cassette of master tape-recorded in 1963.

37   Jackson, *Mixing Musics*, 169.

to Shearith Israel, moreover, Seattle hazzanim historically "did everything," until, after the first rabbinical ordination in the community (Solomon Maimon at Yeshiva University in New York City in 1940), the Seattle congregations for the first time distinguished separate positions for rabbi and hazzan.[38] Nonetheless, the position of the hazzan appears to have maintained its liturgical significance within Seattle congregations, despite its often "semi-professional" or underpaid status.[39]

Religious reform among Ottoman Jewry in the nineteenth century can illuminate the ongoing pride of place granted to hazzanim and orally transmitted monophonic renditions in subsequent diaspora communities like Seattle's. While extensive intellectual interchange thrived between Ottoman and European Jewish thinkers by the nineteenth century, Ottoman religious scholars generally followed their own path to reform, making religiously progressive rabbinical rulings while simultaneously conserving institutional structures and musical liturgies that, in contrast to pre-nationalizing European synagogues, were already well-integrated into Ottoman society.[40] A relatively decentralized Ottoman imperial and Jewish religious system, moreover, cultivated locally autonomous congregations. Among early Seattle Sephardim, arriving as they did from diverse Ottoman regions, these localizing tendencies led to the failure of unified worship and to the division, by 1915, of the Seattle community into three congregations based on customary local liturgical practices. Such divisions further distanced the congregants from the unified European ideal of the Union of Sephardic congregations and cultivated a measure of cultural autonomy through, for example, the reproduction of melodies remembered from diverse historical points of departure (Tekirdağ, Marmara, and Rhodes).[41] Members of a congregation or prior informal hazzanim from the city

---

38 Solomon Maimon, personal interview, 2001. "Doing everything" meant such activities as including serving as rabbi, hazzan, Talmud Torah teacher, visitor to the sick and dying, community mediator, and ritual slaughterer.

39 For example, Samuel Benaroya worked as the congregation's bookkeeper to make ends meet (Benaroya, interview with Eric Offenbacher, 1985). Retired hazzan Isaac Azose worked full time for Boeing while serving Ezra Bessaroth (www.ezrabessaroth.com). By "semi-professional," I mean lack of professional credentialing, not lack of ability or status through expertise or experience.

40 On Ottoman Jewish intellectual exchange, see Julia Phillips Cohen and Sarah Abrevaya Stein, "Sephardic Scholarly Worlds: Toward a Novel Geography of Modern Jewish History," *The Jewish Quarterly Review* 100, no. 3 (2010): 349–84. On alternative reform trends among Ottoman rabbinical scholars, see Norman A. Stillman, *Sephardi Religious Responses to Modernity* (Luxembourg: Harwood Academic Publishers, 1995).

41 As Rosa Berro (b. 1899, Rhodes), a community member, notes, even a single Rhodes congregation in Seattle represented a reduction of diversity: "Take Rhodes, for example, we

of origin consistently instructed newly hired "outsider" hazzanim in the distinctive melodies of their congregation. David Behar, for instance, born and educated in Beirut, learned the specific Rhodes tunes of the Ezra Bessaroth congregation from Haim DeLeon, an early immigrant from Rhodes to Seattle,[42] while Morris Scharhon (arrived from Rhodes, 1907) learned the respective melodies of the now disbanded Marmara congregation (Ahavath Achim), and later by the Tekirdağ congregation where he served as hazzan.[43] Beginning in the 1960s, Hazzan Azose, who grew up in one synagogue (Sephardic Bikur Holim) and served as hazzan for approximately thirty-four years in another (Ezra Bessaroth), acquired the tunes and practices of his new congregation, enabling him to produce a CD of liturgical music containing melodic variants.[44]

Such lack of institutional and liturgical unity among the relatively new Ottoman Jewish immigrants was the major difference highlighted by the Spanish-Portuguese leadership in New York as negatively distinguishing the new immigrants from their own community and motivating the leadership to unite the diverse Sephardi population nationwide through shared religious texts.[45] In the words of de Sola Pool, the rabbi of Shearith Israel from 1907–1956:

> The Sephardi newcomers at the beginning of the twentieth century . . . organized themselves at first into demographic religious, burial, and benevolent associations made up of those who had come from a particular town such as Salonica or Janina in Greece; Constantinople, Adrianople (Edirne), Rodosto (Tekirdag), Gallipoli, or Monastir in Turkey; or Aleppo in Asia Minor. Time, of course, blurs and rapidly erases such initial Landsmannschaft lines of demarcation.[46]

---

are all one community in . . . [Seattle], but there are many synagogues on Rhodes. That doesn't mean anything, just because we are Sephardic we have to be all in one synagogue. I don't believe in that" (Rosa Berro, interview with Fannie Roberts, 1974). For a study of the relationship of Salonikan Jewish immigrants to their city of origin, see Devin E. Naar, "From The 'Jerusalem of the Balkans' to the *Goldene Medina*: Jewish Immigration from Salonika to the United States," *American Jewish History* 93, no. 4 (2007): 435–73.

42 Elazar Behar, interview with Howard Droker, 1982.

43 Sephardic Bikur Holim 70th Anniversary History, 1984.

44 Isaac Azose, *The Liturgy of Ezra Bessaroth*. Bellevue, WA, 1999 (2 CD set).

45 Eastern Mediterranean Jewry also made efforts at institutional unification of their relatively small numbers. See, for example, the enlargement of the Salonika Brotherhood of America, established in 1915, into the Sephardic Brotherhood of America in 1922. Naar, "From the 'Jerusalem of the Balkans,'" 468–69.

46 de Sola Pool, *An Old Faith*, 439.

Such a perspective reflects the discourse in de Sola Pool's history of Shearith Israel—a mix of socio-religious values related to Northern European administrative centralization, the privileging of an ancient European homeland in Spain, and the American ideal of "e pluribus unum" projected onto a diverse Jewish immigrant community, with the aim of increasing strength in numbers among a small Jewish sub-minority.[47] Elsewhere, de Sola Pool questioned the "Sephardi-ness" of Turkish and Balkan immigrants, asserting that the appellation, "Sephardi" was a "most objectionable term" for them, and requesting that they change the names of their social service agencies from "Sephardic" to "Oriental."[48] In a similar vein, a report commissioned by the New York Jewish Federation in the 1920s frames the differences between Jewish immigrants from the Middle East/North Africa and established American Jewry in terms of racial segregation in the United States at the time:

> These facts will provoke some curiosity. In New York City's population of some 1,500,000 Jews, there are 40,000 souls who are almost as alien to their kinsmen as are the Negroes to the average white Southerner. These 40,000 Jews are set apart from New York Jewry by religious, linguistic and psychological differences that vitiate any attempts at mutual understanding.[49]

After World War II, the rabbi made efforts at reconciliation, geographically stretching the term to include the eastern Mediterranean, but maintaining a European civilizational perspective, as can be observed in his history's celebration of those Middle Eastern immigrant members who had graduated with a "Western outlook" from Alliance Israélite Universelle schools.[50] Even with a measure of elasticity, de Sola Pool's Sephardi ideal hinged on a cultural genealogy extending as far as

---

47   In fact, in the context of rising Ashkenazi membership, New York's Spanish-Portuguese community itself was motivated to consolidate a Sephardi religious rite. Ben Ur, *Sephardic Jews in America*, 85.

48   Joseph M. Papo, *Sephardim in Twentieth Century America: In Search of Unity* (San Jose: Pele Yoetz Books, 1987), 54.

49   Louis M. Hacker, "The Communal Life of the Sephardic Jews of New York City," *Jewish Social Service Quarterly* 3, no. 2 (1926): 26. This report was commissioned by the New York Jewish Federation and published by the Bureau of Jewish Social Research to study the social problems of immigrant Sephardim. The report goes on to distinguish these "Sephardim" from the Jewish majority through their language differences (speaking a polyglot assortment of Ladino, Greek, Turkish, and Arabic), social habits (neglecting the home in favor of the coffeehouse), and extreme provincialism (organizing religious and welfare institutions based on Ottoman hometown). For additional examples of attitudes toward Sephardi newcomers in New York in this period, see Naar, "From the 'Jerusalem of the Balkans'." 437n6.

50   de Sola Pool, *An Old Faith*, 489.

a Western European heartland (Northern Europe and Spain) but not as far as a Mediterranean world shared by Ottoman and Moroccan coreligionists historically viewed as authorities on liturgical matters. Like European-centered historical narratives, such a "Western" genealogy relied on a coherent notion of "Europe" emerging in the nineteenth century and generating a previously unarticulated "East-West" bifurcation.[51] In the push for Sephardi unity across the North American continent in the mid-twentieth century, this constructed ancestry had an impact on policy and publication decisions as immigrant communities, such as those in Seattle, came into an unequal institutional relationship with the more well-endowed and established congregation in New York.

Seattle, an Alternative Liturgical Hub

By the 1950s, when Samuel Benaroya came to Seattle, two synagogues (Seattle Bikur Holim and Congregation Ezra Bessaroth) representing immigrant families from Tekirdağ and Rhodes, respectively, served the Seattle Sephardi community, as the struggling Marmara congregation (Ahavath Achim) united for economic reasons with the "Turkish" (Tekirdağ) congregation. While Benaroya further elevated Ottoman art music styles in services, liturgical music and texts of the diverse Seattle community had developed relatively autonomously from Spanish-Portuguese Sephardim on the east coast through the use of regionally-specific melodies and Ottoman-era prayerbooks in the hands of first and second generation hazzanim through the 1930s and early 1940s.[52] It is true that when de Sola Pool and his colleagues moved to nationally standardize the textual dimension of liturgies, the Union of Sephardic Congregations published a Daily and Sabbath Book of Prayers aimed at establishing liturgical uniformity nationwide through dissemination to immigrant congregations across the United States.[53] De Sola Pool's history, however, erroneously claims that the prayer book became standard, with his pastoral tour of the Pacific coast and subsequent visits confirming a "unity of faith and tradition."[54] In fact, the Syrian, Lebanese, and

---

51 The relatively recent rhetorical construction is evidenced by its inapplicability to other historical periods, for example the Christian Byzantine empire (in the "East") and Arab Spain (in the "West"). For further discussion, see M.E. Yapp, "Europe in the Turkish Mirror," *Past & Present* 137, no. 1 (November 1992): 134–155.

52 Isaac Azose, Speech, Nov 2, 2014.

53 Papo, *Sephardim in Twentieth Century America*, 63.

54 de Sola Pool, *An Old Faith*, 444. Ben-Ur echoes this assumption: "The *Book of Prayers*, published by the Union for Sephardic Congregations, is today in its twelfth impression (1997) and remains one of the most enduring legacies of the merging of the two communities." Ben-Ur, *Sephardic Jews in America*, 103.

FIGURE 3.4. Hazzan Isaac Azose. Sephardic Studies Digital Collection, University of Washington. Courtesy of Isaac Azose.

Egyptian synagogues, located primarily in the vicinity of New York, declined to use the prayerbook, and even though Greek and Turkish immigrant congregations were generally persuaded to acquire it, their modified usage of the publication belies de Sola Pool's claims.[55] As the "book of choice" for the Seattle community and replacement for Ottoman prayerbooks in use, the *siddur* nonetheless required significant oral alteration by hazzanim and young men called to read specific passages, in order to adapt its order of prayers to local practice. As Isaac Azose recalls from his youth,

> The hazzanim that I heard in the synagogue, as I'm following along in the prayerbook, I'd notice, hey, he didn't say that. He left out these three words. I'd just lock it up here in my memory. . . . I noticed that it was on a consistent basis. He'd leave out two or three words, or didn't say this phrase or added a different phrase altogether. The hazzanim knew it all by heart.[56]

55 According to Isaac Azose, the Seattle synagogues acquired the de Sola Pool series of prayerbooks (Daily and Sabbath, the Festivals, Rosh Ashana, and Yom Kippur) in the late 1940s and early 1950s. Speech, Nov 2, 2014.

56 Azose, personal interview, 2002.

Such ongoing oral modification continued in Seattle, despite the national prayer-book's reported incorporation of Eastern Mediterranean practices, resulting in prayerbooks interleafed with locally produced and copied texts pasted between their pages.[57] Both synagogues also printed festival booklets based upon their own practices. Because of the significance of the textual differences in the siddur, the congregations made several unrequited appeals to the Union for the publication of a more usable prayerbook. Noting with alarm in the late 1970s and early 1980s that the younger generation of men were no longer making the necessary oral changes, Isaac Azose, then hazzan of Congregation Ezra Bessaroth, initiated a project in 1994 to compile a Daily and Sabbath siddur incorporating the "Turkish" and Rhodes customs not contained in de Sola Pool's publication.[58] After nearly a decade-long process of modifying one computerized Ashkenazi siddur based on personal and collective memory, in March 2002 the *Siddur Zehut Yosef* of the Seattle Sephardic Community replaced the de Sola Pool Daily and Sabbath prayerbook in both Sephardic Bikur Holim and Ezra Bessaroth synagogues.[59] Funded by the non-profit Sephardic Traditions Foundation set up by a member of the community and by a dedication to the same member's father, *Siddur Zehut Yosef* distinguishes between Rhodes and Turkish traditions throughout the text through editorial codes and contains Hebrew, English, and extensive Ladino sections.[60] Among the significant additions made which were not contained in the de Sola Pool edition is the inclusion of all Monday and Thursday Torah readings, the name list for use at the conclusion of the *amidah* (lit. "standing," the central prayer of the Jewish liturgy), collections of *pizmonim*, or hymns, portions of the service traditionally recited in Ladino, and instructions (in Ladino) for the selling of the *mitzvot* (the Sephardi custom of auctioning the honors of taking out the Sefer Torah during services).[61]

Alternate editions of the prayerbook published two years later extended its practical use locally, as well as to other congregations in the United States. In 2004, Azose produced an all-Hebrew version as a lighter-weight edition for congregants not needing the English translation. In the same year, a synagogue in Rockville, Maryland (Magen

---

57   These incorporations have led to assumptions about the utility and success of the prayer-book in eastern Mediterranean Sephardi communities.

58   Azose, personal interview, 2002.

59   Azose, personal interview, 2002.

60   Editorial codes in the siddur are {R} and [T] for Rhodes and Turkish practices, respectively.

61   Other variations include ritual instructions and changes in vowels, phrases, and specific verses.

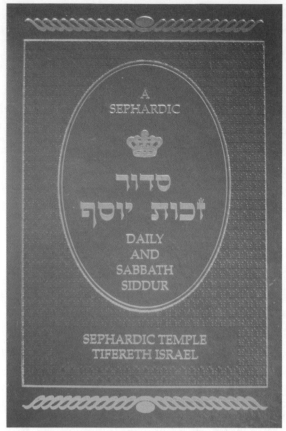

FIGURE 3.5. *Siddur Zehut Yosef: A Sephardic Daily and Sabbath Siddur* edited by Isaac Azose. Seattle, Washington: Sephardic Traditions Foundation, 2002. Courtesy of Isaac Azose.

David Sephardic Congregation) with members of Iraqi, Syrian, and Moroccan descent ordered a shipment of prayerbooks with an English rather than Ladino translation of Pirke Avot ("Sayings of the Fathers"), a request that led to yet another alternate edition and the beginnings of wider sales and dissemination of a siddur originally characterized in purely local terms as "precisely [adhering] to the unique Turkish and Rhodesli *minhagim* as historically practiced in Seattle Washington."[62] In the following years, the prayerbook, which went into a second edition in 2012, filled liturgical needs of congregations in other states such as California, Georgia, Indiana, Oregon, and Maryland that collectively include Ladino-speaking Sephardim as well as Moroccan, diverse North African, Levantine, Iranian, Iraqi, and Yemeni members.[63]

---

62   Isaac Azose, *Siddur Zehut Yosef* (Seattle: Sephardic Traditions Foundation, 2002).

63   Isaac Azose, personal communication, 2014; Emily K. Alhadeff, "Closing the Circle: Seattle's Sephardic Liturgy is Complete," *Jewish Transcript News*, November 14, 2014.

These congregations often represent complex layers of successive Jewish immigration, particularly after WWII and the establishment of the State of Israel, representing the increasing diversity of "American-Sephardim" and the eclipse of eastern Mediterranean Jews by Jewish immigrants from the Middle East and West Asia.[64] Based on their mixed memberships, these congregations have been less well-positioned than Seattle's to produce prayer texts of a coherent liturgical practice. In this context, through its relative communal autonomy in the Pacific Northwest, Seattle's new religious press does not simply represent an provincial particularity, but rather has benefited even newer immigrants better served by specific eastern Mediterranean practices than a unifying Spanish-Portuguese ethic.[65] In the ensuing years, Isaac Azose edited and published additional prayerbooks for the festivals, fast days, and High Holy Days— *Zichron Rahel* (for the festivals of Sukkot, Passover, and Shavuot), *Mahzor Tefilah LeDavid* (for Rosh Ashana), *Siddur Tefilah LeMoshe* (for the five fast days), and *Kol Yaakov Mahzor* (for Yom Kippur)—with distribution expanding to congregations abroad in Cape Town, South Africa and Rhodes, Greece.[66]

Although New York's Spanish-Portuguese congregation and Union of Sephardic Congregations initially projected superior economic resources, American-assimilated institutions, and self-ascribed national religious authority, they were unsuccessful in nationalizing a Sephardi liturgical ancestry that conceptually ended at the borders of Western Europe. To the Seattle community's advantage, mid-century historical events served to raise the value of their easterly cultural legacies, especially in the area of music. Viewing the melodic within a flexible and changing aesthetic zone—but prayer texts as stable and legally binding—de Sola Pool refrained from judging the musical practices of non-European communities: "Oriental" melodies, after all, were associated with so-called ancient Spanish melodies, and their culture-carriers from Southeastern Europe and the Near East required preservation after communities of origin like Salonika and Rhodes had been destroyed in the Holocaust. Through the networking role of de Sola Pool, the employment Samuel Benaroya—an Ottoman-born virtuoso of Hebrew art music—further elevated the Ottoman legacies already in play through informal chains of lay hazzanim since the

64   Ben-Ur, *Sephardic Jews in America*, 6. The membership of Magen David Sephardic Congregation, for example, was originally from Turkey and Greece with a shift to Moroccan, North African, and Middle Eastern membership after 1940.

65   Ben-Ur refers to the first two prayerbooks of the Seattle community, but because of sustained oral transmission and the wider relevance of the recently published prayerbooks, their representation exclusively as a reassertion of distinctive liturgies is erroneous. Ben-Ur, *Sephardic Jews in America*, 104.

66   Alhadeff, "Closing the Circle."

FIGURE 3.6. Siddurim and Mahzorim compiled and edited by Isaac Azose (Seattle, Washington: Sephardic Traditions Foundation). Courtesy of Isaac Azose.

early twentieth century. The post-war environment thus ameliorated to a certain degree tensions that had existed between the unifying objectives of New York City institutions and the troublesome "Landsmannschaft lines of demarcation" among twentieth century immigrants from the Middle East.

It would be half a century later when the textual dimension of local musical liturgies would find a more fitting prayerbook than the de Sola Pool siddur with the publication of *Siddur Zehut Yosef* in 2002, and by 2014, four more prayerbooks completed the liturgical cycle. According to Azose, "the exact opposite" happened from what de Sola Pool and the Union of Sephardic Congregations expected at its establishment: in place of the homogenization of diverse liturgical practices from the Mediterranean region, historical local diversity is flourishing in the United States.[67] Whereas de Sola Pool's Sephardi-American history, as well as certain recent scholarship, has over-emphasized an evolving, coherent Sephardim in the United States—however textured by new and old immigrants—Seattle's prayerbook publications reflect the ongoing cultivation of a regionally specific Ottoman heritage on American soil, pointing to relations with the Union that arguably resemble in some respects their historical "outsider" relationship to majority Ashkenazi institutions and identities in the United States. Textual developments over the past decade in Seattle testify to the significance of persisting local oral practices, often assumed to be tenuous in a literate society—practices that have combined individual initiative with relatively new institutional resources to produce local texts of increasing relevance beyond local contexts. Unique to Turkish and Rhodes congregations and intended exclusively

---

67   Isaac Azose, personal communication, 2005.

for use in Seattle, the publications unexpectedly met the demands of other Middle Eastern and North African congregations in the United States, as well as abroad, all together representing the increasingly diversified mix of Jewish immigrant communities across the twentieth and twenty-first centuries. Documented, published, and distributed since 2002, oral liturgical practices have expanded beyond the local, positioning Seattle as a siddur supplier for a wide swath of linguistically and regionally diverse, but culturally simpatico, congregations, effectively braiding themselves into an eastern Mediterranean line of descent, reinforcing Seattle as an emergent religious press and Sephardi cultural center in the Pacific Northwest.

Bibliography

Alhadeff, Emily K. "Closing the Circle: Seattle's Sephardic Liturgy is Complete." *Jewish Transcript News*, November 14, 2014.

Azose, Isaac. *Siddur Zehut Yosef.* Seattle: Sephardic Traditions Foundation, 2002.

———— *The Liturgy of Ezra Bessaroth*. Bellevue, WA, 1999 (2 CD set).

Ben-Ur, Aviva. *Sephardic Jews in America: a Diasporic History*. New York: New York University Press, 2009.

Bodian, Miriam. "Amsterdam, Venice, and the Marrano Diaspora in the 17th century." In *Dutch Jewish History*, edited by Jozeph Michman, 47–65. Jerusalem: Institute for Research on Dutch Jewry-Hebrew University, 1989.

Eisenstein, Judith K. "Medieval Elements in the Liturgical Music of the Jews of Southern France and Northern Spain," *Musica Judaica* XIV (1999), 15.

Hacker, Louis M. "The Communal Life of the Sephardic Jews of New York City." *Jewish Social Service Quarterly* 3, no. 2 (1926): 26.

Israel, Shearith. *Music of the Congregation Shearith Israel: Songs of the Sabbath*. New York, NY. Cassette of master tape-recorded in 1963.

———— *Music of the Congregation Shearith Israel: The High Holy Days and the Festivals*. New York, NY. Cassette of master tape-recorded in 1963.

Jackson, Maureen. *Mixing Musics: Turkish Jewry and the Urban Landscape of a Sacred Song*. Stanford: Stanford University Press, 2013.

———— "Reaching Beyond the Local: The Itineraries of an Ottoman-Sephardic-American Minhag." *Contemporary Jewry* 35, no. 1 (2015): 89–105.

Lehmann, Matthias B. "Introduction: Sephardi Identities." *Jewish Social Studies: History, Culture, Society* 15, no. 1 (2008): 1–9.

Naar, Devin E. "From the 'Jerusalem of the Balkans' to the *Goldene Medina*: Jewish Immigration from Salonika to the United States." *American Jewish History* 93, no. 4 (2007): 435–73.

Papo, Joseph M. *Sephardim in Twentieth Century America: In Search of Unity*. San Jose: Pele Yoetz Books, 1987.

Phillips Cohen, Julia and Abrevaya Stein, Sarah. "Sephardic Scholarly Worlds: Toward a Novel Geography of Modern Jewish History." *The Jewish Quarterly Review* 100, no. 3 (2010): 349–84.

Pool, David de Sola. *An Old Faith in a New World: Portrait of Shearith Israel 1654–1945*. New York: Columbia University Press, 1955.

Seroussi, Edwin. *Spanish-Portuguese Synagogue Music in the 19th Century Reform Sources from Hamburg: Ancient Tradition in the Dawn of Modernity*. Jerusalem: Magnes Press-Hebrew University, 1996.

———— "Introduction." In *Maftirim*, edited by Karen Gerson Şarhon, 43–77. Istanbul: Gözlem, 2009.

Shire Yisrael be-Erets ha-Kedem. Istanbul: Benjamin Raphael B. Joseph, c. 1921.

Slobin, Mark. *Chosen Voices: The Story of the American Cantorate*. Urbana & Chicago: University of Illinois Press, 1989.

Stillman, Norman A. *Sephardi Religious Responses to Modernity*. Luxembourg: Harwood Academic Publishers, 1995.

Tietze, Andreas and Yahalom, Joseph. *Ottoman Melodies Hebrew Hymns: A 16th Century Cross-Cultural Adventure*. Budapest: Akademiai Klado, 1995.

Turisky, Yoss, director. *The Story of Two Synagogues*. VHS. Tel Aviv: Museum of the Jewish Diaspora/ Beth Hatefutsoth, 1992.

Yapp, M.E. "Europe in the Turkish Mirror." *Past & Present* 137, no. 1 (November 1992): 134–155.

Zerubavel, Eviatar. *Anncestors and Relatives: Genealogy, Identity, and Community*. Oxford: Oxford University Press, 2012.

CHAPTER FOUR

Walking Through a Library:
Notes on the Ladino Novel and Some Other Books

LAURENT MIGNON

Who would have thought that the author of one of the most popular songs of the Paris Commune[1] would have appeared on the bookshelves of Ladino-reading households in Ottoman Turkey and the Balkans? A novel by Alexis Bouvier (1836–1892), whose lyrics for "La canaille" (The Rabble, 1865) were instrumental in turning this rousing anthem into a revolutionary favourite, is among the books in the Elazar Behar collection held at the Sephardic Studies Collection in the University of Washington, Seattle.[2] Entitled *La mujer del muerto* (The Wife of the Dead Man, 1912) and translated into Ladino by Isaac Gabay (d. 1931), who was none other than the chief-editor of the *El Telegrafo* daily, this book was the first volume of Bouvier's cycle of adventure novels, *La grande Iza*. Published originally in French in 1878 with the title "La femme du mort," the novel was not meant to provide moral guidance to aspirational young women. The heroine of the novel, Iza, was described by one of the characters, as "not born to be a virgin or a martyr"[3] in the French edition, though readers of the Ladino version would search in vain for this passage. [4] As far as he could, Gabay chose to edit out and rewrite parts of the novel, which he considered too outrageous for his audience. He was not behaving in an exceptional way within the Ladino literary field, or, indeed, within the broader

---

1   The Paris Commune was a revolutionary socialist government, which ruled the French capital from 18 March 1871 to 28 May 1871 in the aftermath of the French defeat in the Franco-Prussian war, which led to the collapse of the Second French Empire and the establishment of the Third Republic.
2   All collections referenced in this article are located in the Sephardic Studies Collection, University of Washington, Seattle, unless otherwise specified.
3   Alexis Bouvier, *La femme du mort* (Paris: Jules Rouff Editeurs, 1879), 42.
4   Alexis Bouvier, *La Mujer del muerto*, trans. Isaac Gabay (Istanbul: Benyamin ben Yosef, 5672 [1912]), 31.

Ottoman literary field. Most translators adapted the texts, which they translated in accordance with their ideological leanings and the expectations of their readers. Olga Borovaya notes in *Modern Ladino Culture: Press, Belles Lettres, and Theatre in the Late Ottoman Empire,* her ground-breaking study of the development of Judeo-Spanish print culture, that Ladino novels, whether translations, adaptations, or original works, are best described as "rewritings," because they rely to various degrees on foreign, mostly French, fiction.[5]

Bouvier was not mentioned on the book cover, though Isaac Gabay was credited with having translated the novel from French. In an introductory note, the editor of *La mujer del muerto* promised an entertaining read. He maintained "that *The Wife of the Dead Man* would please even more than *The Veiled Lady.*"[6] This was a reference to the French popular novelist Emile Richebourg's (1833–1898) *La dame voilée* (1875), which had also been translated by Gabay under the title *La ermoza istorya de la dama del velo* (The Beautiful Story of the Veiled Lady), published in 1906. Significantly, the editor emphasized the importance of the work, not the author of the novel, who remained unmentioned. He noted that "before presenting the author, we present you the translation of his admirable work,"[7] observing that readers would have had the satisfaction of encountering an "unknown author."[8] This is unusual, as the international popularity—being translated into many languages—of an author and his work was a selection criteria for editors of literature in Ladino and a significant selling point.[9]

Whether Bouvier really was an "unknown author" is questionable, as he had been translated into a variety of European languages, even if it was less than other Western European authors translated into Ladino. Nevertheless, Bouvier was one of the masters of the French popular novel and a prolific playwright. He was, in the words of one of his obituarists, "a writer of the people, by the choices of his subject and the nature of his talent."[10] He reached a certain level of popularity in the Ottoman world, having been translated, not only into Ladino but also into Ottoman Turkish. Bouvier's *Le mariage d'un forçat* (The Marriage of a Convict, 1873, reedited 1888), was translated by no other than Ali Kemal (1867–1922), one of the most notorious figures of the Ottoman Turkish publishing world, in 1888

5   Olga Borovaya, *Modern Ladino Culture: Press, Belles Lettres, and Theatre in the Late Otto-man Empire* (Bloomington and Indianapolis: Indiana University Press, 2012), 140–141.

6   Anon, "Nota del Editor," in Alexis Bouvier, *La Mujer del muerto*, 2.

7   Ibid.

8   Ibid.

9   Borovaya, *Modern Ladino Culture,* 148.

10   Frédéric Lollié, "Alexis Bouvier," *La nouvelle revue* 76 (May-June 1895): 845.

under the title *Bir Mahkûmun İzdivacı yahut Istakad Köprüsü Cinayeti* (A Convict's Marriage or The Boom Bridge Crime).[11] The following year *L'armée du crime* (The Army of Crime, 1886) was translated under the title *Caniler* (The Criminals) by a B. Hasan. In addition to the Ottoman Turkish translations, it should be noted that several Bouvier novels, including *La femme du mort*, were also translated into Castilian Spanish, another indication that the French novelist might not have been an "autor diskonosido" after all in the Ladino-speaking world.

The French popular novel was the most translated genre among the many literary traditions of the Ottoman world.[12] Focusing on the Ladino case, Borovaya notes that most Ladino novels can roughly be categorised as either love stories or adventure stories.[13] Gabay's rewriting of Bouvier's novel certainly fitted the bill, as it combined both aspects in an unusually long page-turner for Ladino standards. The book had no less than 367 pages, whereas most *romansos*, as they were called, rarely went beyond 150 pages.[14] One of the selling points of the novel must have been the character of Iza. While she was not a model of moral rectitude, she was a powerful heroine who was unveiled to a Ladino readership who were not used to encountering proactive women figures in traditional or religious literature.[15] This was certainly attractive for the rising number of literate women, while Iza's many charms, as depicted in a famous 1882 painting by the Croatian artist Vlaho Bukovac (1855–1922), were not displeasing for a male readership either.

Perhaps there was another dimension that rendered Bouvier's work attractive. Just like Ahmet Midhat Efendi (1844–1912), the most prolific Ottoman Turkish author of his age, and Eliya Karmona (1869–1935), himself a productive novelist, Alexis Bouvier had come from a modest social background before becoming an immensely successful author. Ahmet Midhat and Karmona were self-made men who had entered the world of labour during their teenage years in order to make ends meet and did not belong to the educated ruling elite. As for Bouvier, his obituarist in the *Nouvelle revue* described him as an *"enfant du people"*—"a child of

---

11 For a discussion of the authorship of the translation, see Faruk Gezgin, "Ali Kemal ve Romanları," in *Türk Dünyasından Halil Açıkgöz'e Armağan*, ed. Hayri Ateş (Istanbul: Doğu Kitabevi, 2013), 243. In this article, as in most publications on Ali Kemal and bibliographies of works in Ottoman Turkish, Bouvier's name spelled in Ottoman Turkish is misread as Pouillet.

12 Johann Strauss, "Who Read What in the Ottoman Empire (19th-20th Century)," *Middle Eastern Literatures* 6, no. 1 (2003): 39–76.

13 Borovaya, *Modern Ladino Culture*, 150.

14 Ibid., 140.

15 Ibid., 151.

the people"—who took pride in his working-class background.[16] Knowingly, in his writings, Bouvier used realist fiction to denounce poverty, which was "synonymous with hunger, with cold, with untidiness, with bitter and merciless humiliations."[17]

This engagement on the side of the poorest might have attracted those among Bouvier's Sephardi readers who took the teachings of Rabbi Elijah Ha-Cohen's (d. 1729) *Shevet Musar* (1712) to heart. In this continuously re-edited popular treaty on ethics,[18] translated into Ladino in 1748 by Abraham Asa (1710–1768), of which an 1860 edition can be seen in the Richard Adatto collection, the writer invites his fellow Jews to show empathy with the poor within their community: "Know that the acts of the poor man seem wrong and reprehensible, but they are just nevertheless; the rich man does not understand the grievance of the poor, for he has not experienced it."[19] While the rabbi's call for magnanimity would probably not have extended to Bouvier's Romani heroine, as her many crimes were too many and their nature too disturbing, there is no doubt that the novelist's engagement for the poor and the destitute, just like the rabbi's concern, hit a chord within a community that had been badly affected by the severe economic depression of the early nineteenth century. In the early twentieth century, despite major transformations, poverty continued to remain an issue. In his short monograph, *Die Juden der Türkei* (The Jews of Turkey), the publicist and Zionist militant Davis Trietsch (1870–1935) wrote, quoting from a report by the *Hilfsverein der deutschen Juden* (Aid Association of German Jews), a humanitarian association promoting better living conditions for Jews in Eastern Europe and Asia, that

> . . . there are about 200.000 Jews who live in today's European Turkey. The great majority of them in quite deprived conditions, even more deprived than the Jews of Eastern Europe. The poor neighbourhoods which we have seen . . ., the accommodation of hundreds of poor people which we have entered, left us with an indescribable impression of poverty.[20]

While Trietsch was worried about poverty among Ottoman Sephardim, as were other Western Europeans writing on the living conditions of Jews in Ottoman

---

16   Lollié, "Alexis Bouvier," 843.

17   Ibid., 845.

18   Matthias B. Lehmann, *Ladino Rabbinic Literature and Ottoman Sephardic Culture* (Bloomington and Indianapolis: Indiana University Press, 2005), 6.

19   Lehmann, *Ladino Rabbinic Literature and Ottoman Sephardic Culture*, 110.

20   Davis Trietsch, *Die Juden der Türkei* (Leipzig: Veit Verlag, 1915), 16.

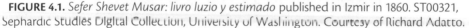

FIGURE 4.1. *Sefer Shevet Musar: livro luzio y estimado* published in Izmir in 1860. ST00321, Sephardic Studies Digital Collection, University of Washington. Courtesy of Richard Adatto.

Turkey, he also showed particular interest in the emergence of a Jewish working class in the Eastern provinces of the Ottoman Empire in his short monograph:

> Already today the Jews do not play an unimportant role in the still little-developed industry of Turkey. In Turkish cigarette factories, Jewish workers are often in the majority. The situation is similar in the blooming Damascene arts and crafts industry. And there are large workshops in Damascus whose Christian entrepreneurs employ exclusively Jewish male and female workers.[21]

However, would impoverished workers have been able to read Bouvier and other novelists? Ladino literacy remains a contentious issue, as there are no statistics pertaining to Ladino literacy rates, even though some scholars, such as Sarah Abrevaya Stein, have stated that Ladino literacy rates were "extraordinarily high".[22] Less enthusiastic

---

21   Ibid., 14.

22   Sarah Abrevaya Stein, *Making Jews Modern: The Yiddish and Ladino Press in the Russian and Ottoman Empires* (Bloomington: Indiana University Press, 2003), 4.

than Stein, Olga Borovaya notes that, while there is no denying that foreign language literacy among men and women had been rising between the 1870s and 1890s in the wake of the establishment of the Alliance Israélite Universelle (AIU) schools in the Empire and that, as a consequence, Ladino literacy must have increased in conjunction, the reading and writing of Ladino was neither being taught in the new schools nor encouraged by the Westernised elites. Moreover, as many elderly illiterate people, especially women, had not been educated in the new schools and were still alive at the turn of the century, literacy rates could not have been very high.[23]

In any case, it seems that the journalistic enterprise, and publishing in general, remained far from being commercially viable ventures. Increased literacy did not necessarily lead to increased sales of print publications, as can be gathered from the following anecdote published in the satirical magazine *El Djugueton* (The Joker) on 26 December 1911:

> **How the Jewish paper is sold:**
> The Turkish paper is sold shouting. The Greek one running. The French one by asking for it and the Armenian one by looking for it. As for the Jewish one: "Can you lend it to me for reading?" When someone buys a newspaper, he has to lend it to his elder brother and his younger brother, to his elder brother's brother-in-law and to the neighbour of his younger brother, to the neighbour next door and the neighbour from across the street, to his daughter's in-laws and to his sister's brother-in-law. And once everyone has lent it to their parents, the newspaper returns to its owner, who after removing the greasiness, adds it to his collection.[24]

The above phenomenon could be partly explained by the fact that people on a tight budget could not afford to buy newspapers and books on a regular basis. Moreover, the important social institution of the *meldado*, the gathering of people in the evening in order to read and have books read to them in a communal setting, survived well into the first quarter of the twentieth century.[25] While originally the aims of those gatherings was to diffuse and discuss religious literature, they prepared the audiences, as shown by Matthias Lehman in his pioneering *Ladino Rabbinic Literature and Sephardic Culture*,[26] for the engagement with secular literature in

---

23 Borovaya, *Modern Ladino Culture*, 52.

24 Anon., "Komo se vende la gazeta Djudia," in *Lo ke Meldavan Nuestros Padres*, ed. Rıfat Birmizrahi (Istanbul: Gözlem Kitap, 2006), 253.

25 Borovaya, *Modern Ladino Culture*, 48.

26 Lehmann, *Ladino Rabbinic Literature and Ottoman Sephardic Culture*, 202–207.

a similar setting in the second half of the nineteenth century.[27] The reception of literature in such a context was not a Sephardic exclusivity. In a striking passage of his still unsurpassed *Ondokuzuncu Asır Türk Edebiyatı Tarihi* (History of Turkish Literature of the Nineteenth Century, 1956, expanded second edition), Ahmet Hamdi Tanpınar (1901–1962), the novelist, poet, and literary scholar, relates how families would gather around the reader in order to listen to the latest instalment of Ahmet Midhat Efendi novels. The Ottoman Turkish novelist, just like Eliya Karmona and other Ladino novelists, would have been conscious of the fact that their books were read aloud, and in many ways performed, and embraced a style that kept the listeners' attention continuously, taking them by the hand through the many exploits of their heroes and, indeed, heroines. Karmona described it as a language that "even children and old women could read".[28] Unsurprisingly, the *meldado* was also the context in which new plays—theatre being another new genre emerging in the second half of the nineteenth century—could be read. In an editorial note for the Ladino translation of Molière's *Le médecin volant* (translated anonymously as *El Mediko Djugueton* [The Playful Doctor], 1863), the publisher hoped that "families would perform them in their own homes and have a good time."[29]

"Pasar el tyempo" is the expression used by the publisher, and there is no doubt that religious scholars would have raised eyebrows. At the onset of printed vernacular literature in Ladino, rabbis wanted to make sure that people were able to study in a language which they understood and did not spend their free time with trivialities. In his introduction to the *Meam Loez* (From a People with a Strange Language), the popular Ladino commentary of the Tanakh, Rabbi Yaakov Kuli (d. 1732) explained that he had undertaken his enterprise of translating the Gemara and the Midrash to edify his readers who would otherwise be unable to understand the Hebrew and Aramaic texts of the sacred scriptures and commentaries. Furthermore, he claimed that he wished to entertain them during long winter nights and dark winter mornings which would otherwise be "wasted in trivial matters of daily life."[30] Yet Kuli's hopes seem not to have been fulfilled, since rabbis in the nineteenth century would complain that people did not read the *Meam Loez* in their free time, but opted for

---

27　Ahmet Hamdi Tanpınar, *Ondokuzuncu Asır Türk Edebiyatı Tarihi* (Istanbul: Çağlayan Kitabevi, 1997), 459.

28　Eliya Karmona, *Komo Nasyo Eliya Karmona* in *Lo Ke Meldavan Nuestros Padres*, 508.

29　Quoted by Elena Romero, *El teatro del Sefardíes orientales*, Vol.1 (Madrid: Instituto Arias Montano, 1979), 339. See also Borovaya, *Modern Ladino Culture*, 98, 99.

30　Quoted in Alisa Meyuḥ Ginio, *Between Sepharad and Jerusalem: History, Identity and Memory of the Sephardim* (Leiden: Brill, 2014),101.

secular literature, the latter being mostly novels.[31] The Ladino press, as well as the rise of the *romanso*, were a serious challenge to the authority of the Rabbinate, as they often promoted Westernisation and a secularised worldview.

Yet there had been attempts before that to introduce Western secular literature to a Sepharad readership in the Ottoman Empire. In 1778, the Livornese merchant David Attias published *Guerta di Oro* (The Golden Garden), which he intended as a guide to secular knowledge, including information about European languages such as Italian and Greek and literature, because in a changing world "not everyone is inclined to [study] the Torah, and to always hear the same thing."[32] While the impact of Attias' book in the development of secular Ladino literature was negligible,[33] it was indicative of the struggle to come. In the second half of the nineteenth century, the new literary genres—the novel and theatre—beside the Ladino press, in which *romansos* were often serialized, promoted secular knowledge and Westernization, openly challenging the religious authorities' moral monopoly on ethics and lifestyle in a development echoed among all ethno-religious communities from Ottoman lands. The books in the collections here assembled bring together the two sides of the conflict. This proves how, for most book owners, reading Rafael Hiya Pontrémoli's *Meam Loez* commentary on the book of Esther, published in Izmir in 1864, was by no means an obstacle to also reading a "*romanso dramatiko i de amor*" such as Sami Namer's *El mansevo sin kulpa* (The Blameless Young Man), published in Istanbul in 1923, both of which can be found in the Adatto collection.

The rabbis were not the only ones who nurtured concerns about the development of Ladino literature. Some within the Francophile secularist elites, too, spoke of the emerging new literature without hiding their disdain. In his milestone *Essai sur l'histoire des Israélites de l'Empire ottoman depuis les origines jusqu'à nos jours* (Essay on the History of the Israelites of the Ottoman Empire From the Origins to the Present Day, 1897), Moïse Franco (1864–1907) acknowledges the emergence of secular literature encompassing novel translations, drama, biographies, didactic scientific works and even works of philosophy.[34] While recognising that such works had been challenging the authority of the rabbis by giving ethical guidance and educating the

31   Lehmann, *Ladino Rabbinic Literature and Ottoman Sephardic Culture*, 67.

32   Quoted in Matthias B. Lehmann, "A Livornese `Port Jew` and the Sephardim of the Ottoman Empire," *Jewish Social Studies*, New Series 11, no. 2 (Winter, 2005): 52.

33   Olga Borovaya, *The Beginnings of Ladino Literature: Moses Almosnino and His Readers* (Bloomington: Indiana University Press, 2017), 238.

34   Moïse Franco, *Essai sur l'histoire des Israélites de l'Empire ottoman depuis les origines jusqu'à nos jours* (Paris: A. Durlacher, 1897), 269.

FIGURE 4.2. *El mansevo sin ḵulpah: romanso dramaṭiḵo i de amor* by Sami Namer, Istanbul, 1923. ST00501, Sephardic Studies Digital Collection, University of Washington. Courtesy of Richard Adatto.

public, he denied Ladino writers the right to call themselves authors: "Leaving aside the editors of Judeo-Spanish newspapers, the remaining authors are, for the most part young men, active in the field of commerce, who spend their leisure time composing or translating some book or other." Indeed, he stated that "the profession of author does not exist among the Israelites of Turkey."[35] This claim would not have come as a surprise to those who were familiar with Franco's active pursuit of the AIU's francocentric mission. Franco, who had attended the Ecole normale israélite orientale, a Paris-based teacher training college set up by the AIU, had denounced Ladino as a "barbaric jargon" which had deformed the "beautiful Castilian language".[36] The issue, however, was not simply a matter of language, but also of the nature of the Ladino novel, which catered to the tastes of a readership thirsting for adventure, love, and increasingly historical and crime novels. This was not high-brow literature. Indeed, in parallel with the transformation of the Ladino press, which initially addressed a

---

35   Ibid., 270.
36   Ibid., 39.

mainly elitist male readership but broadened its audience, the new genre of the novel aimed at a popular readership that also included women.[37] An interesting collateral development of the presence of women as the intended audience of Ladino literature and press was that religious authorities also had to start writing for women.[38]

The most prolific authors of the time reflected on the question of what to read. Alexandre Benghiat (1862–1924), whose "rewritings" are well represented in the collections, established a list of novels that needed to be translated into Ladino for the edification of readers for the Passover supplement of his newspaper *El Meseret* in 1914. This attempt to establish a modern canon of European literature is characterized by a fusion of the popular and the classical: Eugene Sue's (1804–1857) *Les mystères de Paris* (The Mysteries of Paris, 1843), eventually translated and published in Ladino in Salonica in 1922, coexists with Fénélon's (1651–1715) global bestseller *Les aventures de Télémaque* (The Adventures of Télémaque, 1699), which was never translated into Ladino. Strikingly, the list, which also included Victor Hugo (1802–1885), Alexandre Dumas (1802–1870), his son, also named Alexandre (1824–1895), and Daniel Defoe (1660–1731), was representative of what was being translated into every language and transliterated into every alphabet in the Ottoman Empire, a convincing example of the common literary culture among the peoples of the Empire in the age of Westernisation, as discussed by Johann Strauss.[39]

Like in the Ottoman Turkish case, the Ladino novel was conceived both as an instrument of modernization and reform and as the product of a modern society. By writing a *romanso*, authors would educate the readership about modern ways, while showing that they themselves were modern, as they actively promoted new literary genres.

When looking at the genesis of the *romanso*, it should not be forgotten that their serialization was part of a strategy implemented by newspapers wishing to broaden their readership and thus their circulation. As seen above, economic viability was a vital problem for the Ladino press from its inception onwards and a continuous source of complaint for newspaper owners. Eliya Karmona, the novelist and chief editor of the satirical *El Djugueton* (The Joker), describes his engagement with the genre as a way to solve his continuous money problems. In what seems to be a humorous response to the criticism addressed at Ladino literati regarding their amateurishness by the likes of Moïse Franco, Karmona reveals in his memoirs

---

37   Borovaya, *Modern Ladino Culture*, 144.

38   Lehmann, *Ladino Rabbinic Literature and Ottoman Sephardic Culture*, 68–69.

39   Strauss, "Who Read What in the Ottoman Empire (19th-20th Century)."

entitled *Komo Nasyo Eliya Karmona* (How Eliya Karmona Was Born, 1926) that it was his mother who proposed the job of the novelist to him and that she played a central role in the development of the Ladino novel: "I will tell you little stories and you will print them and sell each booklet 10 paras. You will be successful because you know typography and will be able to produce them cheaply,"[40] she told him.

After initial doubts, the novelist started writing down and publishing his mother's little stories or *konsejikas,* which apparently sold quite well. This unexpected success enabled him to set up his own small press, with the financial support of the AIU, within a larger printing workshop belonging to Alexandros Numismatidis. This was one of many instances in Karmona's life which shows, as argued by Marie Christine Varol, that professional solidarities transcended ethnoreligious boundaries.[41] Once his mother had run out of ideas, Karmona turned to the stage of the Armenian theatre director Mardiros Minakyan (1839–1920) for inspiration. Among the stories he claims to have written was *La ija de la lavandera* (The Daughter of a Washerwoman, 1922), to be seen in the collection of Richard Adatto. Of course, one needs to read Karmona's autobiographical text with a pinch of salt, as Karmona was known to have a complex relationship with the truth. Indeed, published on the occasion of the eighteenth anniversary of *El Djugueton, Komo Nasyo Eliya Karmona,* which can be found among the books of the Al Maimon collection, has troubled its scholarly readers again and again with respect to defining its genre, which is somewhere in between memoir and the picaresque novel. Nevertheless, while ridiculing his own contribution to Ladino literature and somewhat "disenchanting" the literary profession, he has drawn the portrait of a literary world where people from different ethnoreligious backgrounds were communicating and supporting each other. Minakyan, a towering figure in the development of the Ottoman Turkish theatre, and, if we are to believe Karmona, one of the progenitors, beside his mother, of the Ladino novel, shared one more characteristic which is not irrelevant when looking at the books collected here. As an actor, a director, and a translator, he promoted the works of William Shakespeare (1564–1616) in Ottoman Turkey. That the Ladino reading public and theatre goers were not insensitive to the art of the Bard is shown by the existence of a Ladino translation by the educator and translator Ben Zion Tarragan (1870–1953) of *A Comedy of Errors,* renamed *Los Buchukes* (The Twins), published in Jerusalem in 1909, in the Adatto collection. The play is described on the cover as "one of the most beautiful comedies of the famous sage Shakespeare."

---

40   Eliya Karmona, *Komo Nasyo Eliya Karmona,* 507.

41   Marie Christine Varol, "L'Empire ottoman à travers la biographie picaresque d'Eliya Karmona," *Cahiers balkaniques* 36–37 (2008), [http://journals.openedition.org/ceb/1576].

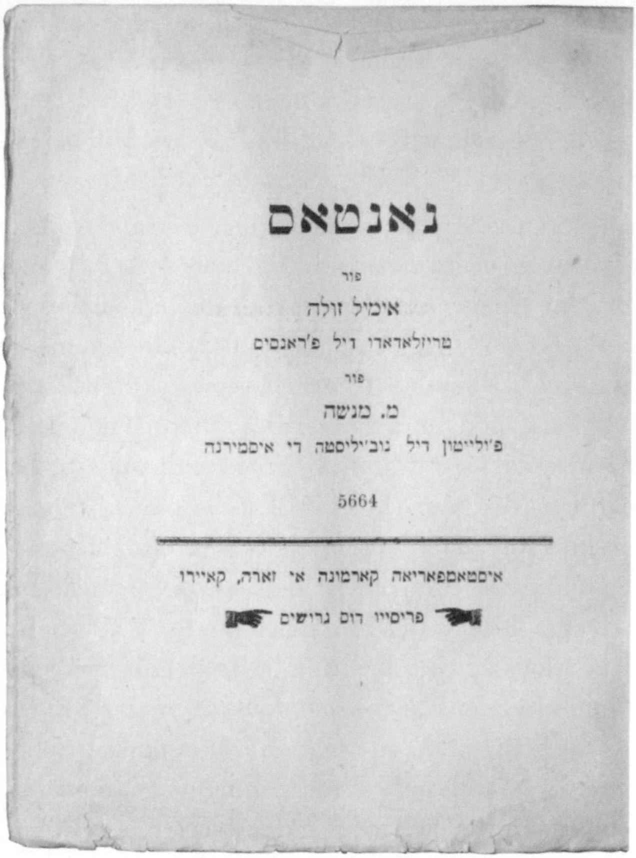

נאנטאם

פור

אימיל זולה

מריזלאדארו דיל פ'ראנסים

פור

מ. מנשה

פ'וליימון דיל נוב'יליסטה די איסמירנה

5664

איסטאמפאריאה קארמונה אי זארה, קאיירו

פריטיזו דוס גרושים

FIGURE 4.3. Emile Zola's novella *Nantas*, translated by M. Menashe, published in Cairo in 1904. ST00478, Sephardic Studies Digital Collection, University of Washington. Courtesy of Richard Adatto.

There is, however, a significant exception among the *romansos* collected here: a translation of Emile Zola's (1840–1902) novella *Nantas* by M. Menashe, published in Cairo in 1904. The text is a quasi-literal translation in a gallicized Ladino by a translator who was attempting to establish a literary language, in sharp contrast to earlier translations and rewritings, which aimed to bridge the gap between the needs of solitary readers and communal listeners of literature.[42] Zola might seem an odd name among the likes of Xavier de Montépin (1823–1902), Alexandre Dumas (1802–1870), and Alexis Bouvier, who are the masters of the popular novels represented in the collection. While *Nantas*'s plot, the rise of a young man from the province in the Parisian *société* and political world, overshadowed by unhappy

---

42 Olga Borovaya makes a detailed analysis of Menashe's translation and language in Borovaya, *Modern Ladino Culture*, 187–191.

love, would have appealed to the readers of the usual fare supplied by the likes of Karmona and Benghiat, Zola's approach to the novel might have been indigestible for many.

And yet the existence of an Emile Zola translation into Ladino is no surprise. The novelist was seen by many in the Sephardic community as a hero who upheld virtue and truth against the bigotry of his contemporaries. For the two generations of readers who emerged from the AIU schools, and who were led to believe that France was the promised land of freedom, equality, and fraternity, the Dreyfus affair, which revealed the depth of anti-Semitic sentiments within French institutions and society and divided the country between 1894 and 1906, came as a deep shock. Readers of the Ladino press knew that Captain Alfred Dreyfus (1859–1935) had been unjustly condemned "*al nombre del puevlo franses*" (in the name of the French people) as Jak Loria (1860–1948) would put it in his 1903 play *Dreyfus*.[43] This was by far not the only Ladino literary work that dealt with the affair. Beside several plays, a whole range of narratives, some original, some translated, explored the issue—they represented examples of a new genre gaining popularity in the Ladino literary world in the early twentieth century: the historical narrative with a Jewish theme. *Sinko anyos de mi vida* (Five Years of my Life), Dreyfus' memoirs, based on the diaries he kept in the penal colony of Cayenne, translated by Isaac Gabay and published in Istanbul in 1901, Shmuel Saadi Halevi [Sam Lévy]'s (1870–1959) *Istorya del Kapitan Alfred Dreyfus* (The Story of Captain Dreyfus), published in Belgrade in 1898, reprinted with Jean Florian as its author's name under the title *Dreyfus o el martiryo de la Isla del diavlo* (Dreyfus or the Martyr of Devil's Island) in Salonica in 1929, and Eliyahu Şem Tov Arditti's *Dreyfus o el romanso de un innosente* (Dreyfus or the Novel of an Innocent), published in Salonica in 1901 were some of those works published throughout the Ottoman Sephardic world and indicative of a need to engage with this traumatic experience. One *romanso* in particular, however, showed that some intellectuals were very conscious that antisemitism was not simply something that happened in Christian Europe. Constant accusations that Jews were "ingrates" and "not true patriots", as Aron de Yosef Hazan (1848–1931) put it in a piece for *La Buena Esperanza* (The Good Hope) in 1891, were a source of concern.[44] In *Millet-i İsrailiye* (The Israelite Nation, 1890), a short monograph

---

43 Jak Lorya, *Dreyfus: Drama en sinko aktos i un apoteos,* transcribed by Olga Borovaya, https://web.stanford.edu/dept/jewishstudies/programs/sephardi/borovaya_texts_files/dreyfus/Dreyfus.Transcription.pdf.

44 Quoted in Julia Phillips Cohen, *Becoming Ottomans: Sephardi Jews and Imperial Citizenship in the Modern Era* (Oxford and New York: Oxford University Press, 2014), 54.

whose general tone prepared the ground for his later anti-Semitic outbursts, Ebüzziya Tevfik (1849–1913), echoing European anti-Semitic propaganda,[45] declared the Jews "to be deserving of spite [*tahkir*] from a political point of view, even though they constituted a case worth pondering from a philosophical perspective."[46] Thus, it was not a surprise that the above-named Shmuel Saadi Halevi also published a work entitled *El Dreyfus Otomano* (The Ottoman Dreyfus) in Salonica in 1909. The novel dealt with the case of Yosef Karmona, a military physician who was unjustly accused of poisoning two soldiers and was expelled from the Ottoman army in 1886, before being rehabilitated 22 years later—a reminder of the universality of antisemitism. In the novel, Yosef Karmona affirms, just like Dreyfus, that his only crime is to be a Jew.[47]

Despite occasional incidents of an anti-Semitic nature, the great majority of Ottoman Turkish intellectuals seem to have been on the side of the *Dreyfusards* throughout the Dreyfus affair.[48] Babanzade İsmail Hakkı (1876–1913) and Ali Reşat (1877–1929), two young Ottoman intellectuals, published a 420 page long volume on the affair with the title *Dreyfüs Mes'elesi ve Esbâb-ı Hafiyesi* (The Dreyfus Affair and its Secret Causes, 1899), a staunch condemnation of antisemitism. Beside letters of thanks from Dreyfus and his lawyer Fernand Labori (1860–1917), it also included a letter by Emile Zola. The novelist was not an unknown figure in the Ottoman Turkish intellectual and literary world either, as debates on Zola's brand of naturalism had contributed to splitting it between opponents around Ahmet Midhat Efendi and his disciples, who condemned the French novelist's apparent focus on misery and depravity, and younger intellectuals such as Beşir Fuat (1852–1887) and Nabizade Nâzım (1862–1893), who espoused his ultra-realism and the worldview which underpinned it.

Antisemitism takes many forms. Christian missionary activities among Jews is arguably one of them. The evangelization of Jews essentially signifies a delegiti-

---

45 For a study of this essay, see Özgür Türesay, "Osmanlı İmparatorluğu'nda Antisemitizmin Avrupalı Kökenleri Üzerine Birkaç Not: Ebüzziya Tevfik ve *Millet-i İsrâiliye* (1888)," *Tarih ve Toplum: Yeni Yaklaşımlar* 6 (Spring 2007–Winter 2008): 97–105.

46 Ebüzziya , *Millet-i İsrailiye* (Istanbul: Matbaa-ı Ebüzziya, 1890), 3.

47 On the Dreyfus case in Ladino literature, see Eva Belén Rodríguez Ramírez, *El caso Dreyfus en la literatura sefardí: Edición y estudio de Cinco años de mi vida. Alfred Dreyfus (Constantinopla, 1901)* (PhD diss., University of Granada, 2006), 27–48 and Nitsa Dori, "The Dreyfus Affair and its Reflection in Ladino Literature," *International Journal in Emerging Trends in Social Sciences* 3, no. 2 (2018): 57–64.

48 Özgür Türesay, "L'affaire Dreyfus vue par les intellectuels ottomans," *Turcica: Revue d'études turques* 47 (2016): 250.

FIGURE 4.4. *El Dreyfus Otomano* by Shmuel Saadi Halevi, published in Salonica in 1909. ST00139, Sephardic Studies Digital Collection, University of Washington. Courtesy of Sephardic Bikur Holim.

mization of Judaism as a religion and an attempt to assimilate them. Reflections of such activities among the Ottoman Jews can also be found among the books of the collection. Noteworthy examples are the German missionary William Gottlieb Schauffler's (1798–1883) translation of the Psalms, *Tehilim o los Salmos trezlada-dos del leshon ha-kodesh en la lingua Sefaradit* (*Tehilim* or The Psalms Translated From the Holy Tongue into the Sephardic Language), published at G. Griffiths, a missionary press in Izmir, in 1852 and his Hebrew–Ladino dictionary titled *Otsar Divrei leshon ha-kodesh o Diksionaryo de la lingua santa kon la deklarasyon de kada vierbo in la lingua Sefaradit* (*Otsar Divrei Leshon ha-Kodesh* or Dictionary of the Holy Tongue With the Declaration of Each Word of the Bible in Sephardic Language), published in Istanbul in 1855. Striking is his reference in both cases to the "Sephardic language" to refer to Ladino.[49] However, his endeavour to convert the Jews of Ottoman Turkey was not met with overwhelming enthusiasm by the local Sephardim. Having settled in Ortaköy, at the time a small village on the European bank of the Bosphorus, he noted that "intercourse with the people was difficult and perilous to a high degree," not least because of the plague which was raging in the Ottoman capital in the early 1830s. Rather disheartened, he wrote in his posthumously published autobiography that, "My work among the Jews seemed to be hopeless. The Jews at Ortakeuy seemed to be most hardened in heart, and are so to this day. None came near me."[50] Nonetheless, Schauffler's attempts to develop a language to translate the sacred texts deserve mention. Looking at an earlier missionary translation of the Old Testament, he criticized it as a mistranslation, for having a corrupt style and for "Hebraizing more strongly" than necessary,[51] an indication that he faced challenges not unlike those of early novelists and newspapermen in search of a language that could seduce a broad readership.

However, at the turn of the century, that readership was growing thirsty for a new genre—that of the historical novel and historical narratives with a Jewish twist. This was the reflection of an increased national consciousness and the growth of Zionism in very unstable times. Jak Lorya's *La sangre de los matsos* (The Blood of the Matzot, 1910) is a case in point. From the Adatto collection, it is subtitled as a "Jewish national novel full of love and action." Other *romansos* too, such as the anonymously published *Los dos melisyos: Romanso de la vida Judya en Austrya* (The Two Twins: Novel of Jewish Life in Austria) from the same collection, are indicative of this new trend.[52] Isaac Gabay's *Yıldız i sus sekretos i el reyno di Abdülhamid* (Yildiz and its Secrets and the Reign of Abdülhamid, 1909), also in the Adatto collection, was one of the many books published in all the languages of the Empire, dealing

---

49   In the introduction that he wrote for Schauffler's memoirs, Edwards A. Park quotes the missionary, saying that "after reviewing and printing in Hebrew and Hebrew-Spanish the Psalms for the Jews here, I have begun already and carried on to considerable extent the revision of the whole Old Testament in that dialect. I am engaged in the construction of a Lexicon in Hebrew and Hebrew-Spanish, which is pretty extensive; and of a vocabulary in the same languages." Edwards A. Park, "Introduction," in William G. Schauffler, *Autobiography of William G. Schauffler: Forty-Nine Years a Missionary in the Orient*, edited by his sons (sic.) (New York: Anson D. F. Randolph and Company, 1887), XXI.

50   Schauffler, *Autobiography of William G. Schauffler*, 77.

51   Ibid., 129.

52   On the development of historical prose and an extensive list of novels and history books in Ladino, see Ana Maria Riaño Lopez, "La prosa histórica en lengua sefardí," in *Sefardíes: Literatura y lengua de una nación dispersa*, eds. Iacob M. Hassán, et al. (Cuanca: Ediciones de la Universidad de Castilla, 2008), 397–420.

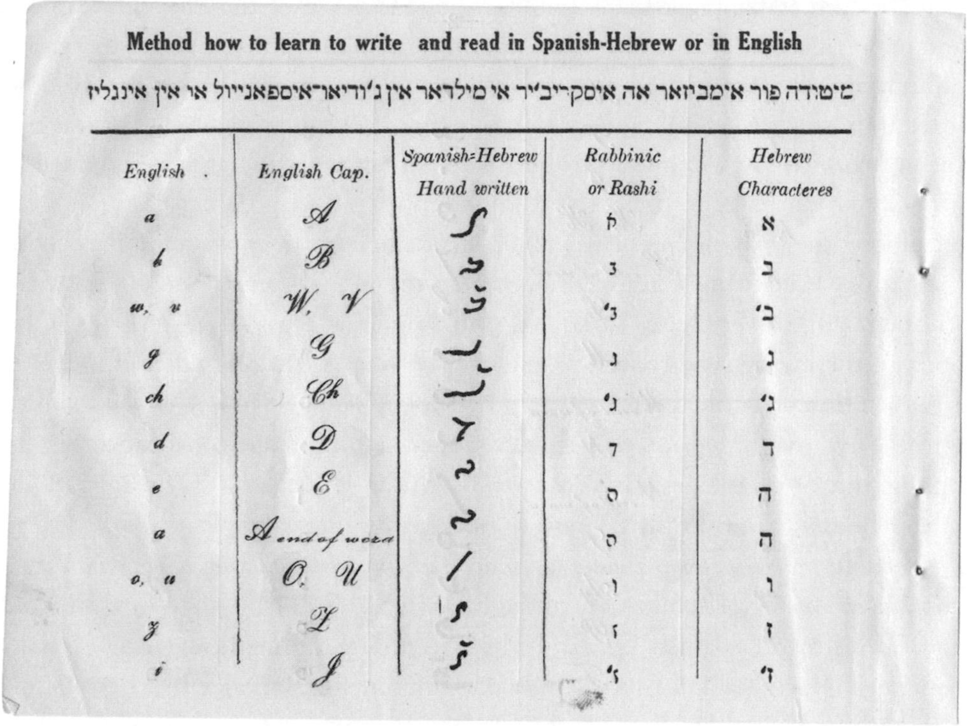

Method how to learn to write and read in Spanish-Hebrew or in English

מיטודה פור אימביזאר אה איסקרייבﬞיר אי טילדרﬞאר אין גﬞ׳ודיאו־איספﬞאנייול אי אין אינגליז

English	English Cap.	Spanish=Hebrew Hand written	Rabbinic or Rashi	Hebrew Characteres
a	$\mathscr{A}$		פ	א
b	$\mathscr{B}$		ב	ב
w, v	$\mathscr{W}$, $\mathscr{V}$		׳ב	׳ב
g	$\mathscr{G}$		ב	ב
ch	$\mathscr{Ch}$		׳ב	׳ב
d	$\mathscr{D}$		ד	ד
e	$\mathscr{E}$		ה	ה
a	$\mathscr{A}$ end of word		ה	ה
o, u	$\mathscr{O}$. $\mathscr{U}$		ו	ו
z	$\mathscr{Z}$		ז	ז
i	$\mathscr{J}$		׳ז	׳ז

FIGURE 4.5. *Livro de embezar las linguas Ingleza i Yudish Muy premorozo i provechozo para todos los Djudyos Espanyoles imigrados o ke pensan imigrar aki en Amerika* by Moise Gadol, 1916. Sephardic Studies Digital Collection, University of Washington.
Courtesy of Isaac Azose.

with what would later be called the "era of oppression," including the spy networks and censorship during the ruthless rule of Abdülhamid II. The repressive publishing laws were the reason why Zola's *Nantas* ended up being published in Cairo at the Estamparia Karmona i Zara. Indeed, Eliya Karmona had to move to Egypt to remain a novelist and publisher, as these professions had become difficult to pursue in the Ottoman mainland. Having been informed by the Ministry of Education, the authority responsible for censorship, that he would not be allowed to write about love, theft, and murder in his novels anymore, Karmona emigrated to Egypt, but soon found out that there was little interest for Ladino literature among the Jews of Egypt.[53] We learn that the issue of censorship and antisemitism were not necessarily disconnected from the writings of İsak Ferera Efendi (1877–1933), a poet and essayist who wrote in Turkish. In a piece that he published in *Mir'ât* (The Mirror, 1909), the first Jewish literary magazine entirely in Ottoman Turkish, he suggests

---

53   Eliya Karmona, *Komo Nasyo Eliya Karmona*, 510.

that İbrahim Hıfzı Efendi (1862–1905), the then head of the Press Directorate and main figure in charge of censorship, prevented him from publishing because of his animosity toward Jews. Ferera's friends told him that all obstacles would be lifted if he used a Muslim name, which he refused.[54] He was aware that he was not the only one to be a victim of prejudice. He noted that "the flames of oppression [*istibdâd* –a reference to the era of Abdülhamid II], have scorched the Jews who are among the weakest creatures."[55] Not surprisingly, many Jewish families chose the path of exile in these uneasy times, even though, as Ferera noted, Jews were still better off in Ottoman Turkey than in Romania, Russia, or Germany. One book in the Isaac Asoze collection tells the story of longing for a better life. It is a 1916 edition of a guidebook, prepared by Moise Gadol (1874–1941), the founder of the New York-based *La Amerika* newspaper, aiming to help Ladino-speaking immigrants or people preparing to cross the Atlantic Ocean to get ready for life in the United States. Entitled *Livro de embezar las linguas Ingleza i Yudish: Muy premorozo i provechozo para todos los djudyos espanyoles imigrados o ke pensan imigrar aki en Amerika* (Book to Learn the English and Yiddish Languages: Suitable and Useful for all Spanish Jews and Those Who Think of Immigrating Here in America), it included information on topics ranging from an idealized description of life in the United States to workers' rights. In many ways, this book, too, just like the *romansos* about love and adventures and the religious tractates, reflected the deepest longings of those who authored and read them. And, indeed, of those who walk through a Ladino library, fascinated by the fact that in the early years of the twentieth century, Alexis Bouvier and his lethal heroine spoke in Ladino.

Bibliography

Abrevaya Stein, Sarah. *Making Jews Modern: The Yiddish and Ladino Press in the Russian and Ottoman Empires*. Bloomington: Indiana University Press, 2003.

Anonymous. "Nota del Editor." In *La Mujer del muerto* [Alexis Bouvier].

Anonymous. "Komo se vende la gazeta Djudia." In *Lo ke Meldavan Nuestros Padres*, edited by Rıfat Birmizrahi, 253. Istanbul: Gözlem Kitap, 2006.

Borovaya, Olga. *Modern Ladino Culture: Press, Belles Lettres, and Theatre in the Late Ottoman Empire*. Bloomington and Indianapolis: Indiana University Press, 2012.

———— *The Beginnings of Ladino Literature: Moses Almosnino and His Readers*. Bloomington: Indiana University Press, 2017.

Bouvier, Alexis. *La femme du mort*. Paris: Jules Rouff Editeurs, 1879.

---

54   İsak Ferera, "İsminden Utanan Yahudiler," *Mirat* 2 (17 Şubat 1324), 22–23.

55   Ibid., 21.

[Bouvier, Alexis]. *La Mujer del muerto*, translated by Isaac Gabay. Istanbul: Benyamin ben Yosef, 5672 (1912).

Dori, Nitsa. "The Dreyfus Affair and its Reflection in Ladino Literature." *International Journal in Emerging Trends in Social Sciences* 3, no. 2 (2018): 57–64.

Ferera, İsak. "İsminden Utanan Yahudiler." *Mirat* 2 (17 Şubat 1324), 22–23.

Franco, Moïse. *Essai sur l'histoire des Israélites de l'Empire ottoman depuis les origines jusqu'à nos jours.* Paris: A. Durlacher, 1897.

Gezgin, Faruk. "Ali Kemal ve Romanları." In *Türk Dünyasından Halil Açıkgöz'e Armağan*, edited by Hayri Ateş, 237–256. Istanbul: Doğu Kitabevi, 2013.

Ginio, Alisa Meyuḥ. *Between Sepharad and Jerusalem: History, Identity and Memory of the Sephardim.* Leiden: Brill, 2014.

Karmona, Eliya. *Komo Nasyo Eliya Karmona.* In *Lo Ke Meldavan Nuestros Padres*, edited by Rıfat Birmizrahi, 479–544. Istanbul: Gözlem Kitap, 2006.

Lehmann, Matthias B. "A Livornese `Port Jew` and the Sephardim of the Ottoman Empire." *Jewish Social Studies*, New Series 11, no. 2 (Winter, 2005): 51–76.

——— *Ladino Rabbinic Literature and Ottoman Sephardic Culture.* Bloomington and Indianapolis: Indiana University Press, 2005.

Lollié, Frédéric. "Alexis Bouvier." *La nouvelle revue* 76 (May-June 1895): 845.

Lorya, Jak. *Dreyfus: Drama en sinko aktos i un apoteos*, transcribed by Olga Borovaya, https://web.stanford.edu/dept/jewishstudies/programs/sephardi/borovaya_texts_files/dreyfus/Dreyfus.Transcription.pdf.

Park, Edwards A. "Introduction." In William G. Schauffler, *Autobiography of William G. Schauffler: Forty-Nine Years a Missionary in the Orient,* edited by his sons (sic.). New York: Anson D. F. Randolph and Company, 1887.

Phillips Cohen, Julia. *Becoming Ottomans: Sephardi Jews and Imperial Citizenship in the Modern Era.* Oxford and New York: Oxford University Press, 2014.

Riaño Lopez, Ana Maria. "La prosa histórica en lengua sefardí." In *Sefardíes: Literatura y lengua de una nación dispersa*, edited by Iacob M. Hassán, et al., 397–420. Cuanca: Ediciones de la Universidad de Castilla, 2008.

Rodríguez Ramírez, Eva Belén. *El caso Dreyfus en la literatura sefardí: Edición y estudio de Cinco años de mi vida. Alfred Dreyfus (Constantinopla, 1901).* PhD dissertation, University of Granada, 2006.

Romero, Elena. *El teatro del Sefardíes orientales*, Vol. 1. Madrid: Instituto Arias Montano, 1979.

Strauss, Johann. "Who Read What in the Ottoman Empire (19th-20th Century)." *Middle Eastern Literatures* 6, no. 1 (2003): 39–76.

Tanpınar, Ahmet Hamdi. *Ondokuzuncu Asır Türk Edebiyatı Tarihi.* Istanbul: Çağlayan Kitabevi, 1997.

Ebüzziya *Millet-i İsrailiye.* Istanbul: Matbaa-ı Ebüzziya, 1890.

Trietsch, Davis. *Die Juden der Türkei*. Leipzig: Veit Verlag, 1915.

Türesay, Özgür. "Osmanlı İmparatorluğu'nda Antisemitizmin Avrupalı Kökenleri Üzerine Birkaç Not: Ebüzziya Tevfik ve *Millet-i İsrâiliye* (1888)." *Tarih ve Toplum: Yeni Yaklaşımlar* 6 (Spring 2007-Winter 2008): 97–105.

———— "L'affaire Dreyfus vue par les intellectuels ottomans." *Turcica: Revue d'études turques* 47 (2016): 235–256.

Varol, Marie Christine. "L'Empire ottoman à travers la biographie picaresque d'Eliya Karmona." *Cahiers balkaniques* 36–37 (2008), http://journals.openedition.org/ceb/1576.

CHAPTER FIVE

Sephardic Soldiers in the Late Ottoman Army

ÖZGÜR ÖZKAN

A key, yet largely unexamined, aspect of the late Ottoman Sephardim experience is military service. In light of new evidence from local archives and ordinary Jewish soldiers' memoirs and testimonies, this chapter first provides a brief history and significance of universal military service in the Ottoman Empire and contextualizes it within the broader framework of the *Tanzimat* reforms. Second, it elucidates what compulsory military service meant for the Ottoman Jews, what kind of challenges and opportunities it offered them as a "model minority," and how it affected their daily lives, relations with the imperial center, and the rest of the society in a rapidly changing imperial context. Finally, the chapter discusses the Jewish attitude toward the military service in the politically turbulent late Ottoman social and political context.

Military service was universalized to include non-Muslim male subjects shortly after the Young Turk Revolution of 1908. The Conscription law of 1909 (*Ahz-ı Asker Kanunu*) compelled all male citizens of the empire irrespective of their ethnic or religious background to serve in the military for the first time. Under the influence of Ottomanism, the dominant governing ideology of the early Second Constitutional Period, Ottoman political elite embraced the idea of a citizen army through universal conscription as a mechanism to promote a common imperial identity. As much as the introduction of universal conscription was part of Ottoman military reforms that sought to revive the empire's military capabilities, it incurred far-reaching social implications. It offered a radical change for Ottoman society's organization, especially for religious minorities, who had been exempt from military service in return for paying a poll tax or a fee—called Jizya until 1856 and *bedel-i askerî* later.[1] The universalization of compulsory military service in 1909 was the final concrete step of the process that marked the end of the Ottoman millet system, which had organized social life and intercommunal relations, as well

---

1   See Erik Jan Zürcher, *Arming the State: Military Conscription in the Middle East and Central Asia 1775–1925* (London, New York: Taurus, 1999).

as each religious community's ties with the palace since the fifteenth century. As the view of Jihad was replaced by the defense of the homeland, the conception of the *millet-i müsellehe*—nation-in-arms, envisioned as the primary instrument of this transition—faced many challenges. The issue of how non-Muslims would be incorporated into the newly conceived Ottoman nation in practice appeared as a major paradox to the modernization and nationalization process of the empire and its society. Unsurprisingly, despite widespread positive attitudes towards military service early on during the Second Constitutional Period, the military service quickly became a source of discontent, exposing the limitations of the idea of Ottomanism, which sought to unify all subjects through civic patriotic attachment to the empire.

Turkish historiography has generally attributed unfavorable references to Jewish and Christian experiences in the military, often highlighting their unwillingness to join the army, and therefore, their disloyalty. Based on a preliminary survey of sources presented by academic and non-academic works in recent years, and my own findings from local and official archival sources, I would argue that the recurrence of reference to non-Muslim soldiers suggests that the presence of Jews and Christians in the ranks of the Ottoman army was much higher than has long been presumed. Especially during the Balkan Wars and First World War, the dynamics underlying the response of Ottoman non-Muslims to mobilization and military service seem not to be significantly different than that of Muslim subjects. Indeed, the rates of Jewish and Christian participation in the Ottoman army reached levels high enough to contradict prevailing views. The enhanced use of and access to sources like memoirs, diaries, notebooks, testimonies, and visual material due to the increasing number of local archives and private collections, as well as new opportunities for collaboration and sharing through social media, blogging, and microblogging, have helped demonstrate non-Muslim experience in Ottoman wars and mobilizations in a more positive and objective light at both the community and individual levels.

The increasing amount of new evidence disseminated across hitherto inaccessible personal records and non-state archives, which I explore further below, is highly valuable. As I argue in this chapter, accessibility to new sources helps scholars uncover new layers of historical truth, as well as reinvigorating debates about dominant and official narratives about the past. Also, the sources leverage new research to challenge linear state- and elite-centric historical perspectives, especially in the area of military history, which has been subjected to little critical revisionism. Last but not least, the abundance of personal documentation, narratives, and visual material in the sources shed light on the diversity of historical experiences of each social group and each individual and social class within these social groups. Especially with respect to the experiences of ordinary soldiers or middle and low-grade officers, about which official archives are of little use, local sources are vitally important. Two significant examples of local archives are the newly established collection at the University of Washington in Seattle and the city museum and municipal archives in Çanakkale, where I uncovered various useful materials offering details about the military service of Jews and their influential legacy on local culture during my research in 2016 and 2017.[2]

The Genesis of the Ottoman Citizen Army

Along with other Ottoman reform projects, early discussions of universal conscription among Ottoman statesmen and intelligentsia dates to the 1820s.[3] While the main premise of a citizen army relying on universal conscription of the male population was the elimination of ideological, cultural, and social differences and inculcation of a shared identity, it is hard to identify a consensus among the early nineteenth century Ottoman reformers pertaining to the creation of a civic imperial identity, despite steps taken toward the introduction of equal citizenship. Although these reformers were aware of the need to address the issue of inequality among Ottoman subjects, especially arising from military service, and introduced a set of legal regulations in that sense, the solution largely sought to respect the differences of each religious community rather than eliminate them. This was visible in Sultan Mahmud II's (1808–1839) vision, which highlighted the necessity of keeping "Muslims in the mosque, Christians in the church, and Jews in the synagogue."[4] This perception highly contradicted the social and political reasoning behind the idea of a citizen army as an intellectual and organizational product of the nineteenth century. Because of this tension, it took a long time for the Ottoman administration to conceptualize the ranks of the military, barracks,

2   Özgür Özkan, "Reimagining Sephardic Çanakkale and Its Ties to Seattle," Stroum Center for Jewish Studies, University of Washington, May 1, 2017, https://jewishstudies. washington.edu/sephardic-studies/sephardic-canakkale-seattle/.

3   Gültekin Yıldız, "Ottoman Military Organization (1800–1918)," *The Encyclopedia of War*, ed. Gordon Martel (Blackwell Publishing Ltd., 2011), accessed June 2020, doi:10.1002/9781444338232.wbeow466. A thorough account of the origins of the modern Ottoman army and Mahmud II's military reforms, precursor of the transition to the compulsory military service, can be found in Gültekin Yıldız, *Neferin Adı Yok: Zorunlu Askerliğe Geçiş Sürecinde Osmanlı Devleti'nde Siyaset, Ordu ve Toplum (1826–1839)* (Istanbul: Kitabevi, 2009).

4   Enver Ziya Karal, "Non-Muslim Representatives in the First Constitutional Assembly, 1876–1877," in *Christians and Jews in the Ottoman Empire: The Functioning of a Plural Society*, eds. Benjamin Braude and Bernard Lewis, Vol.1 (New York: Holmes & Meier Publishers Inc., 1982), 388.

and the battlefield as institutional frameworks and spaces where an assimilation and a formation of a common identity could be promoted. Conservative circles in Ottoman politics also seemed resistant to the idea of Christians and Jews serving in an "army of Islam," while paradoxically resenting their exemption from military service, which, according to them, had undermined the socio-economic standing of the Muslim masses. Challenges in reconciling the requirements of modernizing the state, the military, and society with the ambivalences of Ottoman statesmen and the resistance of traditional circles stalled transition to universal compulsory military service which would integrate Jews and Christians into the Ottoman army. Sporadic efforts of the state fell short of eliminating non-Muslim's exemptions and ensuring ethnic and religious integration in the military.

The first concrete step toward universal military service came after Sultan Abdülmecid's imperial decree (reform edict of the Rose Chamber) of 1839, which prescribed new ways of imagining equality and belonging for all social groups in the empire. The imperial edict of the Rose Chamber introduced a 5-year military service obligation, followed by the issuance of the Drawing Lots Law (*Kur'a Nizamnamesi*) in 1848, marking the beginning of a fairer recruitment system based on drawing lots. However, it excluded a regulation regarding the integration of Christians and Jews into the military. The edict of 1839 focused primarily on organizing military service time and recruitment practices. Yet, on the other hand, it reflected the ambivalence of the Ottoman state toward non-Muslim military service by excluding a formal regulation requesting Jews or Christians to enlist for military service.

1856 was another watershed year for the emergence of a citizen army. The Imperial Reform Edict of 1856 (*Islahat Fermanı*) brought up the issue of military service obligation for non-Muslim subjects, as it effectively abolished the *Jizya*, which had long been imposed on non-Muslim subjects in exchange for their exemption from military service. The reform edict has brought non-Muslim subjects one step closer to become equal citizens by terminating the practice of *Jizya* tax and *dhimmi* status of Jews and Christians, who, as per Sharia law, were granted legal protection and exemption from military.[5] However, in terms of the military service of non-Muslims, what happened in practice was just a change in naming the military fee imposed on Jews and Christians, rather than completely abandoning the practice of exempting them from the draft.[6] The Ottoman administration was content with introducing "*İane-i Askerî*—later named *Bedel-i Askerî*—(military fee) to replace the *Jizya*.

---

5   Ufuk Gülsoy, *Cizyeden Vatandaşlığa: Osmanlı'nın Gayrimüslim Askerleri* (Istanbul: Timaş Yayınları, 2010), 63.

6   Ibid., 59–61.

Hüseyin Avni Pasha's extensive military reforms in 1869 and the New Conscription Law *(Yeni Kur'a Kanunnamesi)* of 1870 introduced several sets of reforms to the organization of the army, restructuring it into regulars, reserves, guards, and active reserves *(Nizamiye, Redif, Mustahfız,* and *İhtiyat),* yet, they too disregarded the integration of the non-Muslims into the Ottoman military. Despite increasingly pronounced complaints within the public and the army that the military service burden was unfairly shared, the conscription of Christians and Jews remained, in Eric J. Zürcher's words, "a theoretical option" until the Young Turk Revolution.[7] Even during critical wars like the Crimean War (1853–1856) and Turco-Russian War (1877–1878), when there was increasingly dire need for new recruits, the Ottoman administration largely maintained its stance. Unlike many domains of the Ottoman bureaucracy, the army remained mostly a religiously homogenous and highly exclusive institutional space until the Second Constitutional Period.[8]

Despite being often timid and half-hearted, there were also some unsuccessful attempts to draft non-Muslims that need to be mentioned here. In the 1830s, in the late 1840s, and during and before the Crimean War, Istanbul ordered the conscription of some non-Muslims into the Ottoman navy and army, but without much success.[9] These attempts, which targeted mostly Christian communities, met with high resistance. Both community representatives and individuals resisted the idea, despite added incentives introduced by Istanbul. Many Christian men requested passports or protection from Russian and Greek Consulates or just deserted, fled abroad, or went into self-imposed exile in the mountains.[10] Interestingly, Jews, probably because of the relatively smaller size of their population, were rarely subject to these practices and were rarely seen as a source of soldier recruits by Ottoman statesmen. In summary, the ambivalence of Ottoman statesmen, the opposition of conservative circles, and the reluctance and resistance of non-Muslims to serve in the military led to the delay of the integration of Jewish and Christian subjects into the Ottoman military. We might add that the Ottoman administration shied away from depriving the state of an important tax income by abolishing the military exemption fee. In short, military service remained a source of discontent until

---

7   Erik J. Zürcher, "The Ottoman Conscription System, 1844–1914," *International Review of Social History* 43, (1998), 447.

8   Amit Bein, "Politics, Military Conscription and Religious Education in the Late Ottoman Empire," *International Journal of Middle East Studies* 38 (2006): 283–301.

9   Ufuk Gülsoy, *Osmanlı Gayrimüslimlerinin Askerlik Serüveni* (Istanbul: Simurg Yayınevi, 2000), 174–9.

10   Ibid., 174–9.

the end of the late nineteenth century, not only for Muslims, who, according to Michelle Campos, perceived it as a source of inequality during a period when the balance of economic, social, and demographic power gradually shifted in favor of non-Muslims,[11] but also for non-Muslims, who had long been exempt and alienated from military duty and were unenthusiastic about joining the military.

The Promises and Challenges Offered by Military Service

The early years of the second constitutional period represents a time when differences among Ottoman religious communities regarding their views on imperial identity, equal citizenship, and a fair military service system were minimized, and a consensus emerged regarding the need for a new egalitarian and inclusive military service law. The Conscription Law of 1909 was an early embodiment of this consensual understanding, namely the realization of the civic ideals of the Young Turk revolution, marked by the slogans of the revolutionaries: liberté, égalité, and fraternité. The introduction of universal conscription illustrated the significant shift in the stance of both the Ottoman statesmen and non-Muslim religious communities toward the idea of non-Muslim soldiers in the Ottoman army. For all the optimism and popular support, however, the implementation of the universal conscription law encountered several difficulties. As the prospects of Ottoman social and territorial unity diminished following the Turco-Italian Wars and Balkan Wars between 1911 and 1913, and as ethnic nationalism quickly replaced the civic and liberal spirit of the revolution as the dominant political phenomenon, it became harder to gather the various ethnic, religious, and linguistic groups under the Ottoman military banner. Convincing the Ottoman citizens, Muslim or non-Muslim, to join the military to defend their newly imagined yet collapsing "patria," in which they could no longer envision themselves enjoying equal rights and fair representation, became more challenging than ever. The military service, therefore, marked the boundaries of both the Ottoman citizens' and the Ottoman state's attachment to the idea of Ottomanism. It exposed not only the contours and limits of non-Muslim communities' loyalty but also the Ottoman state's tolerance toward religious minorities. As Campos points out, military service "quickly became a source of rivalry and contention in the Ottoman Empire—a marker of the limits and boundaries of Ottomanization."[12]

---

11   Michelle U. Campos, *Ottoman Brothers: Muslims, Jews, and Christians in Early Twentieth-Century Palestine* (Stanford, CA: Stanford University Press, 2011), 151.

12   Ibid., 87.

What did military service mean for Christians and Jews in the empire? What did it offer? Conscription meant both a new right for non-Muslim citizens and communities to join in the army, a core apparatus of the Ottoman bureaucratic system, as equal citizens, yet also a difficult obligation, considering incessant mobilizations in response to the internal rebellions and the external belligerence that the empire had long been experiencing. The barracks and the battlefield are seen by many scholars as essential platforms through which underrepresented groups gain admittance to the state apparatus. From this perspective, military service could be said to have offered non-Muslim groups in the Ottoman empire a new venue for integration with the state and other segments of society and for increasing their representation in state bureaucracy through upward social mobility.[13] This new practice also presented new possibilities for less confrontational forms of relations among religious communities, through shared struggles, sacrifices, and grievances for the common goal of defending the homeland.

At the same time, universal conscription offered enormous challenges for non-Muslims at both the individual and community level. Firstly, universal military obligation indicated a significant stride toward a homogenous Ottoman imperial identity. Compulsory military service was an ultimate form of the modern state's new, direct form of relations with its population through the elimination of intermediaries and local identities and belongings. It would require communal leaders to give up significant power and authority, while forcing each community to transform its deeply entrenched religion-based communal identity. Thus, although religious leaders were very supportive of military service, they were concerned about maintaining their status and preserving the religious identities of young recruits.

Lastly, joining the army was a challenging decision to make for Ottoman individuals at a time when returning home alive was highly unlikely. The last decade of the Ottoman empire from 1908 until 1918 was a period defined by the army's constant engagement in military campaigns. First the revolt in Yemen, and then the Albanian Revolt of 1910, the Turco-Italian War of 1911, the Balkan Wars in 1912 and 1913, and, finally, World War I between 1914 and 1918 left a significant mark on Ottoman society's relations with the military. Because of the unending mobilizations and shortage of manpower, an entire generation was deployed from one front to another, spending an important portion of their lifetimes under uniform.

---

13   Eyal Ginio, "El Dovér El Mas Sànto: The Mobilization of the Ottoman Jewish Population During the Balkan Wars (1912–13)," in *Conflicting Loyalties in the Balkans: The Great Powers, the Ottoman Empire and Nation-Building*, eds. Hannes Grandits, Nathalie Clayer and Robert Pichler (London, New York: Taurus, 2011), 162.

This was highly discouraging for the young men who had to enlist. Also, worsening financial circumstances in the empire were hitting the military very hard. Many of the under-rationed and under-equipped soldiers were dying of epidemics even before firing a single bullet during campaigns. Under these circumstances, every young man and his family knew that being drafted meant, in most cases, never returning home.[14] All in all, while the military service offered Christians and Jews some opportunities to better integrate into Ottoman politics and bureaucracy, and was therefore promoted by communal elites for a while, joining the army met with increasing resistance, as it was highly costly for Ottoman men who were often the only breadwinners in the Ottoman traditional family structure.

Jews and Military Service

For the Jews, the late nineteenth and early twentieth centuries witnessed major changes that, in the Ottoman case, culminated during the Second Constitutional Period. The Jews' identities, connectivity, social networks, and relations to their respective states and other communities were subject to extensive transformations. The gradual destruction of imperial umbrellas, which hitherto had provided Jews some religious and economic autonomy and allowed for the maintenance of their local identities, accompanied two parallel processes toward the emergence of the concepts of citizenship and nationalism. Unprecedented state penetration and militarization in public and private life accelerated the pace and expanded the extent of transformations in Jewish identity and social life. These processes, which led to the genesis and progress of democratic rights in Europe and the Ottoman Empire, forced Jewish communities and individuals to revise their allegiances to the state. As a modern phenomenon, citizen armies became institutional spaces where these transformations were both incentivized and also tested.

For Ottoman Jews, the wars of the early twentieth century offered an opportunity not only to show their allegiance to the empire but also to prove that they possessed the physical and moral qualities of modern citizens. Military service came to be increasingly viewed by Jews as an essential step toward becoming a modern citizen. This idea was primarily motivated by the Jewish community's bottom-up modernization efforts that spread from the Alliance Israélite Universelle Schools.[15] In sum, along with classrooms, barracks also came to be seen as agents

---

14   Erik Jan Zürcher, "Between Death and Desertion: The Experience of Ottoman Soldier in World War 1," *Turcica* 28 (1996), 255.

15   See Paris Papamichos Chronakis, "Global Conflict, Local Politics: The Jews of Salonica and World War I," in *World War I and the Jews: Conflict and Transformations in Europe, the*

of modernization. On the other hand, although the Jewish elite encouraged youth to enlist, they were very particular about maintaining their communal sense of belonging and religion. Religious leaders were especially concerned that military service in Muslim-dominant units could weaken religious identity among young Jewish recruits. For example, an important concern for community elders was that young Jews would not be able to maintain a Kosher diet.[16]

The barracks, battlefield, and home front became contexts in which Jews' transnational, local, and newly forming national identities were challenged, competed against, and reshaped by each other. Many of the familiar certainties and anxieties that had governed Jewish lives were under revision. These spaces exposed the contours and boundaries of belonging in Jewish communities and the limits and extent of Jewish patriotism in a period in which the meaning of equal citizenship and civic patriotism was challenged by rising ethnic and religious nationalism.[17]

Ottoman efforts to incorporate non-Muslim citizens into Ottoman bureaucracy, military, and political life in the early years of the revolution were quickly replaced by the policies of ethno-religious exclusion in the wake of the Balkan Wars. This rapid change in attitude towards non-Muslims led to the reproduction of starker differences, stricter social hierarchies, and deeper social cleavages. Literature offers bifurcating views about Jewish experience with military service. While some scholars optimistically overemphasize the high prospects of ethnic and religious pluralism in the military, as well as in political life, and state bureaucracy, others paint a highly gloomy picture, emphasizing that Ottomanism had already been a dead project long before the Balkan wars. However, a closer investigation reveals a much more complex reality about the Jewish experience with Ottoman military service. Although we need to acknowledge that a significant shift occurred during the Balkan wars, which Eyal Ginio sees as the genesis moment of the Ottoman "culture of defeat,"[18] there was still a significant non-Muslim presence, including Jewish, in the Ottoman army, which contradicts the common scholarly perception.

Middle East and America (New York: Berghahn Books, 2017) and Aron Rodrigue, *French Jews, Turkish Jews: The Alliance Israelite Universelle and the Politics of Jewish Schooling in Turkey, 1860–1925* (Bloomington, Indiana University Press, 1990).

16 Julia Phillips Cohen, *Becoming Ottomans: Sephardi Jews and Imperial Citizenship in the Modern Era* (New York: Oxford University Press, 2014), 73–74.

17 Marsha L. Rozenblit and Jonathan Karp, *World War I and the Jews: Conflict and Transformations in Europe, the Middle East, and America* (New York: Berghahn Books, 2017), 2–5.

18 Eyal Ginio, *The Ottoman Culture of Defeat: The Balkan Wars and Their Aftermath* (New York: Oxford University Press, 2016), 162.

Although many Jews and Christians were relegated to labor battalions,[19] the number of those who served in the combatant units or medical corps, as well as those who were killed and wounded in action, was not insignificant. How authorities decided who would be allowed to be combatant and who would be sent to labor battalions is still a mystery and requires further research.

Beyond that, no research or official document provides comprehensive statistical evidence to reveal the complete demographic landscape of Ottoman military service, which would present figures on how many non-Muslims served in the military, in what roles and ranks, how many deserted, avoided service, or conversely volunteered, were wounded, or killed in action. The number of works focusing solely on non-Muslim military service is very limited. Particularly, there is no in-depth analysis of non-Muslim reserve officers, some of which, in Beşikçi's words, were in a "schizophrenic" situation during the Great War between the state oppression their communities faced and their individual patriotism and sacrifices in the Ottoman army.[20] Most accounts are fixated on dichotomies focusing on the patriotism or disloyalty of non-Muslim individuals or communities and the inclusiveness or discriminatory attitude of the state. These accounts ignore the diversity of the non-Muslim experience and significant temporal and intra-community variation pertaining to military service.

The Jewish Response to Military Service: Between Patriotism and Expatriation

It is hard to generalize and suggest a "typical" Jewish experience in the Ottoman military or a "typical" Jewish attitude toward military service. The Jews' response to conscription varied over time and within the Jewish community, based on various social, economic, and political factors at the community and individual level.

From the promulgation of the imperial edict of 1856 until the end of the Balkan Wars, the greater Jewish community appears to show increasing interest in joining the ranks of the Ottoman army. The literature generally acknowledges that the response of Jews to military service was relatively more favorable compared to other non-Muslim

---

19   Devi Mays, "Recounting the Past, Shaping the Future: Ladino Literary Representations of World War I," in *World War I and the Jews: Conflict and Transformations in Europe, the Middle East, and America,* eds. Marsha L. Rozenblit and Jonathan Karp (New York: Berghahn Books, 2017).

20   For a detailed account of reserve officers in the Ottoman army, see Methmet Beşikçi, "İhtiyat Zâbiti"nden "yedek subay"a: Osmanlı'dan Cumhuriyet'e bir zorunlu askerlik kategorisi olarak yedek subaylık ve yedek subaylar, 1891–1930," *Tarih ve Toplum Yeni Yaklaşımlar,* Sayı 13, (Güz 2011): 83.

religious groups, especially after the introduction of the Conscription Law of 1909. However, both claims lack substantive evidence. Although draft-dodging and desertion were thought to be quite common among Jews, there were several examples of voluntarism as well. On the other hand, although many young Ottoman Jewish men were unenthusiastic about joining the army, the reluctance was not limited to non-Muslims, as opposed to what Turkish official historiography typically emphasizes. Turkish military records state that the perception of military service was so negative in the early days of the Balkan Wars that only 290,000 enrolled out of 812,663 eligible men,[21] which shows that opposition to conscription can hardly be accounted for solely by non-Muslims resistance. In World War I, the estimated number of deserters in the Ottoman army reached 300,000 by 1916[22] and 500,000 by 1918,[23] while the French military saw approximately 21,000 deserters, even during the height of well-known mutinies, in 1917.[24] The resistance to the draft was extraordinarily high, especially in urban areas and in regions where feudal and nomadic social structures were more resilient.[25] In the Balkans, Bosnians and Albanians[26] and, in Iraq and Syria, Kurds, Druzes, and Alawites[27] were groups who showed significant opposition to the draft.[28] In Anatolia, as Reşat Kasaba shows, the Ottoman administration's attempts to draft nomadic groups had long been unsuccessful.[29] Resistance to the draft was not low

21   See *Türk Silahlı Kuvvetleri Tarihi, Balkan Harbi (1912–1913), III. Cilt, 2nci Kısım* (Ankara: Genelkurmay Basımevi, 1993), 709.

22   Emin Ahmed Yalman, *Turkey in the World War* (New Heaven: Yale University Press, 1936), 255.

23   See Edward J. Erickson, *Ordered to Die: A History of the Ottoman Army in the First World War* (London & Westport, Connecticut: Greenwood Press, 2001), 243. Yalman, *Turkey in the World War*, 255; Lucassen and Zürcher, Introduction, "Conscription and Resistance: The Historical Context," in *Arming the State: Military Conscription in the Middle East and Central Asia 1775–1925*, ed. Erik Jan Zürcher (London, New York: Tauris, 1999), 14.

24   Leonard V. Smith, "Remobilizing the Citizen-Soldier through the French Army *Mutinies of Spring 1917*," in Home State, Society and Mobilization in Europe during the First World War, ed John Horne (NY: Cambridge University Press, 2002), 79–92.

25   Zürcher, "The Ottoman Conscription System," 449.

26   Odile Moreau, Bosnian Resistance against Conscription in the Nineteenth Century, in *Arming the State: Military Conscription in the Middle East and Central Asia 1775–1925*, ed. Erik Jan Zürcher (London, New York: Tauris, 1999), 129.

27   Dick Douwes, "Reorganizing Violence: Traditional Recruitment and Conscription in Ottoman Syria," in *Arming the State: Military Conscription in the Middle East and Central Asia 1775–1925*, ed. Erik Jan Zürcher (London, New York: Tauris, 1999), 120.

28   Zürcher, "The Ottoman Conscription System," 441.

29   Reşat Kasaba, *A Moveable Empire: Ottoman Nomads, Migrants, and Refugees*, Studies in Modernity and National Identity (Seattle: University of Washington Press, 2009).

among Sunni-Turkish groups. For instance, in his work on battalion imams, Beşikçi emphasizes how these religious officials became an important component of efforts to prevent draft evasion, desertion, self-maiming, and suicide, which were common issues undermining the combat capabilities of the army.[30] These historical figures and evidence indicate that resistance to military service was an empire-wide issue rather than one of a certain religious community.

Given the rudimentary conditions in the under-equipped and poorly-rationed Ottoman army, brutal conditions on the early twentieth century battlefield due to the increased killing capacity of firearms and widespread fatal epidemics and famines often put Ottomans, Muslim or non-Muslim, in a position to choose "between death and desertion," at the decisive moment to enlist or not.[31] Those who put on uniform were usually the ones who had no alternatives or who could not afford any method of evasion—in the form of buying a medical exemption report, a journey abroad, foreign citizenship, or paying bribes. In other words, the repertoire of alternatives at the disposal of conscripts increased the significance of social status. In short, the decision to comply with the Ottoman state's request for military service was, to an important extent, associated with the social and economic background of the conscript, his repertoire of choices, and personal and even household matters, as well as local social and political dynamics. Unsurprisingly, those who ended up serving were mostly boys from rural areas, especially from Anatolia;[32] those who had no or few other alternatives.

Notwithstanding the gloomy circumstances of the Ottoman military and generally negative attitude toward military service, there were several instances of Jewish participation in the Ottoman military service. However, due to the long-standing disinterest in the social history of war and disregard for the voices of ordinary soldiers, the relative scarcity of memoirs and diaries in the highly illiterate Ottoman army, and, finally, the Turkish state's strict control over military archives, the contributions and experiences of Jews and Christians have remained largely unexamined. Although the evidence regarding non-Muslim reluctance to

---

30 Mehmet Beşikçi, Askeri Modernleşme, Askeri Disiplin ve Din: Düzenli Kitle Orduları Çağında Osmanlı Ordusu'nda Tabur İmamları, *Akademik İncelemeler Dergisi*, 11/1 (2016): 1–33.

31 Zürcher, "Between Death and Desertion," 256.

32 Mehmet Beşikci, *The Ottoman Mobilization of Manpower in the First World War: Between Voluntarism and Resistance*, (Leiden: Brill, 2012), 20; Virginia Aksan, "Ottoman Military Recruitment Strategies in the Late Eighteenth Century," in *Arming the State: Military Conscription in the Middle East and Central Asia 1775–1925*, ed. Erik Jan Zürcher (London, New York: Tauris, 1999), 22; Zürcher, "The Ottoman Conscription System," 449; Gülsoy, *Osmanli'nin Gayrimuslim Askerleri*, 172–3.

serve in the military has been prevalent and over-focused, new scholarship relying on, especially, local sources indicates that Jewish and Christian presence in the Ottoman ranks was much higher than has long been presumed. For instance, some scholars, like McCarthy, point to a higher rate of Jewish presence in the Ottoman army by suggesting that significant decline in the Ottoman Jewish population between the Balkan Wars and the end of the Greco-Turkish War cannot be explained solely by migration.[33] They imply that it was the enormous death toll of Jews in the Ottoman ranks during this war-ridden period that led to the decimation of the Jewish population in the Ottoman lands. Burgeoning literature regarding Ottoman Jewish soldiers in the Balkan and First World Wars bolsters these claims and provides some evidence.

For example, as Gülsoy notes, Sergeant Mishon, a son of a wealthy Jewish family from Kocamustafapasa, who successfully commanded a platoon in the Balkan Wars, is a significant example of Jewish voluntarism.[34] Glenda Abramson examines the experiences of Haim Nahmias, who served in various locations in Anatolia, and Yehuda Amon, who was deployed to both Palestine and Western Anatolia, during World War I in Ottoman uniform based on their diaries.[35] Additionally, Beki Bahar notes in her memoirs that the legs of her mother's uncle had to be amputated due to frostbite, that her grandmother helped soldiers with sewing work, and that her grandfather was killed in action on the Çanakkale front.[36] Similarly, Nissim Benezra reports in his memoirs that his father died in Gallipoli.[37]

Recent findings further undermine the commonly-held views. For instance, Devin Naar and Oscar Aguirre-Mandujano uncovered a diary in Seattle that belonged to Leon Behar, who signs his diary as an artillery officer in the Ottoman Army.[38] The

---

33 Justin McCarthy, "Jewish Population in the Late Ottoman Period," in *The Jews of the Ottoman Empire*, ed. Avigdor Levy (Princeton: The Darwin Press, 1994), 37–397.

34 Gülsoy, *Osmanlı'nın Gayrimüslim Askerleri*, 174.

35 See Glenda Abramson, *Soldiers' Tales: Two Palestinian Jewish Soldiers in the Ottoman Army during the First World War* (Oregon and Middlesex: Valentine Mitchell Press, 2013).

36 See Beki Bahar, *Ordan Burdan: Altmış Yılın Ardından* (Istanbul: Gözlem Gazetecilik Basın ve Yayın A.Ş., 1995). Leyla Neyzi, "Trauma, Narrative and Silence: The Military Journal of a Jewish 'Soldier' Turkey During the Greco Turkish War," *Turcica* 35 (2003): 291–313.

37 See Nissim Benezra, Une Enfance juive à Istanbul, 1911–1929, op. in Leyla Neyzi, "Trauma, Narrative and Silence: The Military Journal of a Jewish 'Soldier' Turkey During the Greco Turkish War," *Turcica* 35, 2003, 291–313.

38 Hannah Pressman, "A Soldier's Ladino Poems of Ottoman-Jewish Pride," Stroum Center for Jewish Studies, University of Washington, November 10, 2014, http://jewishstudies.

songs recorded in the diary show Behar's enthusiasm about the Ottoman victories during the Balkan Wars. His experience contradicts the prevailing perception about Jewish attitude toward military service. The patriotic tones in Behar's diary are a reflection of changing Jewish identities and varying attitudes toward military service in the late Ottoman context. These two examples challenge the common perception emphasizing Jewish avoidance from military service in the last decade of the Ottoman Empire. Similar examples can shed new light on elite-centric military historiography, as well as help to understand the diversity of non-Muslim experiences in the late Ottoman Empire. For example, Mithat Atabay, a professor of history at Çanakkale 18 Mart University, identifies 558 non-Muslim soldiers who fought in the Ottoman army on the Çanakkale/Gallipoli front alongside Muslim soldiers.[39] Army officers David Hakohen and Meir Bogdanovski, Private Yako Kohen, Master Sergeant Nesim Avram Eskinazi, Lieutenant Abdullah Abut Abigadol, Pepo Levi, Efraim Varon, and Mordehay Efendi were some of them who served in the Ottoman army on various fronts during World War I.[40] These examples can surely be expanded through research in local archives where Ottoman Jewish immigrants originated or settled. The Turkish Military archive (ATASE) has become more accessible to researchers over the past decade and is also an important source, despite problems of digitization and cataloguing.

In order to exemplify the practical contributions of local archives and the advances in communication and internet technologies, I want to share a few of my personal experiences. In a short essay in 2018, I examined the sources of the peaceful historical narrative and pluralist culture embraced by Çanakkale, a small coastal town in southern Marmara, despite its heroic reputation, which has been almost exclusively associated with the defensive battles that took place in the Dardanelles and the Gallipoli peninsula during World War I. After the publication of this essay, I received several emails and comments through social media platforms. Perhaps the most important aspect of these emails and comments sent from various states in the U.S. were that they mentioned family members whose names never appear in the existing lists in the literature. Some were asking for help to find records of relatives fallen or gone

washington.edu/sephardic-studies/soldier-ladino-poems-ottoman-jewish-pride/.

39 Mithat Atabay, "Gayrimüslim Osmanlı Tebaası'nın Askere Alınması ve Çanakkale Savaşları'nda Hayatını Kaybeden Gayrimüslim Osmanlı Askerleri," *Yeni Türkiye* 65 (2015): 1342–54.

40 These names were collected in the 500th Year Foundation Jewish Museum of Turkey and in an exhibit named "Sephardic Soldiers in the Ottoman Army during the World War I," in Çanakkale, Turkey.

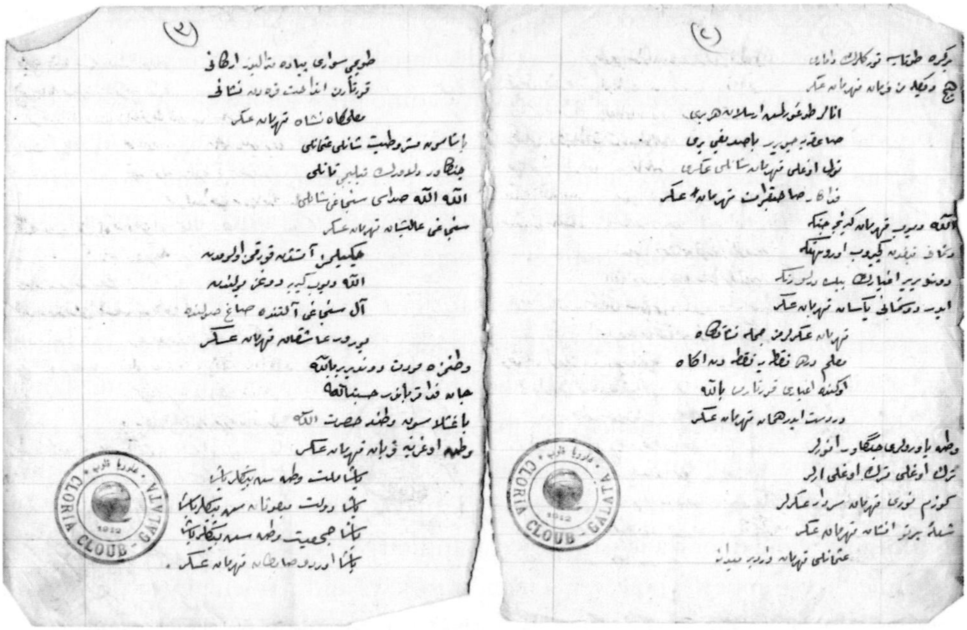

FIGURE 5.1. Leon Behar's notebook. Sephardic Studies Digital Collection, University of Washington. Courtesy of Josie Agoado.

missing in action; some were sharing the photographs or letters they had. For instance, in one of these messages, Victor Gabay stated that his father Joseph, who was from Edirne, served as a lorry driver in the Ottoman army during the Great War. In another, Andrea L. Leal shared that her grandmother's brother, David Aldoroty, was killed in action on the Gallipoli front. This correspondence shows how new diaries, memoirs, and letters, cooperation, and the collaborative environment generated by new communication technologies increase interest in personal and family histories and the willingness to share sources and findings. Most importantly, newly accessible local collections can play an important role in providing sources that can put dominant narratives into question and stimulate new debate about them.

We observe several instances of Jewish and Christian voluntarism before the introduction of universal conscription in 1909, as well. In dire situations, Jews, like Greeks and Armenians, volunteered to serve in the army and support the Ottoman Empire's military struggles. Unlike other religious communities, the Jews' willingness to join the imperial army noticeably increased over time. Until the Russo-Turkish war of 1877–1878, the Jews seem to be almost absent in most state-led projects. This was due in part to their disinterest in participating in the state bureaucracy and the army, partly because of the Ottoman state's neglect of Jews, as well as any motivation to integrate them. The Jewish elite made significant efforts to overcome this "benign neglect" and worked very diligently so that Jews would count in imperial politics. They saw military service as an essential platform for increasing Jewish influence in imperial politics. The nascent Ladino press joined the Jewish leaders' efforts to encourage young Jewish men to volunteer for the army.[41] A new wave of patriotism replaced Jews' initial resistance to *Islahat* reforms and mobilization during the Crimean War, as the Jewish community repositioned itself and adapted to the rapidly changing conditions of the empire.

Early indications of change in Ottoman Jews' relations with the state can be observed in the late 1870s during the Ottoman-Russian War, when some multi-confessional guard units were established for the defense of Salonica and Izmir. One of the two Salonican infantry companies, which were composed of around two hundred young volunteers, including approximately sixty Jewish recruits, visited Istanbul. In 1893, under the leadership of Chief Rabbi Moshe Halevi, the Jewish community applied for their acceptance to military service. Sultan Abdülhamid II welcomed these appeals; however, a request to Jews and Armenians in this regard was never made.[42] During the Greco-Turkish War (Domokos) of 1897, the number of Jewish soldiers in the Ottoman army seemed to be even greater. The Ottoman state rewarded many Jews for their sacrifice during the war of Domokos. For instance, Ishak Samuel Feraci from Salonica, who served in the Eğirdir Reserve Battalion, was decorated for his combat service.[43] Similarly, Sultan Abdülhamid II recognized the Salonican Jews Mibahu, Ekber Avram, and Avram, Lodin, and Salamon, who volunteered in the Greco-Turkish War, with medals for their service in the Ottoman army.[44] The Jews' contribution to the Ottoman struggle against enemy forces was not limited to joining the ranks of the army. Various Jewish foundations and associations also offered help to the families of soldiers and orphans during the wars.[45]

Conclusion

General Jewish attitudes to military service were more favorable compared to that of other non-Muslim religious groups in the late nineteenth and early twentieth

---

41   Cohen, *Becoming Ottomans*, 74–85.

42   Ibid., 164–5.

43   Directorate of State Archives, Ottoman Archives, Archive Code Y. MTV, Folder Number 179, File Number 129, Date 1316 S.

44   Directorate of State Archives, Ottoman Archives, Archive Code I. TAL., Folder Number 121, File Number 60, Date 1315 Ca.

45   Directorate of State Archives, Ottoman Archives, Archive Code Y. PRK. AZN, Folder Number 17, File Number 27, Date 1314 Za.

centuries. It is clear that Jewish elites and the Judeo-Spanish press were convinced that military service was an important instrument in the path for Jews to gain greater representation in the Ottoman state apparatus and to better integrate into imperial politics. They saw military service as an opportunity for Jews to show their patriotism and loyalty.

Notwithstanding a relatively positive attitude towards conscription, we should note that the position of the Jews, like that of other religious groups, was neither singular nor rigid. It changed over time, depending on political developments inside and outside the Ottoman empire. As the euphoria of early revolutionary days and the "popular image of the romantic heroism of the Ottoman military" wore off, most non-Muslim youth became increasingly disinterested in the idea of enlisting, which bore significant risks for them and their families. Given the marked shift in the Jewish attitude toward military service after the Balkan Wars, it is fair to suggest that the Ottoman authorities' attitude and prospects regarding the "survival" of the empire affected the Jews' positionality as well. We have to add that burgeoning Zionism added new layers of complexities to the dynamics of Jewish participation in the Ottoman army. Overall, the Jewish military service appears as a critical social experience that vividly illustrates how the barracks, battlefield, and home front together remodeled Jewish identity and unveiled the ways in which transnational, local, and newly formed nationalist layers of Jewish identity interacted and reshaped each other.

As this volume shows, extant archives formed by late Ottoman Jewish migrant communities at their destinations, as well as their places of origin, are increasingly crucial sources for new material that sheds light on the experience of so-called "ordinary soldiers" and non-Muslims in the Ottoman army. As I mentioned before, the discovery of Leon Behar's diary is significant for showing the importance of non-traditional archives, precisely like the one formed in Seattle at the University of Washington. It is important to note that the Sephardic Jewish community which settled in the American west during the early twentieth century after leaving their homes in Ottoman towns like Tekirdağ, Marmara Island, Gelibolu, and Kala-i Sultaniye (Çanakkale) has made significant contributions in the formation of these archives. Another example is the city museum and municipal archives in Çanakkale where I located various useful materials on the military service of Jews and their influential legacy in relation to the local culture during my research in 2016 and 2017. Non-state archives of this sort can offer invaluable sources for scholars and help reveal new layers of truth about the past and also change static and singular perceptions and perspectives. Especially with respect to the experiences of ordinary soldiers or middle-ranking officers, which can rarely be found in official archives, local collections are highly important. Visual and textual documents, like photographs, anecdotes, memoirs, and diaries, that belong to ordinary soldiers can help expand scholarship, providing instances and details of Jewish voluntarism and such resistance strategies as draft-dodging and desertion.

Bibliography

Abramson, Glenda. *Soldiers' Tales: Two Palestenian Jewish Soldiers in the Ottoman Army during the First World War.* Oregon and MiddleSex: Valentine Mitchell Press, 2013.

Aksan, Virginia. "Ottoman Military Recruitment Strategies in the Late Eighteenth Century." In *Arming the State: Military Conscription in the Middle East and Central Asia 1775–1925,* edited by Erik Jan Zürcher, 21–39. London, New York: Tauris, 1999.

Atabay, Mithat. "Gayrimüslim Osmanlı Tebaası'nın Askere Alınması ve Çanakkale Savaşları'nda Hayatını Kaybeden Gayrimüslim Osmanlı Askerleri." *Yeni Türkiye* 65 (2015): 1342–54.

Bein, Amit. "Politics, Military Conscription and Religious Education in the Late Ottoman Empire." *International Journal of Middle East Studies* 38, no. 2 (2006): 283–301.

Beşikçi, Mehmet. "'İhtiyat Zâbiti'nden 'Yedek Subay'a: Osmanlı'dan Cumhuriyet'e Bir Zorunlu Askerlik Kategorisi Olarak Yedek Subaylık ve Yedek Subaylar, 1891–1930." *Tarih ve Toplum Yeni Yaklaşımlar* 13 (Güz 2011): 45–89.

——— *The Ottoman Mobilization of Manpower in the First World War: Between Voluntarism and Resistance.* Leiden: Brill, 2012.

——— "Askeri Modernleşme, Askeri Disiplin ve Din: Düzenli Kitle Orduları Çağında Osmanlı Ordusu'nda Tabur İmamları." *Akademik İncelemeler Dergisi* 11, no. 1 (2016): 1–33.

Campos, Michelle U. *Ottoman Brothers: Muslims, Jews, and Christians in Early Twentieth-Century Palestine.* Stanford, CA: Stanford University Press, 2011.

Chronakis, Paris Papamichos. "Global Conflict, Local Politics: The Jews of Salonica and World War I." In *World War I and the Jews: Conflict and Transformations in Europe, the Middle East and America,* edited by Marsha L. Rozenblit and Jonathan Karp, 175–200. New York: Berghahn Books, 2017.

Cohen, Julia Phillips. *Becoming Ottomans: Sephardi Jews and Imperial Citizenship in the Modern Era.* New York: Oxford University Press, 2014.

Douwes, Dick. "Reorganizing Violence: Traditional Recruitment and Conscription in Ottoman Syria." In *Arming the State: Military Conscription in the Middle East and Central Asia 1775–1925,* edited by Erik Jan Zürcher, 111–128. London, New York: Tauris, 1999.

Directorate of State Archives, Ottoman Archives.

Erickson, Edward J. *Ordered to Die: A History of the Ottoman Army in the First World War*. London and Westport, Connecticut: Greenwood Press, 2001.

Ginio, Eyal. "El Dovér El Mas Sànto: The Mobilization of the Ottoman Jewish Population During the Balkan Wars (1912–13)." In *Conflicting Loyalties in the Balkans: The Great Powers, the Ottoman Empire and Nation-Building*, edited by Hannes Grandits, Nathalie Clayer ve Robert Pichler, 157–181. London, New York: Taurus, 2011.

———— *The Ottoman Culture of Defeat: The Balkan Wars and Their Aftermath*. New York: Oxford University Press, 2016.

Gülsoy, Ufuk. *Cizyeden Vatandaşlığa: Osmanlı'nın Gayrimüslim Askerleri*. Istanbul: Timaş Yayınları, 2010.

———— *Osmanlı Gayrimüslimlerinin Askerlik Serüveni*. Istanbul: Simurg Yayınevi, 2000.

Karal, Enver Ziya. "Non-Muslim Representatives in the First Constitutional Assembly, 1876–1877." In *Christians and Jews in the Ottoman Empire: The Functioning of a Plural Society*, Vol 1, edited by Benjamin Braude and Bernard Lewis, 387–400. New York: Holmes & Meier Publishers Inc., 1982.

Kasaba, Reşat. *A Moveable Empire: Ottoman Nomads, Migrants, and Refugees*. Seattle: University of Washington Press, 2009.

Mays, Devi. "Recounting the Past, Shaping the Future: Ladino Literary Representations of World War I." In *World War I and the Jews: Conflict and Transformations in Europe, the Middle East, and America*, edited by Marsha L. Rozenblit and Jonathan Karp, 201–221. New York: Berghahn Books, 2017.

McCarthy, Justin. "Jewish Population in the Late Ottoman Period." In *The Jews of the Ottoman Empire*, edited by Avigdor Levy, 375–397. Princeton: The Darwin Press, 1994.

Moreau, Odile. "Bosnian Resistance against Conscription in the Nineteenth Century." In *Arming the State: Military Conscription in the Middle East and Central Asia 1775–1925*, edited by Erik Jan Zürcher, 129–138. London, New York: Tauris, 1999.

Neyzi, Leyla. "Trauma, Narrative and Silence: The Military Journal of a Jewish 'Soldier' Turkey During the Greco Turkish War." *Turcica* 35 (2003): 291–313.

Özkan, Özgür. "How the Turkish 'City of Peace' Remembers its Sephardic Veterans." Stroum Center for Jewish Studies, University of Washington, April 16, 2018, https://jewishstudies.washington.edu/sephardic-studies/canakkale-city-of-peace-turkey-sephardic-veterans-exhibit/

———— "Reimagining Sephardic Çanakkale and Its Ties to Seattle." Stroum Center for Jewish Studies, University of Washington, May 1, 2017.

Pressman, Hannah. "A Soldier's Ladino Poems of Ottoman-Jewish Pride." Stroum Center for Jewish Studies, University of Washington, November 10, 2014, http://jewishstudies.washington.edu/sephardic-studies/soldier-ladino-poems-ottoman-jewish-pride/.

Rodrigue, Aron. *French Jews, Turkish Jews: The Alliance Israelite Universelle and the Politics of Jewish Schooling in Turkey, 1860–1925*. Bloomington: Indiana University Press, 1990.

Rozenblit, Marsha L. and Jonathan Karp, ed. *World War I and the Jews: Conflict and Transformations in Europe, the Middle East, and America*. New York: Berghahn Books, 2017.

Smith, Leonard V. "Remobilizing the Citizen-Soldier through the French Army Mutinies of Spring 1917." In *Home State, Society and Mobilization in Europe during the First World War*, edited by John Horne, 79–92. New York: Cambridge University Press, 2002.

Türk Silahlı Kuvvetleri Tarihi, Balkan Harbi (1912–1913), Vol. III, Section 2. Ankara: Genelkurmay Basımevi, 1993.

Yalman, Emin Ahmed. *Turkey in the World War*. New Heaven: Yale University Press, 1936.

Yıldız, Gültekin. "Ottoman Military Organization (1800–1918)." *The Encyclopedia of War*. Edited by Gordon Martel. Blackwell Publishing Ltd, 2011. doi:10.1002/9781444338232. wbeow466.

——— *Neferin Adı Yok: Zorunlu Askerliğe Geçiş Sürecinde Osmanlı Devleti'nde Siyaset, Ordu ve Toplum (1826–1839)*. Istanbul: Kitabevi, 2009.

Zürcher, Erik Jan. "Between Death and Desertion: The Experience of Ottoman Soldier in World War 1." *Turcica* 28 (1996): 255.

——— "The Ottoman Conscription System, 1844–1914." *International Review of Social History* 43, no. 3 (1998): 437–449.

———*Arming the State: Military Conscription in the Middle East and Central Asia* 1775–1925. London, New York: Taurus, 1999.

PART THREE

Reflections: Ottoman Pasts, Private Collections, and Family Memories

Artifacts and their Aftermath: The Imperial and Post-Imperial Trajectories of Late Ottoman Material Objects

BENJAMIN C. FORTNA

> We are that strange species that constructs artifacts intended
> to counter the natural flow of forgetting.
>
> —William Gibson[1]

For historians, a three-dimensional object can be a good place to start. Willard Sunderland opens his evocative history of late Romanov Russia, *The Baron's Cloak: A History of the Russian Empire in War and Revolution*, with a physical description of a single, arresting object.[2] By introducing his wide-ranging account with the baron's cloak of his book's title, the garment that Baron Ungern Sternberg takes off before being shot by a Soviet firing squad in 1921, Sunderland highlights the effectiveness of an artifact as an historical opener. The baron's cloak affords Sunderland the opportunity not only to draw the reader's attention to the turbulent history that led up to the baron's execution but also to allude to the aftermath of that violent act. Holding the garment in the historian's hands provides the opening to delve into the ways in which the Baron and his execution have been remembered to the present day.

A few years ago, I was fortunate to have the chance to examine materials left behind by a most intriguing figure named Kuşçubaşı Eşref (1883–1964), an Ottoman insurgent and special operations officer of Circassian ancestry. Like that of Ungern Sternberg, Eşref's dramatic life story played out in the tumultuous final years of another sprawling, multi-ethnic empire supplanted by an ideologically-driven, uncompromising new regime. Unlike the Baron, Eşref died of old age after a long

---

1   William Gibson, *Distrust That Particular Flavor* (London: Penguin, 2012), 37.
2   Willard Sunderland, *The Baron's Cloak: A History of the Russian Empire in War and Revolution* (Ithaca: Cornell University Press, 2014), 1.

period of exile and returned to Anatolia, now in the Turkish Republic, at a much later stage of his life. In exile and after his return, Eşref had ample time to write and organize his papers and other memorabilia. He produced a massive autobiography which, unfortunately, perished when the house of his literary executor went up in flames. Therefore, the trunk of papers, which I consulted due to the generosity of his descendants, took on special significance. To adapt Gibson's phrase, they represent the otherwise lost attempt of an important if controversial historical character to "counter the natural flow of forgetting." Since Eşref had, as we shall soon see, fallen foul of the official historiography of this period in Turkey, due to his break with the fledgling Ankara government and its rising leader Mustafa Kemal (Atatürk), his efforts were aimed at combatting more than simply historical amnesia. They represent his determination to reassert himself into the historical mainstream so as to claim what he felt to be his rightful place at the center of political and military activity in the final years of the Ottoman Empire and the first year of the fighting that led to the establishment of the Turkish Republic.

Even before I had the chance to look into Kuşçubaşı Eşref's trunk, I encountered another, less dramatic artifact that remained from his remarkable career spanning the final decades of the Ottoman Empire and its equally tumultuous aftermath. Prior to examining Eşref's papers, his daughter very kindly opened an old pouch and poured out its contents onto a table in the living room of the family's summer house. Out tumbled a collection of seals and stamps. As she explained, they proved to be all in Bulgarian. Eşref had, as his descendants understood, taken the seals after the Ottoman recapture of Edirne at the start of the Second Balkan War, a turn of events that the contents of his trunk would soon illuminate. Had Eşref used the seals and stamps to forge documents during his time behind Bulgarian lines in preparation for off-the-books raids into Bulgarian territory? If so, they were, like much of Eşref's documents and, indeed, his career, connected with clandestine activity and a checkered history. More important for the subject of this volume, they represented physical evidence that, like his chest of papers, embodies a condensed distillation of a broad imperial to post-imperial trajectory that had led him from his childhood in the imperial capital of Istanbul to a number of military schools, exile in Arabia, service as an officer working closely with İsmail Enver Bey, subsequently Enver Paşa, who would become the most important Ottoman military figure in the years leading up to and during the First World War. Numerous missions followed before, like many of his fellow fighting men, Eşref joined the "national movement" aimed at restoring sovereignty to the Muslim majority of Anatolia as the war effort and the empire collapsed. After breaking with the Ankara movement and its leader

Mustafa Kemal, the future Atatürk, Eşref went into two extended phases of exile, first in Greece and then in Egypt, before returning to Anatolia as an old man. There, far from the center of things, he worked on his memoirs and arranged the papers that he would keep in a trunk for decades.

Eşref's materials are particularly important for the passage of history linking the late Ottoman Empire and its tortuous demise to the national era. Given the strong degree to which the newly established states used history—zealously controlled and even manufactured it—to buttress their newfound and therefore inherently shaky legitimacy, many aspects of the story were sidelined. Like many newly created states, the Kemalist republic wanted to tell its own version of its history. Mustafa Kemal (Atatürk)'s famous historiographical intervention, delivered in thirty-six-and-a-half hours over six days in October 1927 and referred to simply as The Speech (*Nutuk*) in Turkish, provided the founding text for the history of the republic that he and his partisans established. That proclamation and much that followed in the creation of an official history was, of course, particularly self-serving. It proceeded by both emphasis and exclusion. He dedicated a large part of the lengthy oration to criticizing the role of a long list of individuals who would later be sidelined in Turkish historiography. Eşref's papers are thus simply one in a series of alternative accounts that the official historiography sought to sideline or deny. The most famous (or infamous, depending on one's point of view) is the memoir of Kâzım Karabekir, the key military figure in eastern Anatolia during the fighting that established an independent Turkey. His work was prevented from being published until 1968.[3] Although in many cases what Eşref has to say is complimentary of his colleague Mustafa Kemal, the fact that Eşref split from the Ankara movement when Mustafa Kemal was consolidating control over it inevitably meant that their rift would become significant and take on a degree of animosity and suspicion that echoes to the present day. Atatürk and his supporters thus saw Eşref's papers as a challenge to the official line. They had the potential to fill in some gaps that were intentionally left unfilled.

And yet, Eşref's papers themselves are far from systematic. As I began to examine them, it quickly became clear to me that they contained their own gaps and silences, some of them almost deafeningly conspicuous. Eşref was stunningly silent about some of the most crucial and, indeed, controversial episodes of his life. The materials he left behind give no explanation as to why, for example, he felt compelled to break

---

3   Erik Jan Zürcher, "Young Turk Memoirs as a Historical Source: Kazim Karabekir's *İstiklal Harbimiz*," *Middle Eastern Studies* 22 (1986), 562–570.

with the *Kuvâ-yi Milliye* ("National" Movement) in 1920 or why he took up arms against it. In other words, Eşref's papers, while helping to fill in some important gaps in the official story, also leave crucial questions unanswered. In this respect, they are not unlike the broader state of private papers in Turkey relating to the late Ottoman era. Private papers dating to this period turn up from time to time, but their availability is inevitably haphazard. Given the change in script and language effective in many areas of the former Ottoman Empire, it is understandably not uncommon for those who have private, often family, collections not to know the import of what they hold in their possession.

In retrospect, Eşref's pouch of seals and stamps turned out to be a harbinger of a long and fascinating investigation into Eşref's life and its many episodes, nearly all of which were shot through with more than a modicum of controversy. The trunk would eventually yield a remarkable trove of materials. Sources of varying types and importance emerged from its deceptively modest confines, which would collectively form the starting point for my attempt to recreate Eşref's colorful life story. While working through the contents of the trunk, I drew simultaneously on published and archival materials in order to test the information that Eşref's materials presented. They produced their own, largely textual, story.[4] But the physical dimension of Eşref's legacy is worth considering here at greater length, particularly in light of the emphasis that the Trajectories project places, rightly, in my view, on the material aspect of the late Ottoman collections analyzed in this volume. In what follows, I comment on Eşref's sources, both two- and three-dimensional, in terms of how they help us expand our view of late Ottoman history, how they function as a "charged site" for the study of that period and its national aftermath, and what they contribute to a discussion of imperial (and post-imperial) lives. Choosing the period of the Balkan Wars as an example relevant to this volume, I focus on Eşref's activities in that highly contentious conflict. I conclude with some broader reflections on the ways in which personal or "private" sources can enrich our approach to this history.

Eşref's Trunk

Let's start with Eşref's trunk. The sheer physicality of the collection of papers that he assembled is especially important in relation to any claims they might make *vis-à-vis* the established history of the late Ottoman and early Republican periods, especially given Eşref's controversial and largely marginalized presence in the his-

---

4   Benjamin C. Fortna, *The Circassian: A Life of Eşref Bey, Late Ottoman Insurgent and Special Agent* (New York: Oxford University Press, 2016).

tory of that era. Apart from its material persistence, perhaps the most striking thing about the collection he left behind is its rather modest appearance. A simple wooden trunk, the only distinguishing feature of which was some colored floral painting on the exterior, Eşref's physical legacy is far from imposing. It hardly deserves to be considered as an archive. The term "archive" as we have come to understand it in recent centuries connotes solidity, officialdom, and, indeed, monumentality. In the words of Nicholas Dirks,

> . . . the archive, that primary site of state monumentality, is the very institu-
> tion that canonizes, crystalizes, and classifies the knowledge required by the
> state even as it makes this knowledge available to subsequent generations in
> the cultural form of a neutral repository of the past.[5]

Against the voluminous mass of the Ottoman archives, Eşref's papers are a mismatch of colossal proportions. Compared with millions of documents, they contain perhaps only several thousand. They command no budget and have as yet no permanent, that is to say, institutional, home, and certainly no staff to "keep" them. And yet they contain things that the Ottoman archives and, indeed, no other archive, can supply. That is because, in spite of the impression of completeness and finality that archives seek to create, no archive is ever exhaustive. Indeed, as Christine Philliou demonstrated several years ago when examining the collections of the Gennadius Library in Athens while working on the nineteenth century Ottoman diplomat Musurus Paşa,[6] archives can exhibit remarkable gaps. As we will see shortly, Eşref's papers, though much smaller in scope, contain some breathtaking omissions of their own. As Dirks says, archives intend to impose neutrality; Eşref's papers are inevitably depicted as partisan, as supporting his own particular historical and, indeed, historiographical agenda. But we should of course be suspicious of any source's claim to absolute neutrality. Whether public or private, all source collections can be shown to have their own advantages and disadvantages, illuminating vantage points and blind spots. A clue to the unique perspective that Eşref's papers offer is found in the term "private" which is frequently attached to such unofficial source collections.

---

5   Nicholas B. Dirks, *Castes of Mind: Colonialism and the Making of Modern India* (Princeton: Princeton University Press, 2001), 107.

6   Christine Philliou, "The Paradox of Perceptions: Interpreting the Ottoman Past through the National Present," *Middle Eastern Studies* 44, no.5 (September 2008): 661. As Philliou explains, 800 pages of Constantine Musurus Paşa's correspondence that had been unknown to the curators came to life following a request based on a reference in the library's catalogue.

FIGURE 6.1. Eşref's trunk.

The contents of Eşref's trunk are "private" in two main senses of the term. The first is simply that they were not collected, maintained, or displayed by any government or institution, local or national, but rather were created as a collection by one individual, namely, Kuşçubaşı Eşref himself. There are indications that this might have been otherwise. According to his descendants, Eşref attempted during his final years to give the papers to the Turkish Historical Society (*Türk Tarih Kurumu*), an organization founded by Mustafa Kemal and closely associated with the Turkish state. These offers were rebuffed, but after Eşref's death, the same institution apparently came calling in order to obtain the papers. Due to the family's suspicions, these efforts were rejected. And so Eşref's trunk remained in his family's possession. Perhaps someday its contents will make their way into an official archive or library collection, but for now they remain in private hands. As a result, they are sadly not open to the public and thus remain private in that sense of the word as well. Because Eşref's papers bear no official attestation or provenance, there are those who have been skeptical of their contents. I have encountered such distrust on several occasions, with colleagues naturally wanting to see the evidence themselves, especially the corroboration of official, that is to say, properly archival, sources. In many cases that has been easy to supply but in other cases impossible, given the silence of the archival record on many, but hardly all, of Eşref's far-flung activities. In this respect, the physicality of Eşref's trunk and its contents has proved crucial. Whether it was the Bulgarian seals, the medical record of Eşref's physical examination conducted by a German army doctor in Libya, the photographs of Eşref with various colleagues, the sheaf of telegrams that Eşref saved from the period which he spent reconnoitering the Sinai peninsula in preparation for the Ottoman attempt to cross the Suez Canal in World War I, the souvenirs exchanged by fellow inmates of the British prison camp on Malta, or the hefty stack of papers relating to his legal case for restitution of his estate in Salihli that had been confiscated by the Turkish Republic, Eşref's trunk delivered a large and diverse collection of indisputably original material.

Another, and historiographically more relevant, meaning of Eşref's papers *qua* private papers lies in what they reveal about the unofficial side of his activities. As an officer in the Ottoman gendarmerie and military, Eşref kept numerous official papers and wrote about the official duties that he undertook. But he also kept a number of papers that shed light on his family, his friends, and his business dealings. They thus offer fascinating insights into what we might think of as his "private life." Such a term, however, implies a false dichotomy between Eşref's official and unofficial dealings. In practice, as his papers reveal, the reality was much more complex, reflecting blurred boundaries between the personal and the official aspects of his life. For example, the telegrams that Eşref exchanged with a variety of correspondents when on assignment in the field, sometimes in very remote areas of the empire or beyond its borders, often mixed family and official business. We learn from Eşref's second wife's account of this period (one of the most engaging personal documents to emerge from the trunk) that Eşref had had a telegraph machine installed at their private residence, reflecting the practical imperative for operational overlap. Likewise, we also learn that when Eşref returned to Istanbul from imprisonment on Malta during the war years, he was in the process of reconnecting with his former associates in the Ottoman Special Organization (*Teşkilât ı Mahsusa*) who were then mobilizing for the resistance movement against Allied occupation and the division of Ottoman lands. He divided his attention between paramilitary business and family obligations. For example, on one occasion, Eşref felt obliged to pay a social call on the mother of two of his fellow officers because she had made it clear that she would consider it an egregious lapse in etiquette if Eşref and his wife failed to visit. As is often the case, the limits between work life and social life were almost impossible to define. These blurred boundaries point to what is one of the most important advantages of private papers, namely, the clues they offer to aspects of life that rarely appear in official accounts or government records. As recent studies by Yiğit Akın and Elif Mahir Metinsoy have demonstrated,[7] the military front and the home front were often intensely intertwined, even if most sources reveal only the official side of the story.

---

7   Yiğit Akın, *When the War Came Home: The Ottomans' Great War and the Devastation of an Empire* (Stanford: Stanford University Press, 2018); Elif Mahir Metinsoy, *Ottoman Women during World War I: Everyday Experiences, Politics and Conflict* (Cambridge: Cambridge University Press, 2017).

Eşref's Papers as a "Charged Site"[8]

Although he died in 1964, the mention of Kuşçubaşı Eşref's name still elicits strong emotions today. Although not a household word outside of Turkey, inside its borders he retains a certain degree of notoriety. Some have lionized him as an unrecognized hero of the "Turkish" nation, conveniently overlooking his Circassian roots and Ottomanist proclivities. Nationalist Turks have claimed him as a hero *manqué* who was marginalized in Turkish historiography but deserves a place among the heroes of the nation for his exploits. He has been called a "Turkish Lawrence of Arabia," due to his combat service against the Arab Revolt and, surpassing even the level of hyperbole frequently found on the Internet, "the world's greatest spy." An anonymous individual with apparently insightful knowledge of the Turkish "deep state" has established a Twitter account in his name through which Eşref appears to "tweet" from beyond the grave. Others have condemned him as a ruthless killer and, for some far worse, an individual who turned against Mustafa Kemal Atatürk during the War of Independence and thus became *persona non grata* in the young Turkish Republic. As someone who remained loyal to Enver, whose reputation the early Republic did so much to besmirch, Eşref was further distanced from those honored in the new Turkey. The fact that Eşref's younger brother Selim Sami fought with Enver when he was killed in Central Asia and later died in an apparent attempt to infiltrate the Turkish coastline on a mission to assassinate Mustafa Kemal did little to reduce suspicions of Eşref in Ankara.

Because Eşref's career never ventured far from one controversy to another, it is important to understand the source of the political and historical contestations that he, his career, and therefore his papers represent, and why he is still a contested figure in our day. Over the course of a highly eventful and far-flung career, Eşref engaged in a long list of activities, including many clandestine operations, but it is for two broad reasons that he garnered a controversial reputation. First, as an important member of the far-flung institution known as the Special Organization, Eşref has been linked to a number of nefarious activities. Established by Enver as his own *force spéciale* with intelligence, warfare, and propaganda capabilities, the Special Organization was involved in a wide range of actions both inside and outside the Ottoman Empire's borders. Its agents grew in prominence after the Balkan Wars and were particularly active before and during the Great War. Eşref considered himself to be a key player in the organization and, indeed, one of the most committed of

---

8   Ann Laura Stoler, *Along the Archival Grain: Thinking Through Colonial Ontologies* (New Jersey: Princeton University Press, 2009), 47.

the inner group known as the "self-sacrificing officers" (*fedaî zabitan*) that formed around Enver. The Special Organization has been linked to the Armenian deportations of 1915 and thus has earned a particularly negative reputation. Although my research turned up no direct connection between Eşref and the destruction of the Ottoman Armenians, for many he is simply guilty by association. Secondly, in the eyes of Kemalists (devotees of Mustafa Kemal and the secular republic he founded in 1923), Eşref is guilty of having crossed the future Atatürk at a particularly sensitive time during the passage of history that led to the establishment of the Turkish Republic. By breaking with his erstwhile colleague and comrade-in-arms and the Ankara movement over which Mustafa Kemal was steadily consolidating under his rule, Eşref condemned himself to personal banishment and historiographical opprobrium. The fact that he then created, together with his fellow Circassian and fellow former colleague of Mustafa Kemal "Çerkes" Edhem, an armed organization aimed at overthrowing the Ankara government sealed his fate. He was labeled a "traitor to the nation" (*vatan haini*) of the early Turkish Republic and, along with another 149 men who formed the list of the "150," banned from the country when it was created in 1923 during the negotiations with the Allied powers at Lausanne.

Given the seriousness of the events in which Eşref was involved and the gravity of the charges laid against him, whether legitimate or not, and the legends and counter-narratives that have grown up around him, Eşref's personal papers doubtless qualify as what Ann Laura Stoler terms a "charged site."[9] While they provide much information about his colorful life, they somewhat frustratingly leave many of its long-standing issues unresolved. What they offer is a wealth of personal detail and contextual texture. For example, if we are to focus on Eşref's involvement in the Balkan Wars, we get a good sense of the individual connections and contingencies that are often overlooked when history is seen from above. To take only one example, Eşref's papers contain personal correspondence between Eşref and Enver during the crucial period when the Ottoman high command considered pressing the advantage gained after the recapture of Edirne (Adrianople) in 1913. To the hawkish faction, Bulgarian weakness was an invitation to press on beyond Edirne in order to retake territory that had recently been lost and where the Muslim population had suffered horrific violence and displacement during the First Balkan War. In Eşref's telling, the matter was touch-and-go. He was involved in heart-to-heart talks with Enver and other senior members of the Ottoman military. The relationships described here were personal and the decisions laden with emotion.

9   Ibid.

Eşref's account involves tears and anguish. Another dimension it reveals is the tension between the regular army command and the paramilitary ranks. The former was often highly suspicious of the irregular forces who operated outside the chain of command and who could frequently rely on their personal relationships with leaders such as Enver for special treatment. Such tensions are not only important to understand the dynamics of the time but also the ways in which the history of this period has subsequently been written, largely from the official point of view.

The links between Enver and men such as Eşref were echoed among Eşref and his colleagues. Eşref's papers provide lively accounts of differences in temperament and self-control. To take another example from the Balkan Wars, Eşref describes the ways in which one of his associates, a fellow Circassian man named "Çerkes" Reşid, had to be reined in when he "ran amok," committing atrocities against the non-Muslim civilian population in Western Thrace. At one point, Süleyman Askerî, Eşref's close colleague and fellow organizer of the short-lived Independent Government of western Thrace, asked Eşref to take a hand-propelled railroad side car to fetch Reşid and to use force if required to prevent further atrocities.[10] This was precisely the kind of rogue behavior which the rank-and-file military had been afraid of as paramilitary forces were increasingly relied upon in the bellicose final decades of the empire's history.

For a brief period of time at the end of the Second Balkan War, the rogue Ottoman view seemed to be getting the upper hand. Once the decision was made, over the objections of several high-ranking Ottoman officials, to press on with the Ottoman advance into Bulgarian territory after the capture of Edirne, Eşref and his close associates established the short-lived Independent Government of Western Thrace in what is now part of northern Greece and southern Bulgaria. Eşref and his personally selected force of 115 men were only too happy to proceed. While the Ottoman government demanded deniability, claiming that this was the unsanctioned activity of irregular troops, Eşref and his colleagues quickly established a mini-state, replete with its own flag, anthem, and postage stamps. Their attempt at *fait accompli* politics lasted only a couple of months. Eventually, Istanbul negotiated away the rogue statelet in return for the right to hold on to Edirne and in order to avoid a larger and potentially costly diplomatic row with the European Powers. The Western Thrace episode came to a quick, and for Eşref, a disheartening end. After leading the effort to capture the territory, Eşref had served, along with his brother Selim Sami, his close friend Süleyman Askerî, and his former schoolmate Sapancalı Hakkı, as the key figures in the mini-state. When it was forced to break

10   Eşref Kuşçubaşı Papers, EK2 Scan 298.

FIGURE 6.2. Eşref's stamps.

up, Eşref and his close associates were distraught; their emotions color the account of the period that he left behind in his trunk.

Conclusion

It is ultimately impossible, perhaps, to consider Eşref outside of politics, but despite the politically charged nature of what he and his trunk represent, the materials he left behind speak volumes about imperial lives and their post-imperial fate. His collection of stamps and seals is not dissimilar in some respects to the Baron's Cloak, a sign of vital imperial remnants in what has become a largely national—and nationally defined—history. Following Sunderland's lead, we can see the imperial individual when holding Eşref's stamps or looking through the papers in his trunk. These and other tangible remnants provide important reminders of the individual stories (the rivalries, the personalities, the affinities) that inevitably become submerged in the collective history, the imperial trajectories amid the imprinted records that are archived and understood in national collections and now perforce interpreted in non-imperial ways. Delving into this material offers a partial (in both senses of the word) corrective to the prevailing story.

Bibliography

Akın, Yiğit. *When the War Came Home: The Ottomans' Great War and the Devastation of an Empire*. Stanford: Stanford University Press, 2018.

Blouin, Francis X. and William G. Rosenberg, eds. *Archives, Documentation, and Institutions of Social Memory: Essays from the Sawyer Seminar*. Ann Arbor: The University of Michigan Press, 2007.

————*Processing the Past: Contesting Authority in History and the Archives.* Oxford: Oxford University Press, 2012.

Dirks, Nicholas B. *Castes of Mind: Colonialism and the Making of Modern India.* Princeton: Princeton University Press, 2001.

Endelman, Judith E. "'Just a Car': The Kennedy Car, the Lincoln Chair, and the Study of Objects." In *Archives, Documentation, and Institutions of Social Memory: Essays from the Sawyer Seminar,* edited by Francis X. Blouin and William G. Rosenberg, 245–252. Ann Arbor: The University of Michigan Press, 2007.

Eşref Kuşçubaşı Papers.

Farge, Arlette. *The Lure of the Archives.* New Haven: Yale University Press, 2013.

Fortna, Benjamin C. *The Circassian: A Life of Eşref Bey, Late Ottoman Insurgent and Special Agent.* New York: Oxford University Press, 2016.

Gibson, William. *Distrust That Particular Flavor.* London: Penguin, 2012.

Metinsoy, Elif Mahir. *Ottoman Women during World War I: Everyday Experiences, Politics and Conflict.* Cambridge: Cambridge University Press, 2017.

Philliou, Christine. *Biography of an Empire: Governing Ottomans in an Age of Revolution.* Berkeley: The University of California Press, 2011.

————"The Paradox of Perceptions: Interpreting the Ottoman Past through the National Present." *Middle Eastern Studies* 44, no. 5 (September 2008): 661–75.

Provence, Michael. *The Last Ottoman Generation and the Making of the Middle East.* Cambridge: Cambridge University Press, 2017.

Steedman, Carolyn. *Dust: The Archive and Cultural History.* New Brunswick, NJ: Rutgers University Press, 2002.

Stoler, Ann Laura. *Along the Archival Grain: Thinking Through Colonial Ontologies.* New Jersey: Princeton University Press, 2009.

Sunderland, Willard. *The Baron's Cloak: A History of the Russian Empire in War and Revolution.* Ithaca: Cornell University Press, 2014.

Zürcher, Erik Jan, "Young Turk Memoirs as a Historical Source: Kazim Karabekir's *İstiklal Harbimiz."* *Middle Eastern Studies* 22 (1986): 562–70.

CHAPTER SEVEN

Narrating Sephardic Histories: A Reflection

CHRIS GRATIEN, SAM NEGRI

The following is a reflection piece on the experience of narrating the life of a single Sephardic immigrant in the United States who faced deportation during the Great Depression. It is based on Episode 3 of the Deporting Ottoman Americans investigative series produced by the Ottoman History Podcast, which detailed the life of Leo Negri, a man born in Ottoman Istanbul who died in New York City during the 1960s. Part 1 by Chris Gratien, producer of the Deporting Ottoman Americans podcast series, reflects on how Leo Negri's life fits into the history of migration and race between the former Ottoman Empire and the United States. Part 2 by Sam Negri, a retired journalist and son of Leo Negri, offers a memoir of the Sephardic world of Brooklyn where he grew up and how the experience of making a podcast episode on his father's life influenced that memory.

Producing "Deporting Ottoman Americans"
Chris Gratien

Devi Mays is a professor at the University of Michigan studying the history of Sephardic migration to Mexico and beyond. Towards the end of an interview about her book project, she surprised me with an important lesson for those interested in studying the lives of ordinary, everyday Sephardim. "These are not people who are thinking about 'Who am I? What does it mean to be Sephardic? What does it mean to be Ottoman?'" she said. For merchants and migrants, navigating a complex legal landscape meant engaging with the categories available to them, not necessarily asking the questions of the cultural elite or for that matter the inquiring historian. In many cases, social class and gender played a much more crucial role in their daily lives than less concrete categories of identity. That was good news for me, because I had no idea what it means to be Sephardic. I stumbled into the study of Sephardic lives with a completely different set of questions than anything pertaining to Sephardic identity.

The lessons that Mays draws from her research into the lives of ordinary migrants affirm the value of narrating the history of individual lives, which I have also found researching and producing *Deporting Ottoman Americans*. I began writing and recording material for this investigative podcast series in 2017. It builds on years of experience with the Ottoman History Podcast, a public humanities project that encompasses a large team of contributors who have hosted almost 400 guests since 2011. With *Deporting Ottoman Americans*, I aimed to take our program to a new level by bringing the historian's craft to the podcast medium. Podcasting is more than just history as usual in an audio format. The medium itself brings new things to the narrative by capitalizing on the affective qualities of sound. The human voice, music, and other audio elements can be used to communicate emotion, build mood, and steer a narrative. And as such, storytelling has emerged as one of the main strengths of the podcast medium, which, while considerably more independent, has roots in radio journalism. But historians narrate the past in a very different manner, often with the kind of nuance and context that is lost in mainstream discourses. Scholarly history podcasting is public scholarship made with a sense of responsibility to a much larger and more diverse audience. The idea is to provide new content but also to lay bare the work and methods of scholarly history-writing, a practice that proves how thinking about the past can be relevant to everyday life.

The *Deporting Ottoman Americans* series is based on archival research and interviews with scholarly experts and revolves around the question: how do you deport someone to a country that no longer exists? During the 1920s and 30s, the United States began deporting thousands of people per year at the federal level for the first time. Deportation peaked in the early years of the Great Depression, when migrants were scapegoated for America's economic woes. Throughout that period, as many as a million Mexicans and native-born Mexican-Americans were deported or pressured into "repatriation." In much smaller but still wildly unprecedented numbers, people from all over the world were deported through more formalized legal channels. People born in the Ottoman Empire were a small part of this picture, but because the empire they were born in had since fragmented into many new states with their own stringent nationality laws, deporting Ottoman-born Americans posed particular challenges. The episodes in the series explore the making of modern migration regimes as reflected in the lives and deportation cases of each person studied and, through them, the histories of many migrant groups from the Ottoman Empire like the Sephardic community of late Ottoman Istanbul.

The backbone of each episode comes from the deportation case files of a particular individual. The case files contain legal documents, including transcripts of

FIGURE 7.1. Leo Negri's deportation file included his original Ottoman identity papers. The image above was (probably) taken of Leo in Istanbul while he was in his late teens. RG 84, Turkey (Ankara Embassy), Box 40,855. Negri, National Archives and Records Administration.

deportation hearings, as well as internal and diplomatic correspondence pertaining to their deportation. My main collaborator on the series, Emily Pope-Obeda, a scholar of deportation in the United States, refers to the various bodies of the American state and society that collaborate together on deportation cases as "nesting scales of space and authority."[1] Immigrant lives are documented by different

---

1   Emily Pope-Obeda, "'When in Doubt, Deport!': U.S. Deportation and the Local Policing of Global Migration During the 1920s" (Ph.D. Dissertation, University of Illinois at Urbana-Champaign, 2016), 36.

levels of authority over certain respective spaces involved in the deportation pro-cess: families, communities, police stations, courtrooms, prisons, hospitals, the Department of Labor, Department of State, embassies, consulates, and finally the foreign ministries of other governments. Although these documents offer a skewed perspective on the lives of individuals, usually in their most vulnerable moments, they provide a wealth of detail with which to contextualize a person's life within the larger historical processes of migration and deportation.

Leo Negri was an American immigrant born into the Sephardic community of Istanbul. He left as a young man during the early years of the Turkish Republic, spent years in Cuba, and finally settled in New York City. What initially attracted me to his deportation story was the ways in which his deportation hearings spoke to the issue of class and the injustices of immigration enforcement. For his time, Leo was well-educated, speaking no less than four languages. He stated that he was qualified for work as a translator, clerk, electrician, or painter. Yet he scraped by during the Depression years, working any job he could find—jobs that often took a heavy toll on his body—cleaning streets, draining swamps, shining shoes, or guessing the weight of people outside of the Steeplechase amusement park in Coney Island. Barely able to make ends meet, his family qualified for home relief and relied on it during the years of the Great Depression. In his hearings, he de-scribed his travails in language both matter-of-fact and moving. There was a stigma around not being able to earn a living—Leo had a large family—and being poor was anything but an asset in front of an immigration investigator. The mere fact of receiving social welfare from the state—becoming a public charge—was enough to threaten deportation for non-citizens.

Leo's only other fault in the eyes of the authorities was entering the country on a fake Cuban passport to sidestep the racially-biased immigration quotas. Even though his wife and children were native-born Americans, the authorities followed him right into the years of the Second World War and the Holocaust, using diplomatic channels to try to obtain a Turkish passport for his deportation.

The Negri family's deportation nightmare was inextricable from a context in which mainstream white supremacism had succeeded in overturning America's liberal immigration policies that had allowed millions of migrants from Eastern Europe, Southern Europe, and the Middle East to become U.S. citizens. With the implementation of nationality-based immigration quotas in 1924, people like Leo faced tremendous obstacles obtaining an immigration visa. Jewish immigrants were foremost among the groups that supporters of the quota system sought to limit. Sephardic Jews from Turkey were especially restricted; in the first quotas, implemented around the time Leo Negri left for Cuba, Turkey received just 100 visa slots per year. In a region devastated by the First World War and the fall of the Ottoman Empire, ethnolinguistic minorities had even more impetus to follow in the footsteps of prior generations of migrants. That is why Leo and so many other people like him resorted to illicit channels in order to reach the United States, a process well-studied in Libby Garland's monograph *After They Closed the Gates: Jewish Illegal Immigration to the United States, 1921–1965*.

The story of Leo Negri's brush with the deportation state encapsulated the immigration history of an entire community. In order to tell his story with its numerous facets, I drew on collaboration with a number of scholars to create an episode for *Deporting Ottoman Americans*. To understand the history of the Sephardic community in the United States, I interviewed Devin Naar, chair of the Sephardic Studies program at the University of Washington, Seattle. Naar explained how the Sephardic community maintained a notion of a distinctive "Turkino" identity that reflected their unique position within the larger Jewish-American dynamic with enduring links to the Ottoman Empire and Turkey. The Turkinos were distinguished from other Jewish immigrants in their being Turkino, meaning an Ottoman/Turkish subject or citizen. The second component of Sephardic identity that became relevant in the experience of global migration were Iberian origins; while Sephardic Jews were among the many different ethnolinguistic communities of Ottoman port cities, their use of Ladino, with its close resemblance to Spanish, meant that in the Americas, Sephardic Jews were often read as Hispanic. As Devi Mays explained in an interview, this perceived Iberian heritage presented certain opportunities. In Mexico, Sephardic Jews were seen as favorable immigrants during an interwar period in which governments became more hostile towards Jewish immigrants. And because the U.S. did not implement any visa regime for Latin American countries, Sephardic Jews passing as residents of migration hubs like Mexico or Cuba could sidestep immigration quotas. Leo Negri did so by obtaining a passport indicating that he was a Cuban national named Ramon Franqui, an assertion that would be difficult for a border official to refute based on his appearance and accent alone.

Deporting the husband and father of native-born Americans for violating a regulation that had not existed just a few years prior would have been an expression of the emerging deportation state's cruel persistence. After WWII, immigration authorities relented, and Leo Negri remained in the country for the rest of his life. But trying the follow the outcome of Leo's deportation took the project in a strange direction when I discovered that he had been the victim of a senseless killing decades later in his former New York City neighborhood of Brownsville. While the killing appeared to be a random act of violence, it took on a political dimension in the rapidly changing neighborhoods of Brooklyn during the 1960s. The former immigrant neighborhoods of Brownsville and East New York had become predominantly African-American and Puerto Rican. The most vocal opponents of this change were Italian-Americans and other people from groups who had been on the other side of a nativist backlash decades prior. People once targeted by white supremacists had become both the agents and dissenting voices in the phenomenon of "white flight" and everything that accompanied it. Because Leo Negri's shooter was black, these dissenting voices held his murder up as an example of something larger that was taking place, calling for more policing in local governments where white New Yorkers held disproportionate sway.

Finishing Negri's story involved delving into a separate set of questions in the history of the regions where they settled in the United States, far from the concerns of historians of the Ottoman Empire and modern Turkey. The history of New York and other American cities during the 1960s had little to do with the context from which Leo Negri's migration story began, but it had everything to do with where and how it ended. To understand the intersections of race and politics in America's changing cities, I interviewed Claudrena Harold, Professor of African-American history at University of Virginia. I also drew on the work of Wendell Pritchett, *Brownsville, Brooklyn: Blacks, Jews, and the Changing Face of the Ghetto*, which studied the transformation of the Brooklyn neighborhood where Leo Negri spent much of his life and was ultimately killed.

Leo Negri's death was politicized due to the hotly contested nature of urban space during the period. Archived and searchable digital newspaper collections provided quick access to a perspective on how the different press outlets sought to frame Negri's murder in different ways, allowing me to observe how the spin operated in real time. Articles with nearly identical content based on news services like the Associated Press often appeared with different titles depending on the politics of the newspaper. For example, whereas one South Carolina newspaper adopted the headline "Husband Shot Protecting Wife," a Jackson, Mississippi newspaper published the same article with the headline "Man Killed By Negro Youths' Shot." Whereas the former title focused on the victim's story, the latter sought to underscore the race of the perpetrator.

Talking to Leo Negri's sons, Louis and Sam, further underscored the tension underlying the politicization of individual life stories in which people are held up as representatives of a particular group. Decades later, Louis still remembered bitterly how the mayor of New York, John Lindsay, was eager to keep things quiet surrounding Leo Negri's murder, largely because it was being used by his political opponents who wanted to depict the case as evidence of how the character of Brooklyn's neighborhoods was changing in step with demographic change. Sam, himself a journalist at the time, remembered the politics of the news coverage, especially news outlets which attempted to play up the racial dimension of the killing. In addition to processing the sudden loss of a father, Sam had to see Leo Negri's death used to further a political agenda that he was entirely opposed to as a supporter of the civil rights movement.

Connecting the history of an integral ethnolinguistic community in the late Ottoman capital of Istanbul to the changing neighborhoods of modern Brooklyn was an exciting challenge. Through the experiences of an ordinary Sephardic migrant with an extraordinary life story, we were able to show how white supremacist discourses have governed processes of social change in the United States from the anti-immigrant turn of the 1920s to the era of civil rights during the 1960s. Scholars of race and immigration in America have demonstrated the process by which immigrants labeled as undesirable by the old Anglo-Saxon Protestant elite of the U.S. came to be reimagined and in some cases came to represent anti-integration stances during the post-WWII period.

Leo Negri, from his arrival in the US with a fraudulent passport to his years-long deportation saga to his highly-publicized slaying in East New York decades, later embodied many aspects of this process in a single human life. His story demonstrates the violence and distortion caused by categories imposed on ordinary people who sought to make a life for themselves in the United States. Though the many times and places Leo Negri inhabited could be studied elsewhere, connecting them through a single life revealed for me as a historian the artifice of most of the categories we normally use to describe people. Throughout his life in Istanbul, Cuba, and New York, Leo went by different names, wore many hats, and was identified by others in radically different ways. In Istanbul, he was a member of an important ethnolinguistic minority of Sephardim educated in French schools. In Cuba, he worked as a peddler and passed as a Spanish-speaking Cuban in order to enter the United States. Once there, he was doubly marginalized: as a Jewish migrant belonging to a group maligned by anti-immigration activists and white supremacists and as a Sephardic man living in a city where Ashkenazi culture and institutions dominated the Jewish-American community. When both Brownsville and the status of Jews in America changed after the Second World War, he returned to his former neighborhood as an anonymous white man killed by an African-American teenager. In the context of the Civil Rights battles of the 1960s, many of the same people who would have opposed Jewish immigration decades earlier and supported the deportation of undocumented people like Leo decried his death in an effort to resist the demographic change taking place in America's cities and the integration that came with it. While the story of Leo Negri that we presented defies any attempt to reduce his identity to a stable category, it also laid bare the hypocrisy of those who sought to instrumentalize his murder using racist and segregationist discourses.

Remembering Brownsville

By Sam Negri

When I was a child in the 1940s, I lived in Brownsville, a small but densely populated neighborhood in Brooklyn. The streets were narrow and crowded with stone apartment houses built in the 1920s. Vacant lots were filled with trash. There was a soda factory, a pickle factory and a huge place where they collected and baled rags. That's what I saw on my walk to school.

Brownsville was small, slightly less than two square miles, but its cockroach-infested tenements were packed with roughly 250,000 people, about 80 percent of whom were poor Jewish immigrants. Someone once called Brownsville "Little Jerusalem" because in the 1930s and 1940's, there were 82 synagogues crammed into its crime-ridden streets. For many families, it was the crucible through which they passed on their way to greener pastures in the suburbs of Long Island or New Jersey.

On Belmont Avenue, which was a permanent farmer's market and the main shopping center predating chain supermarkets, Jews owned most of the shops and most of the shop windows had signs in Yiddish, with Hebrew letters. The street was crowded from end to end with pushcarts. You could buy anything from potatoes to beets and brooms and freshly slaughtered chickens. The vendors and customers spoke Yiddish, German, Russian, or broken English, among other languages.

There were few cars in the neighborhood when I was growing up. Hawkers came down our street selling fruits and vegetables from horse-drawn wagons. Apartments had iceboxes, not refrigerators, and blocks of ice were also delivered on horse-drawn wagons. Other solitary vendors pushed metal carts and sold potato or kasha knishes. Still others pushed a grinder for sharpening knives.

Only one kid on the block had a TV. It had a 10 inch black and white screen. Most of the time, we listened to shows on the radio. When I was 13, we still could not afford a TV.

Sephardic Jews were rare in this neighborhood. Without intending to do so, an immigrant woman who lived down the street made an innocent mistake that illuminated the distinction between Ashkenazi and Sephardic Jews.

Mrs. Miller was an Ashkenazi Jew. She was short, round, and had the red cheeks of a Campbell Soup kid. She spoke Yiddish and broken English. She seemed to be constantly concerned about the health of Bernie, her only son, one of my childhood friends who suffered from some sort of skin condition. I usually saw Mrs. Miller only when she interrupted our street games to coat him in what looked like Calamine lotion.

When I was in the third grade, she approached me at the end of one of our games, and asked me to do her a favor. Would I go to her apartment, in a tenement across the street from the one I lived in, and light the stove for her? At the time, I didn't know why she didn't just have her own son do it, but I didn't ask any questions, maybe because she offered to pay me a dime for helping her out.

What I didn't know was that it was Friday, the beginning of the Jewish Sabbath. Mrs. Miller, who was orthodox, was prohibited from lighting the oven on the Sabbath, so she hired a kid she thought was a non-Jew, sometimes called a Shabbos goy in Yiddish. When I told my mother, a Sephardic Jew, about this incident, she became angry and bitter. Then she went down the street to give Mrs. Miller a piece of her mind. It was the first time I learned that we were different from all the other Jews who surrounded us in the teeming ghetto that was Brownsville at the end of World War II.

In retrospect, it seems my mother was not upset by what I had done but by the neighbor's presumption that I was not Jewish, possibly because she had never been exposed to Sephardic Jews. A few years later, when I was enrolled in the United Sephardic Talmud Torah on Malta Street in East New York, adjacent to Brownsville, I encountered another population that had previously been unknown to me, though culturally they were very much like me. Like me, the kids at the Talmud Torah were Sephardic Jews and had family names like Motola, Behar, Levy, Ventura, Morhaim, Franco, Maya, and Arias. Most were from Turkey or, in the case of my mother, descended from immigrants native to Romania and Bulgaria.

All were descended from Spanish Jews exiled from Spain in 1492 who settled in the Ottoman Empire. Eventually, they emigrated to enclaves in America like the Lower East Side of Manhattan, Brownsville, Coney Island, and East New York.

I was born in Coney Island Hospital in 1941, the year the United States entered World War II. We moved to Brownsville around the tail end of World War II, probably in 1944. We were a minority within a minority, a Sephardic family in the middle of a dense community of Ashkenazi Jews, but I knew nothing of that at the time. There were fourteen boys in my age group on my block with last names like Abramovitz, Zavilowitz, Bernstein, Stampnitsky, Turetsky, and Hirschenson, none ending in a vowel. All were children from Ashkenazi families and descended from Eastern European people. I never felt any different from the other kids, but there clearly were cultural distinctions.

Brownsville is located in eastern Brooklyn, between East New York and Canarsie, six miles from Lower Manhattan. It was crowded, populated mostly by impoverished Jews still recovering from the scourge of the Great Depression or war-ravaged Europe. Every so often we would encounter someone with a number tattooed on his or her arm, a sad reminder of the Nazi concentration camps.

Around the time I started junior high school in 1953, there was a day when the bustle of the neighborhood came to an eerie standstill. A few blocks from the junior high, P. S. 165, there was a mortuary, the I.J. Morris Funeral Home, and that day the funeral for Ethel and Julius Rosenberg was conducted there—the climax to an international controversy over a couple convicted of selling secrets to the Soviet Union, later executed in Sing Sing Prison. The Rosenbergs' case dominated headlines across Europe and the United States. Many thought it resulted from blatant antisemitism and anticommunist paranoia, a viewpoint that resonated among the many leftists and Marxists living in Brownsville.

Over the years, I've had many negative thoughts about that neighborhood—mainly because of its poverty and the omnipresent threat of violence—but when my parents moved to Connecticut around the time of my fifteenth birthday, I felt like something important had been ripped from my life. Brownsville had become an almost palpable force in my consciousness, an ethnic and religious cocoon. I knew no other world. I had no choice but to go along, unwilling conscript though I might be, to a place dominated by Roman Catholic families. There were fewer than five Jews in the high school I attended in Bridgeport, CT. There were no Turks or Spanish Jews or anything else that seemed familiar. I was cast adrift in a strange new world. The move to Connecticut was the cultural equivalent of the wheel turning away from itself. Without the religious and cultural safety blanket that Brownsville provided, the links to my Sephardic background grew weaker every year.

The immigrant population in Bridgeport, CT consisted mainly of Italians and people from Slavic countries who worshipped in the city's many Catholic churches. My family differed from that population. We never listened to Christmas carols, and as a child I never heard anyone refer to Jesus or "the Holy Mother," terms used by one of my teachers in my Bridgeport high school. My father and his relatives were called Turks and spoke no Yiddish and very little English. Instead, they conversed in Ladino, a hybrid that included old Spanish words, some Hebrew, Portuguese, and other languages, but no Yiddish. My mother's parents were first cousins from Bulgaria and Romania.

My mother, Flora Gadol, was born in Brooklyn and spoke two languages, English and Ladino. My father, Yuda Leon Negri, was born in Istanbul and came to America illegally, via Cuba, in 1928 when he was 22 years old. He spoke Ladino, Turkish, Greek, and possibly some French. My parents' courtship and marriage depended heavily on their knowledge of Ladino. My mother spoke no Turkish. My three older brothers picked up some of the Ladino, but I was the youngest of four, and as time passed, the Ladino my parents used for shouting and fighting was gradually replaced by English. I could understand it but was never able to speak it.

It took many years and sporadic exposure to the writings of others to understand that, hardships aside, the predominantly Jewish community in Brownsville, and especially my extended family living in the nearby tenements, provided security and comfort that I would never duplicate anywhere else. All of my aunts and uncles, like many other immigrants, had migrated to Brownsville or East New York from the fetid slums of the Lower East Side of Manhattan.

Life in Brownsville was closely integrated with the Jewish calendar, which made no distinctions between Ashkenazi and Sephardic. The year was not only defined by the seasonal change in the weather, but by the flow of Jewish Holidays, beginning with Rosh Hashanah, the Jewish New Year, followed 10 days later by Yom Kippur (the Day of Atonement); then came Succoth, Simchat Torah, Hanukkah, Purim, and Passover, with a variety of other holidays sprinkled in between.

Brownsville's public schools were mostly vacant at Rosh Hashanah and Yom Kippur. Throughout that period, people would appear on the streets dressed in their finest clothes. Life would slow down, and everyone would be seen walking to the many synagogues in the area several times a day. Our never-ending street games, which included stickball, handball, and kick the can, would cease. Most of us walked around or sat on the steps of our tenements all day dressed in starched shirts, pressed pants, and new shoes.

At Simchat Torah, a joyful holiday marking the end of the cycle of reading the Torah and starting the cycle all over on a weekly basis, I would walk to the Sephardic synagogue in East New York, sing songs, and come home with a paper flag. It would have a large Star of David on it and a jelly apple impaled on the top of the stick. All of my Ashkenazi friends went to synagogues closer to home, but everybody ended up with flags and jelly apples.

All of us attended the same elementary school, P. S. 184. It was only a block or two from our street. Along our walk to school, we would pass a rag factory where oddly pungent bales of rags were stacked on the street. Across from the rags was a soda bottle distributor, and about 50 feet beyond that we passed barrels of kosher pickles waiting to be loaded onto delivery trucks. On the street parallel to our route to school, a large commercial bakery exhaled the fragrance of fresh rolls, and so our walk was often redolent with the weird smell of old rags, truck exhaust fumes, pickles, and freshly baked bread.

The Sephardic influence came mostly from my time at the two-story Talmud Torah and the synagogue adjacent to the school. One thing I learned there was that the Sephardim pronounce Hebrew words one way and Ashkenazis another. This obscure fact stuck with me every time I attended the wedding or bar mitzvah of Ashkenazi friends. Throughout my life, I've been sensitive to the sound of language and music, and hearing their dissonant pronunciations was offensive to my ears. That odd prejudice stayed with me well into adulthood.

The Hebrew of our synagogue, on the other hand, was, to my ear, more mellifluous and tuneful, especially when sung. The songs I heard from these Mediterranean and North African Jews were not the painful lamentations I heard in Ashkenazi synagogues. Without any musical accompaniment, Sephardic singing always seemed to transmit a warm climate, soft breezes, and a love of poetry. The singing was neither guttural nor morose. Some of those tunes are still trapped in my brain, and occasionally I feel like singing aloud the few phrases I can remember from the Sabbath services.

I'd forgotten how evocative those melodies could be until recently, when someone posted a YouTube video of a Hanukkah celebration in an old part of Istanbul. Hundreds of people congregated in the square and sang a traditional Hanukkah song called Ma-oz Tzur (to the tune of Rock of Ages). Hearing it brought back vivid memories and sent a chill down my spine. How could I have forgotten? The melody reminded me that I belonged to something, despite all the years I had spent ignoring it. The scene reminded me of the cohesiveness of my parents, my aunts and uncles, and their childhood friends.

Our synagogue was a small but familiar community where, according to Orthodox customs, women sat separate from the men. At the end of my bar mitzvah, I headed a procession carrying the Torah through the aisles and was bombarded with the hard candies that the woman tossed down on me from the balcony.

My friends who sat in the front row reflected the diverse world beyond the synagogue and the world of the Turks. One friend was Cuban, one was black, another Puerto Rican, one was Italian and Catholic, and others came from Ashkenazi families. We all went to school together, played baseball, handball, and stick ball together, and none of them had ever entered a Sephardic synagogue before.

Nor had I until I was around 12 years old, when the time came to prepare for my bar mitzvah. Then, after a day at public school, I would walk to my friend Elliott Israel's apartment, and together we made the long walk to Hebrew School. Elliott was the only Sephardic contact I had outside my immediate family. During one of these walks, Elliott taught me how to whistle. I had a hard time getting it right and continued trying even when I got to my seat at the back of the classroom. This irritated the Hebrew teacher, a Turk named Rabbi Pesah, and for years I nurtured a memory of his slapping my face and upbraiding me for being a wise guy. Strangely, as I grew older, I began to question whether that was an invention of my juvenile mind or whether it had really happened. I do remember that he was furious.

Similarly, doors opened and closed on scenes from childhood that provided glimpses into many of the connections I knew nothing about as a child. For example, on many weekends, many of my aunts and uncles, all Sephardic, would gather at my aunt Sophie's apartment on New Lots Avenue, a busy thoroughfare in East New York. The men played cards in the living room, using the table usually reserved for the annual Passover Seder, and the women played bingo in the kitchen. Kids sat with the women snacking on the spinach and cheese borekas Sophie had baked. The apartment was tiny, four small rooms on the second floor, and when the kids got drowsy, they would be ushered into a bedroom where winter coats had been piled on a bed.

Looking back at those family gatherings, I realized that all of the participants, both friends and blood relatives, had known each other since childhood when they were living in Williamsburg or the Lower East Side. When they left those places, they moved, more or less as a unit, within a few blocks of each other in Brownsville and East New York. This was a great comfort for me, because no matter which direction I walked from my tenement on Watkins Street, there was always an aunt or uncle and cousins I could visit on my way home.

My father's parents and his sister Rica remained on the Lower East Side, as did the coffee houses where Turks congregated to eat, smoke, and play cards. My father was a frequent visitor and occasionally brought me with him. I will never forget the powerful smell of freshly brewed Turkish coffee that was omnipresent the moment the door opened.

More recently, I came upon a passage written by the late Alfred Kazin that resonated with my experiences. Kazin was a famous critic and author who was born in 1915 in the neighborhood where I grew up. Many years after Kazin had moved on to fame and fortune, he reflected on his bar mitzvah. In *A Walker in the City*, one of his many books, he wrote:

Whether I agreed with its beliefs or not, I belonged; whether I assented to its rights over me or not, I belonged; whatever I thought of them, no matter how far I might drift from that place, I belonged. This was understood in the very nature of things; I was a Jew. It did not matter how little I knew or understood of the faith, or that I was always reading alien books; I belonged. I had been expected. I was now to take my place in the great tradition.[2]

Reading that lyrical passage explained why I'd never been able to get my child-hood years in Brooklyn out of my mind.

Collectively, the Jewish kids I knew best were aware of their background, but their Jewish customs were taken for granted and our conversations were more fo-cused on sports, especially the fate of the Brooklyn Dodgers, than anything even remotely connected to religion.

Many years after my bar mitzvah, I returned to the old synagogue to say Kaddish for my father who had been shot to death while walking to a bus stop with my mother late at night. The street where this senseless tragedy occurred was just a few blocks from the synagogue. A group of teens were out partying that night, and one of them tried to snatch my mother's purse. My father was shot in the back and died before the police arrived. The next day, the *Daily News* ran a gruesome picture of his body sprawled in the aisle of a city bus where he had been dragged after the shooting. The following day, my older brother and I went to the morgue at Kings County Hospital to identify the body, a grim scene that lurks forever in memory.

Early in the morning during our week of sitting shiva, we would go back to the synagogue where I'd had my bar mitzvah. The rabbi lit one candle and placed the brass candle holder on the floor facing the ark. There were ten men present to say Kaddish, but things were already changing for this community. Some mornings when my brothers and I got to the synagogue, the rabbi would get on the phone to cajole another two or three men to come in so that we would have a minyan

---

2   Alfred Kazin, *A Walker in the City* (New York: Harcourt Inc., 1979), 45.

NARRATING SEPHARDIC HISTORIES: A REFLECTION | 197

as required for the ritual. So many families had moved to the suburbs that it was becoming increasingly difficult to round up ten men to pray for the deceased.

In the time between childhood and our move to Connecticut, I heard very little about my father's life in Istanbul and knew nothing about his immigration problems. After I moved to Arizona in 1972, the Brownsville stories that intermittently played like a slideshow in my mind had blurred.

The one element that persisted was my negative feelings about my father. I saw him as someone who was given to rages, smoked four packs a day, and fought bitterly with my mother over money. Worst of all, it seemed he could never hold a job for longer than six months.

In short, his values were not my values, but I never gave much thought to why this was so until 2018. At that point, I was 77 years old and enjoying the contented life of a retiree, when out of the blue I received a Facebook message from Chris Gratien, a University of Virginia historian and researcher, which unlocked a trove of factual information about my father's illegal entry to the United States via Cuba and the years of the government's attempts to deport him, an effort that turned out to be unsuccessful.

History, through Gratien's work and the writings of Gerald Sorin, a Brownsville native and professor at the State University of New York, shattered my ignorance and led to an epiphany of sorts in the way I viewed my family's experiences.

Combing through the many transcripts Gratien sent, mostly immigration officials interviewing my parents, I realized I had judged harshly, that my views were built around the effects without any knowledge of the causes. I'd had no information about why my father behaved as he did or how hard he had struggled to make enough money to survive and feed a wife and four sons. None of the details of my parents' daily life had been shared with me. Occasionally, I heard vague references to a work-related injury, and his "case." But details were always absent.

What I learned from Gratien's research was that my father briefly worked for the New York Sanitation Department. In 1937, while working on a truck doing snow removal, he fell and hit his head on the icy asphalt, suffering a concussion that left him hospitalized at Cornell Medical Center and Good Samaritan Hospital off and on for 38 days. He suffered dizzy spells and other symptoms as a result. My older brother remembers my mother being told that the injury would result in occasional rages. His behavior after that was sometimes unpredictable but often combative.

The pictures I carried in my memories were all negative until I saw evidence of his real-life struggles. He never resorted to crime, despite his inability to find permanent employment. When he didn't have a job, he put together a shoeshine box and set up business on the street above a subway station, where he toiled long hours. The vicissitudes he endured were not his alone but a common state of affairs for many who arrived in America in the early twentieth century to pursue the dream of a better life.

The more I read from the historical record, the more my animosity toward him melted away, released by the liberating gift of forgiveness.

FIGURE 7.2. A portrait of Leo c. 1936 from his deportation file. RG 84, Turkey (Ankara Embassy), Box 40,855. Negri, National Archives and Records Administration.

Conclusion

Most people are not accustomed to thinking of their family and friends as historical subjects, and historians often forget that the subjects they study are real people with family, friends, and descendants. In narrating the life and death of Leo Negri, we found a meaningful way of enriching public knowledge of the past that reaffirms the responsibility of scholars towards their subjects and audience. But the story of Leo Negri does not only belong to his time and to his descendants and relatives today. Nor does it belong only to the annals of Sephardic history. In the public-facing podcast format, the story of Leo Negri also became the story of immigrants and immigrant families today. It is the story of undocumented people who fight deportation and exclusion in hopes of keeping their families intact. It is the story of people from the lands of the former Ottoman Empire who face the same types of challenges and prejudices in coming to America that Leo Negri faced nearly a century ago. And it is also the story of America's changing cities, racism, and the politics of policing that remain as pressing today as they were when Leo Negri's murder was suddenly thrust into the middle of a much larger political struggle. Through Leo Negri and his migration experience, the trajectories of Sephardim take on a much wider historical significance. They speak to vital issues of their time and ours.

Bibliography

Kazin, Alfred. *A Walker in the City*. New York: Harcourt Inc., 1979.

Pope-Obeda, Emily. "'When in Doubt, Deport!' U.S. Deportation and the Local Policing of Global Migration During the 1920s." PhD diss., University of Illinois, Urbana-Champaign, 2016.

Further Reading

Episode 3 of Deporting Ottoman Americans podcast entitled "Turkino" is available on the Ottoman History Podcast website at http://www.ottomanhistorypodcast.com/2019/05/turkino.html.

Angel, Marc D. *La America: The Sephardic Experience in the United States*. Philadelphia: Jewish Publication Society of America, 1982.

Ben-Ur, Aviva. *Sephardic Jews in America: A Diasporic History*. New York, N.Y.: New York University Press, 2012.

Garland, Libby. *After They Closed the Gates: Jewish Illegal Immigration to the United States, 1921–1965*. Chicago: University of Chicago Press, 2018.

Gratien, Chris and Emily Pope-Obeda. "Ottoman Migrants, U.S. Deportation Law, and Statelessness during the Interwar Era." *Mashriq & Mahjar*. 5, no. 2 (2018): 125–158.

Hester, Torrie. *Deportation: The Origins of U.S. Policy.* Philadelphia: University of Pennsylvania Press, 2017.

Kanstroom, Dan. *Deportation Nation: Outsiders in American History.* Cambridge, MA: Harvard University Press, 2010.

Mays, Devi. *Forging Ties, Forging Passports: Migration and the Modern Sephardi Diaspora.* Stanford, CA: Stanford University Press, 2020.

Moloney, Deirdre M. *National Insecurities: Immigrants and U.S. Deportation Policy Since 1882.* University of North Carolina Press, 2016.

Naar, Devin E. "Turkinos beyond the Empire: Ottoman Jews in America, 1893 to 1924." *Jewish Quarterly Review* 105, no. 2 (2015): 174–205.

Ngai, Mae M. *Impossible Subjects: Illegal Aliens and the Making of Modern America.* Princeton, NJ: Princeton Univ. Press, 2014.

Pritchett, Wendell. *Brownsville, Brooklyn: Blacks, Jews, and the Changing Face of the Ghetto.* Chicago: The University of Chicago Press, 2003.

Stein, Sarah Abrevaya. *Extraterritorial Dreams: European Citizenship, Sephardi Jews, and the Ottoman Twentieth Century.* Chicago: University of Chicago Press, 2017.

Zolberg, Aristide R. *A Nation by Design: Immigration Policy in the Fashioning of America.* Cambridge, MA: Harvard University Press, 2008.

CHAPTER EIGHT

Amid Galanti's Private Documents: Reflections on the Legacy, Trajectory, and Preservation of a Sephardi Intellectual's Past

KEREM TINAZ

Historian Cecil Roth portrayed Avram Galanti[1] as a "single-handed Jewish Historical Society" on the occasion of Galanti's Jubilee, organized in honor of his eighty-fourth birthday in 1957 by his friend Habib Gerez (1926–).[2] Born in a Sephardic family in Bodrum in 1873, Galanti was a prolific intellectual whose long life spanned from the late Ottoman Empire to the Republic of Turkey. Researching, writing, and publishing stood at the center of Galanti's life. His copious books and articles published in many different journals covered a wide range of subjects about the history and culture of the Sephardim and contributed exceptionally to the studies on Jews in the Ottoman Empire and Turkey.

Roth also emphasized that Galanti's "name was well known in the world of learning" in the twentieth century. Academics and researchers from different parts of the world recognized his expertise in Sephardic history and consulted him often for field-related issues. One of these researchers was Albert Adatto (1910–1996), an intellectual with significant contributions to the foundations of Sephardic Studies in the United States.[3] In his letter to Galanti, dated 21 December 1938, Adatto briefly presented his MA thesis written at the University of Washington, titled "Sephardim and the Seattle Sephardic Community of Seattle." Then, he mentioned his plan to study "the fourteen Sephardic communities in the United States outside

---

1   The name Avram Galanti appears in various formats in different documents (i.e. Avram Galanti, Abraham Galante, Abraham Galanti) depending on the language and origin of the source/publication. Avram Galanti is the format of his name that often appears in his Ottoman and Turkish individual and official documents. Consequently, I have used this spelling of the name throughout the chapter.

2   "A Letter From Cecil Roth to J. Habib Gerez," *The Central Archives for the History of the Jewish People Jerusalem* (CAHJP), P/112, F.1.

3   CAHJP, P/112, F.47.

New York City" and highlighted his eagerness to extend his knowledge about the "Sephardim of the Near East," despite the lack of sources and materials in Seattle at the time.[4] Adatto asked Galanti ten questions to advance his research, namely, a list and corresponding prices of Galanti's works, the names of prominent Sephardic scholars in different parts of the world, the names of leading specialists on Ladino literature, a list of pioneering and available books that would be important to start organizing a Sephardic library, the possibility of obtaining a Ladino grammar and a Ladino dictionary, the estimated Sephardic population in the world, the general Sephardic approach to Zionism in Turkey, and Galanti's opinions about different Sephardic-related issues. I was not able to find evidence of an answer among Galanti's papers. Thus, with the sources we have at hand, it is impossible to know whether Galanti contributed directly to Adatto's intellectual efforts or the organization of his library, which today stands as one of the most valuable components of the Sephardic Studies Collection at the University of Washington. Since Galanti was not indifferent to the requests that he received and generally supported efforts to develop studies on Sephardic history in different parts of the world,[5] we can only speculate on an answer to Adatto's request, now lost to history.[6] In any case, it is clear that Galanti's work was important to Adatto's intellectual curiosity.

Galanti's trajectory was the immediate subject to appear in my mind when a discussion about *Sephardic Trajectories* occurred the first time between me and Oscar Aguirre-Mandujano, the co-editor of this volume. Galanti's life provided a useful yet complex example to think about the different trajectories Ottoman Jews followed as they migrated from the Ottoman Empire to various parts of the world at the turn of the twentieth century. His life, and the documents he left behind, also illustrates the many possible reasons behind these trajectories. Until Avram Galanti moved to Istanbul in 1911, his intellectual and career trajectories were not easily

---

4   In his letter, Albert Adatto remarks "Though my knowledge of Sephardic culture is limited my thirst for additional knowledge is far from quenched." CAHJP, P/112, F.47.

5   For example, see Letters of Salo Baron to Abraham Galante in Julia Phillips Cohen and Sarah Abrevaya Stein, eds., *Sephardi Lives: A Documentary History, 1700–1950* (Stanford: Stanford University Press, 2014), 412–13. For the original letters see CAHJP, P/112, F.45. Also see letters from Cecil Roth to Avram Galanti in CAHJP, P/112, F.52, 57.

6   Today, Albert Adatto's papers are located in the Washington State Jewish Archives (University of Washington). If Adatto received an answer from Galanti, then perhaps that answer might be found in his personal papers. For further information about Adatto, see chapters written by Devin Naar and Ty Alhadeff in this volume. Also see Ty Alhadeff, "Wisdom for politicians from a Ladino poet: Avoiding a nuclear inferno," Stroum Center for Jewish Studies, University of Washington, 1 November 2016, https://jewishstudies. washington.edu/digital-sephardic-treasures/avoiding-a-nuclear-inferno/.

predictable. In the years between 1894–1904, he worked in different institutions located in Rhodes and Izmir as a teacher, an education inspector, and a censor for the Abdulhamid II administration. In 1904, he moved to Cairo and stayed there until 1909. During his years in Cairo, Galanti continued his research and publishing activities as an intellectual and a journalist. He was involved in broader political networks, supported the political activities of Young Turks, and used his newspaper *La Vara* (The Stick) as a means to sharply and sometimes unfairly criticize religious authorities of the community. He also prepared a report to allocate Sudan to the Jews as a homeland.[7] Avner Levi claims that during these years, Galanti also appealed to the kings of England and Spain for employment.[8] Furthermore, following the 1908 Young Turk Revolution, he chose to go to England and Germany rather than return to Ottoman lands, where he would participate in an optimistic intellectual environment in the Empire during the early phase of the Second Constitutional Period. Galanti's accounts and the writer of Galanti's biography, Albert Kalderon, mainly depicted Galanti in these years as an intellectual who consistently struggled for freedom in the suppressive context of the early years of the twentieth century in the Ottoman Empire.[9] However, considering the range of activities that Galanti was involved in, it would be more appropriate to define these years as a period of self-discovery or personal searching in his career.[10] The unpredictability of Galanti's

---

7   For an evaluation of Galanti's years in Egypt, see Avner Levi, "Kahire'de Gazetecilik Yılları ve Avram Galanti," *Tarih ve Toplum* 26, no. 153 (September 1996):13–22. For the handwritten copy of the proposal to allocate Sudan to the Jews, see CAHJP P/112, F.88. For the examination of the proposal, also see Jacob M. Landau, "Due progetti per la colonizzazione del Sudan al principio del secolo XX," *La Rassegna Mensile di Israel* 21, no. 6 (1955): 229.

8   Levi, "Kahire'de Gazetecilik Yılları," 14. Levi does not provide any details about the content or the scope of Galanti's request from the kings of England and Spain.

9   Albert E. Kalderon, *Abraham Galante: A Biography* (New York: Sepher-Hermon Press, 1983), 25–37.

10   Avner Levi and Rifat Bali also interpret these years as a period of searching for Galanti. Levi, "Kahire'de Gazetecilik Yılları," 14–15; Rifat N. Bali, "Avram Galanti'nin Hayatı ve Eserlerinin Bibliyografyası," in *Arabi Harfler Terakkimize Mani Değildir*, by Avram Galanti (İstanbul: Bedir Yayınevi, 1996), 7. Even after Galanti had a relatively settled life in Istanbul in 1911, different opportunities knocked on his door. One of those opportunities could easily take him to the United States. According to his biography, in 1914, the year he started working at *Dârülfünun*, Jewish Organizations in New York offered Galanti a leadership position for the Sephardim Community in New York. The idea behind this position was to find a person that would organize the Sephardic immigrants in New York. They offered him the position again in 1916, yet Galanti did not accept it. The reasons for his rejection of the offer are open to speculation. However, in the chaotic context of the

PROF. A. GALANTI

KINALI ADA   ISTANBUL

ABRAHAM GALANTÉ
Professeur à l'Université

Stamboul

Abraham Galante
Directeur et Rédacteur en chef du Journal " LA VARA".

Le CAIRE, (Egypte).

Abraham Galante
Directeur de l'Ecole Tiféret-Israël

Rhôdes

Abraham Galante
Chef du Comité Israélite Ottoman

AVRAM GALANTİ
Darülfünun müderrislerinden

İstanbul

آورام غلانتى
Abraham Galante
Professeur au Lycée Impérial Ottoman

Rhôdes

آورام غلانتى
ABRAHAM GALANTÉ

CONSTANTINOPLE   استانبول

FIGURE 8.1. Galanti's bussines cards from different phases of his career. Central Archives for the History of the Jewish People (CAHJP).

trajectory in the early phase of his career was not an exception. In the context of the fluid dynamics of the last decades of the Ottoman Empire, we may observe similar experiences. For example, Avram Galanti's brother, Haim Galanti, was also in Egypt almost during the same period as him. However, Haim decided to depart from Egypt to Southern Rhodesia around 1908 and eventually settled in Salisbury, today known as Harare, the capital of Zimbabwe.[11]

Galanti's private documents located in the archives in Israel help us to examine the complexity of his life story. The variety of materials related to his pursuits from the late Ottoman Empire to the Republican era provides insight into the extent and content of his sociopolitical and intellectual efforts. Furthermore, the story behind these documents allows us to extend the scope of our inquiry regarding his intellectual trajectory. Compared to his early years, the last phase of Galanti's life was quiet and isolated. After he acted as the deputy of Niğde in the Grand National Assembly in the years 1943–1946, he settled in Kınalıada and mainly lived there until his death on 9 August 1961. Following the death of Galanti, his private documents and books were donated to the Rabbinate of Turkey. However, parts of his papers in the Rabbinate were lost due to poor preservation conditions. The surviving documents were dispatched to Israel.[12] A portion of Galanti's documents were given to the National Library of Israel in 1969 by the Ben-Zvi Institute. The rest were transferred to the Central Archives for the History of the Jewish People (CAHJP) in 1971.[13]

The story is indeed ironic. He dedicated his life to researching, unearthing, and preserving the past and culture of the Jewish community in the Ottoman Empire and Turkey. In a short autobiographical statement for the records of the Grand National Assembly of Turkey in 1943, he wrote: "In sum, from 1895 up to today I have served Turkey, which is my homeland, with all my strength. While doing this, my only aim has been the rise and greatness of Turkey. As I write these last sentences my conscience is at ease."[14] Although Galanti's intellectual endeavors and

---

Ottoman Empire and Europe, this could easily have been an appealing offer to consider for Galanti. For the details of the offer, see Kalderon, *Abraham Galante*, 44–45.

11 For more information on Haim Galanti, see Hannah S. Pressman's chapter in this volume.

12 Bali, "Avram Galanti'nin Hayatı," 12.

13 E-correspondence between the author and the CAHJP, 17 July 2019. E-correspondence between the Archive Departments of the National Library of Israel and the author, 14 August 2019. Also see "Ownership History," Abraham Galanté Collection National Library of Israel, accessed May, 12, 2020, https://www.nli.org.il/en/archives/NNL_AR-CHIVE_AL002885561/NLI.

14 Avram Galanti, *Türkiye Büyük Millet Meclisi Mebusları İçin Tercümeihal*, TBMM Sicil Arşivi, Dosya no. 1272.

their implications require further scrutiny, his autobiographical comments already reflect how important it was for him to understand his works as acts of service to his homeland and his community. However, no institution or individual in his homeland preserved or catalogued his valuable documents accurately following his death. This story of Galanti's papers cannot be neglected in any attempt to understand Galanti's intellectual trajectory. The contents and fate of the papers shed light on the legacy of Galanti, his relation with society, and features of the intellectual milieu to which he belonged. More importantly, it shapes how we study and understand Galanti today. From a broader perspective, the examination of the dynamics behind the fate of his documents and works helps us reflect on practices to preserve the materials of Jewish intellectuals in Turkey.

In the following pages, I discuss the story of Galanti's private papers and its implications. Then, I analyze the content and features of Galanti's available documents located in archives in Israel and highlight some of the angles that these documents provide us in order to better understand the characteristics of the late Ottoman intellectual world and Galanti's intellectual efforts at the turn of the twentieth century.[15]

Galanti and His Documents

In 2014, I conducted a brief interview with Galanti's friend, artist and poet Habib Gerez (1926–) as a part of my doctoral research. Through this interview, I sought to learn whether Gerez held any private document about Galanti or could give any further information about Galanti's papers. Beyond my interest in more sources, I had a dearer expectation from interviewing a person who had been close to Galanti: I hoped Gerez's memories could extend the depth and breadth of my efforts to comprehend Galanti beyond his intellectual persona.

The letters sent by Galanti to Gerez in the years 1956–1958 show that Habib Gerez was one of the closest persons to Galanti in the last years of his life, despite their age difference. Gerez helped Galanti in some of his activities in the city, including dispatching his books, checking the status of books Galanti had sent earlier, and making payments on his behalf. Moreover, Galanti truly enjoyed their conversations.[16]

---

15 Galanti's available documents in the archives also cover the Republican period. However, in this paper, I mainly reflect on his documents concerning the late Ottoman era.

16 The letters from Galanti to Gerez are located in the CAHJP, P/112. In his letters, Galanti often invites Gerez to the island and shows his appreciation for his friendship. In our discussion, Gerez also mentioned that they were close to each other and enjoyed their friendship. (Habib Gerez, in discussion with the author, March 2014, Istanbul). Also see,

What I learnt from Gerez was not what I expected at the time. None of the correspondence between them was in Gerez's personal archives anymore. Years ago, Gerez handed all the related documents to Dr. Albert E. Kalderon, the writer of Galanti's biography.[17] More importantly, Gerez informed me that he made the transfer arrangements for Galanti's books and documents from his house in Kınalıada to the Rabbinate in Istanbul upon his death. Galanti's private documents were neither recorded nor catalogued. Probably, they were left inside bags and carried to the Rabbinate.[18] The details regarding the rest of the story are not clear. We do not know on whose initiative or exactly why the documents were dispatched to Israel. However, different accounts and historians agreed that the preservation conditions of his documents in Istanbul at the time were poor and inadequate. Sadly, these conditions led to the destruction of some of Galanti's papers while still in Istanbul.[19] Hearing what happened to Galanti's documents was not encouraging for someone hoping to gain access to them. After an initial disappointment, however, what Gerez recounted forced me to think not only about the content of Galanti's private papers, but their story and its many ironies. In a word, it helped me consider the fate of Galanti's documents within the broader legacy of his works.

Galanti was a hardworking intellectual with a high prolificacy. He remained unmarried. He considered marriage a possible obstacle for his intellectual endeavors.[20] His deteriorated eye health in the last years of his life was probably the result of long hours and years of reading and writing. Despite this dedication, however, his works attracted the attention of neither the Jewish community nor the broader audience in Turkey to the extent he desired. Moreover, he did not receive financial and moral support for his efforts in the way he expected. These were sources

---

J. Habib Gerez, "Bir Dost Gözü ile. Prof A. Galante," *Şalom Gazetesi, 27* February 1985, *Yaşam Dergisi* (Newspaper Supplement), 8.

17   Also see Kalderon, *Abraham Galante*, 2. Kalderon passed away in 1983, the same year that his book on Avram Galanti was published. The documents that Gerez handed to Kalderon are in CAHJP today.

18   Gerez, discussion.

19   Ibid. Bali, "Avram Galanti'nin Hayatı," 12. Gerez, discussion. Naim Güleryüz, who has worked for the preservation of Jewish culture and past in Turkey for years, also confirmed other accounts and expressed similar opinions in a discussion with the author in the summer of 2019. (Naim Güleryüz, in discussion with author, July 2019).

20   In the interview, Gerez remarked that Galanti once told him, "You either get married and be a part of family or would become Galanti. I chose to become Galanti". (Gerez, discussion). Also, according to Gerez, Galanti got engaged once when he was young. Yet he eventually broke off the engagement because he was concerned that it would not allow him to work prolifically. (Gerez, "Bir Dost Gözü İle," 8).

of disappointment and resentment, and probably some of the reasons behind his isolation in the last years of his life. Gerez remarks that Galanti opposed the idea of organizing a Jubilee in 1957 because of this state of mind.[21] Likewise, in the letters where Galanti invited Gerez to Kınalıada in the late 1950s, he often added a phrase asking him to come alone.[22] Indeed, the story of his documents echoes Galanti's intellectual efforts throughout his lifetime. In order to understand an aspect of the story of his documents, we should look at the factors that influenced his relationship with both Jewish and general audiences in Turkey.

From the early years of his career, Galanti was concerned with the integration of Jews into the broader society within the official ideological framework promoted by existing political orders.[23] While in the late Ottoman period, his voice was in accordance with Ottomanist principles of the time, in the Republican years, his ideas on education and the promotion of the Turkish language as a part of one's identity mainly remained within the borders of the assimilative strategies utilized by the regime.[24] Likewise, Galanti's political concerns influenced the narratives of his works on the history of the Jewish community written in the Republican period. In his works, he promoted a narrative based on the assumption of uninterrupted positive relations between Jews and Muslim Turks. While in recent years this narrative has been subject to criticism, Galanti, at the time, presented this selective and optimistic picture of the past as evidence for the united futures of these communities.[25] He

---

21 Gerez, "Bir Dost Gözü İle," 8. Yusuf [Josef] Habib Gerez, "Sunuş," in *Türklük İncelemeleri*, by Avram Galanti (Istanbul: Yeditepe Yayınevi, 2005), 10. Gerez, discussion.

22 Obviously, different private reasons might have played a role in his request to Gerez. However, I believe his attitude is also a sign of his isolated life. He had made his funeral adjustments with his own means four years before his death and informed Gerez about his wish to be buried without any pretentious funeral ceremony. (See private letters from Galanti to Gerez located in CAHJP, P/112).

23 Avram Galanti's sociopolitical thoughts from the late Ottoman period to the early Republican era and their relation with his intellectual efforts will be explored in depth in a monograph that I am currently working on.

24 We should note that Galanti was a strong opponent of Romanization of the alphabet. This was one important exception in which he contradicted the premises of the official ideology. See, Avram Galanti, *Arabi Harfler Terakkimize Mani Değildir*, translit. by Fethi Kale (Istanbul: Bedir Yayınevi, 1996).

25 Kerem Tınaz, "An Imperial Ideology and Its Legacy: Ottomanism in a Comparative Perspective, 1894–1928" (PhD dissertation, University of Oxford, 2018), 242–243, 267–268. Also, for a brief evaluation of Galanti's narrative in his works, see Rıfat N. Bali, "Osmanlı/Türk Yahudiliği Tarihi İle İlgili Yayınlar ve İçerdikleri Tarih Söylemi – II," *Tarih ve Toplum*, no. 33 (September 1996): 57.

was either silent or uncritical in the face of traumatic events such as the 1934 Thrace Events and the Wealth Tax in 1942. These were difficult experiences that had deep consequences in the collective memory of the Jewish community. Therefore, it is possible to argue that for members of the Jewish community subjected to unfair sociocultural and political treatments in the early decades of the Republic, the works and narrative of Galanti may not have resonated with their day-to-day realities. Furthermore, as Naim Güleryüz remarks, Galanti's works on the history of Jews were mainly the "compilation of documents" (*belgesel derleme*).[26] His primary concern was the preservation and the transmission of the detailed information that he collected from primary sources on the subject. Likewise, his works on philological issues mostly included detailed technical discussions. Thus, the content and the narrative of his works might not have been appealing for readers outside academia.

General readers' accessibility to Galanti-related studies or his works is another issue to consider in analyzing Galanti's poor relationship with his audience. The first level of this problem is the scope and quantity of the analysis on Galanti's work. Despite the importance of Galanti as an intellectual, we have almost no extensive and analytical study on his efforts.[27] This scholarly gap is an outcome of both ideological and technical problems that have influenced broader historiography. On the one hand, Turkish national historiography in the twentieth century mainly did not include voices from different ethno-religious groups living in the Ottoman Empire and the Turkish Republic. On the other hand, studying figures like Avram Galanti required researchers to face a variety of challenges, such as texts in different languages and alphabets, dispersed sources, and missing materials. These problems, in return, have probably influenced the quantity and quality of the works on Galanti and, thus, prevented the general reader from learning more about him.[28]

Also, a technical issue regarding Galanti's publications hindered the accessibility of his works, at least until recently. Galanti published his works often with his own resources. The books were not adequately distributed and were not sold

---

26 Naim A. Güleryüz, preface [to the first edition] to *Bizans'tan 20. Yüzyıla Türk Yahudileri* (Istanbul: Gözlem Gazetecilik Basın ve Yayın A.Ş.).

27 The two biographies written by Abraham Elmaleh in 1947 and by Albert Kalderon in 1983 are to the day the most complete sources for Galanti's life. Kalderon's use of primary sources and other references offer a useful roadmap for further study of Galanti's life. Yet, both Elmaleh and Kalderon approach Galanti's story with non-critical lenses and an obvious sympathy. Abraham Elmaleh, *Le professeur Abraham Galanté: sa vie et ses oeuvres* (Istanbul: Kagıt ve Basım Isleri AS, 1947); Kalderon, *Abraham Galante*. Tınaz, "An Imperial Ideology," 21.

28 Ibid., 13–14, 22.

widely.[29] The fact that neither the Jewish nor the general reader showed interest in his works might have shaped publishers' decisions regarding the distribution of his books at the time.[30] To overcome this problem, Galanti sent his works to libraries, universities, intellectuals, politicians, and friends for free.[31] Overall, however, this situation limited the visibility and recognition of Galanti's efforts. We need to also note that Galanti published some of his important works in French, despite his efforts to promote Turkish within the Jewish community in the early period of the Republic. This choice might be an outcome of Galanti's aim to reach a broader audience, as he believed that his books were read abroad more than in Turkey.[32] In any case, although some of his works were transliterated into modern Turkish and re-published in recent years, most of his books were not easily accessible for general Turkish-speaking readers for a long time.[33]

Gerez called Galanti an unfortunate author. Considering the indifference of his target audiences, lack of research on his intellectual pursuits, and economic concerns, one may indeed agree with Gerez. However, most of the dynamics mentioned above were hardly experiences exclusive to Galanti as an intellectual.[34] Laurent Mignon has shown that the works and legacy of İsak Ferera, a Jewish poet whose life also extends from the late Ottoman period to early Republican era, had a similar fate with readers, publishers, and researchers.[35] In the late 1950s, Gerez also mentioned in a

---

29 Gerez remarks that a maximum of 15–20 copies of his books were sold in the book-stores. J. Habib Gerez, "Sanatkarı Teşvik Babında [originally published in *La Luz De Turkiya*, 14.11.1956]," in *Örneklerle Türk Musevi Basınının Tarihçesi*, ed. Nesim Benbanaste (Istanbul: Sümbül Basımevi, 1988), 75–76. Gerez, discussion. Also see Bali, "Avram Galanti'nin Hayatı," 13.

30 For example, in a letter written by Ahmet Emin Yalman, the editor of the newspaper *Vatan*, on 6 September 1949, Yalman informs Galanti that the newspaper will not publish the piece sent by Galanti because of the limited space within the newspaper and limited audience that would be interested in the subject. CAHJP, P/112.

31 Galanti's private documents contain many letters sent by different individuals and institutions to thank him for the books that they received from Galanti.

32 Gerez, "Prof A. Galante," 8.

33 Tınaz, "An Imperial Ideology," 21–22. Some of his works that are transliterated: Galanti, *Arabi Harfler*; Avram Galanti, *Türklük İncelemeleri*, ed. and translit. by Önder Kaya (Istanbul: Yeditepe Yayınevi, 2005); Avram Galanti, *Vatandaş Türkçe Konuş*, translit. by Ömer Türkoğlu (Ankara: Kebikeç Yayınları, 2000).

34 Tınaz, "An Imperial Ideology," 12–14.

35 Laurent Mignon, "Türkçe Yahudi Edebiyatının Doğuş Sancıları: İsak Ferera Efendi ve Mirat Dergisi," in *Ana Metne Taşınan Dipnotlar: Türk Edebiyatı ve Kültürlerarasılık Üzerine Yazılar*, by Laurent Mignon (Istanbul: İletişim Yayınları, 2009), 11–14, 18–24.

series of articles his own economic concerns about publishing issues and complained about weak connections between Jewish intellectuals and their audience.[36] Similarly, Galanti also received letters at the time from members of his own intellectual circles informing him about their own difficult conditions. For example, in a letter sent from distinguished professor Samuel Aysoy to Galanti in 1947, Aysoy first suggested him to place an ad in *Journal d'Orient* and other newspapers in Istanbul for his book *Türkler ve Yahudiler.* The ad could publicize the book and improve its sales. He also advised him to send a copy of the book to the director of the National Library in Ankara. He thought the director could read an excerpt of the book aloud in a radio broadcast. Afterwards, Aysoy remarked that he completed a few books during that year; however, he had not published any of them yet. Aysoy was waiting for paper and printing prices to fall.[37] We can assume from this letter that, similar to Galanti, Aysoy also published some of his works with his own resources and faced financial difficulties. Indeed, Galanti's experiences with contemporary readers might be seen as a prelude to the unfortunate end of his private papers. Yet, as we have seen above, we should also consider Galanti's circumstances more broadly and in relation to the status of Jewish intellectuals and their relations with the intellectual world in Turkey at the time. Therefore, it is also necessary to contextualize the story of Galanti's paper with broader questions regarding the preservation of the Jewish community's past in Turkey in the course of the twentieth century.

In the title of an article, Rıfat Bali describes the Jewish community in Turkey as those who prefer to forget.[38] The title attempts to capture the complex identity of Turkish Jews and their relation with the community's recent past in Turkey. According to Bali, the Jewish community in Turkey adopted a low-profile socio-political attitude from the 1940s on. This attitude of the community appeared in relation to unfair political and legal treatments and as a mechanism to cope with sociocultural pressures that the Jewish community was subjected to, particularly in

---

36   J. Habib Gerez, "Türk-Yahudileri Hakiki Vatandaşlıklarını Türkçe Eser Vermek Suretiyle Göstermelidirler," [originally published in *La Luz De Turkiya*, 21.09.1955] in *Örneklerle Türk Musevi Basınının Tarihçesi*, ed. Nesim Benbanaste (Istanbul: Sümbül Basımevi, 1988), 72; J. Habib Gerez, "Okuyucu ve Yazar," [originally published in *La Luz De Turkiya*, 27.06.1956] in *Örneklerle Türk Musevi Basınının Tarihçesi*, ed. Nesim Benbanaste (Istanbul: Sümbül Basımevi, 1988), 73–74; J. Habib Gerez, "Sanatkarı Teşvik Babında," 75–76.

37   ARC. Ms. Var. 411 Abraham Galanté Collection, Archives Department, National Library of Israel, Jerusalem.

38   Rıfat N. Bali, "Unutmayı Tercih Edenler: Türk Yahudi Cemaati" in *Toplu Makaleler - I Tarihin Ufak Bir Dipnotu: Azınlıklar* (Istanbul: Libra Kitapçılık ve Yayıncılık, 2013), 295–303.

the early decades of the Republic.[39] An implication of this position in the context of our discussion was not to mention traumas and unfairness that the community experienced. Accordingly, for years, among members of the community there was either silence or a limited number of historical narratives of Turkish Jews, with a selective focus and non-critical lenses. Consequently, this approach to the past did not encourage or motivate any institution or individual to preserve it. When Galanti passed away, there was no active community, institution, or archive that was interested in or responsible for the proper preservation or cataloguing of materials that recorded the Jewish past in Turkey. Therefore, the fate of Galanti's papers was not the result only of his own personal experience. It should also be contextualized within a larger phenomenon. The complex sociopolitical and cultural background of the Jewish experience in Turkey was conducive to the neglect of Galanti's documents.

The Jewish community's position to preserve and discuss its past in Turkey has changed along with the community's low-profile strategy since the 1990s. Different researchers and institutions, along with broader political developments in the country, have played a role in this transformation. For example, the Quincentennial Foundation has organized many conferences, concerts, exhibitions, and other cultural activities since its foundation in 1989. Gradually, growing efforts of historians and public intellectuals in Turkey contributed to our perspective on Jewish history, as well as to the preservation of Sephardic culture.[40] The scope of academic studies—in Turkey and

---

39   For a detailed discussion of the subject and its consequences, see Rifat N. Bali, *Cumhuriyet Yıllarında Türkiye Yahudileri Bir Türkleştirme Serüveni (1923–1945)* (Istanbul: İletişim Yayıncılık, 2010); Süheyla Yıldız, "Asimile Olma, İçe Kapanma, Kimliklenme Cumhuriyetten Bugüne Türkiye Yahudilerinin Kimlik Stratejileri," *Alternatif Politika* 7, no. 2 (June 2015): 257–290.

40   Among others, Rıfat Bali is one of the most important and prolific historians working on the subject in Turkey today. Since the 1990s, he has published numerous books and articles on Jewish history in Turkey and contributed significantly to our perspective on Jewish experiences in the Republican period. Another important name in Turkey is Naim A. Güleryüz. He was one of the founders of the Quincentennial Foundation and the founding project coordinator and curator of the Quincentennial Foundation Museum of Turkish Jews. He is also a prolific researcher publishing on the history of Jews in Turkey and the Ottoman Empire. At this point, I should also note that the narratives in the works of Güleryüz and Bali represent different trends in the historiography of the Jewish past in Turkey. Clearly, a detailed discussion or assessment of these narratives falls beyond the scope of this paper. My interest here is to highlight their contributions to the visibility of the topic, regardless of the differences in their narratives. For a concise examination of the narratives in their works, see Marc David Baer, "Turkish Jews Rethink 500 Years of Brotherhood and Friendship," *Turkish Studies Association Bulletin* 24, no. 2 (2000): 63–73. In recent years, an important amount of publications in Turkish have

beyond—on Sephardic history has been extended considerably in recent decades and has increased the visibility of the subject within the broader literature.[41] However, we should also note that broader social and institutional change is still in progress. Today, for example, there is still no community library or organized open archive promoting and aiming at the collection and preservation of different memories of Jews in Turkey.[42] As discussed in this volume, new private and personal collections, as well as the increasing relation between universities, scholars, and local communities, are producing archives that have proven to be very important in the emergence of a new cultural and historical consciousness. A single object or document with no apparent historical significance kept in a personal library, when placed together similar objects in a collection, might become an indispensable element in piecing together the communal past. The initiative to put objects of personal significance side-by-side may provide a new dimension or a novel insight for historians and ethnographers hoping to understand the intellectual life, material culture, music, food, language, and politics of a given community. Notably, today's digital developments establish an advantageous ground to pursue such projects. They allow us to preserve varying kinds of materials without necessarily asking the actual owner to hand in the object for good by sacrificing personal, emotional or intellectual attachments. Furthermore, digital developments promote researchers' accessibility to such initiatives considerably.[43] The lack of such efforts in the context of the Jewish community in Turkey for so many years probably led to the extinction of many stories that could have been

---

participated in a dialogue on Jewish past in Turkey. Among others, two intriguing recent examples in the context of the volume's topic are Rita Ender, *Aile Yadigârları* (Istanbul: İletişim Yayınları, 2018) and Raşel Meseri and Aylin Kuryel, *Türkiye'de Yahudi Olmak Bir Deneyim Sözlüğü* (Istanbul: İletişim Yayınları, 2018).

41   The important work of Aron Rodrigue, Avigdor Levy, and Esther Benbassa has been crucial in expanding our understanding of the Ottoman Sephardic past and placing the Ottoman Sephardic experience in Ottoman history and Jewish Studies. Similarly, research by Sarah Abrevaya Stein, Julia Philip Cohen, Devin Naar, Olga Borovaya, Aviva Ben-Ur and others has brought to our attention the complex history of Ottoman Sephardic Jews in the imperial and transnational contexts.

42   For a discussion of available sources or archives to study Jews in Turkey, see Rifat N. Bali, "Osmanlı Türk Yahudileri Araştırmaları: Engeller, İmkanlar, Kaynaklar," in *Toplu Makaleler - I Tarihin Ufak bir Dipnotu: Azınlıklar* (Istanbul: Libra Kitapçılık ve Yayıncılık, 2013), 465–471.

43   For example, recently, Goldstein-Goren Diaspora Research Center of Tel Aviv University launched a digital project that allows researchers to examine 61,022 Jewish tombstones in Turkey. It is indeed a highly valuable initiative that contributes to the efforts to preserve the Jewish past in Turkey. For the details of the project, see "A World Beyond: Jewish Cemeteries in Turkey, 1583–1990," Goldstein-Goren Diaspora Research Center of Tel

FIGURE 8.2. Some of Galanti's materials located in the Archive Departments of the National Library of Israel (ADNLI).

FIGURE 8.3. Avram Galanti's identification card as translator for the Ottoman Red Crescent Society. CAHJP.

added to the memory of contemporary Turkish society and could have also added new dimensions to historians' perspectives. Galanti's example is a helpful case for us to reflect on the scope of this problem and, thus, to acknowledge the essential role that the presence of such initiatives might play.

Fortunately, the story of Galanti's papers does not have a completely sad ending, as his extant documents are preserved in archives in Israel today. CAHJP preserves the bulk of Galanti's remaining materials. Over two hundred thin dossiers with variable amounts of content include a variety of materials, such as notebooks, draft manuscripts, postcards, business cards, pictures, letters, identity papers, press clippings, articles, his will, and other papers from the Ottoman and Republican periods. Additionally, similar materials—less in quantity but the same in importance—are held in the Archive Departments of the National Library of Israel (ADNLI). The materials in both archives provide us with useful channels to delve into Galanti's intellectual endeavors, personal life, and the late Ottoman intellectual milieu.

Inside Galanti's Materials

Galanti was a well-integrated and active member of the late Ottoman intellectual milieu, despite never having risen to become a key figure within the sociopolitical life of the Empire. His available documents show that his language skills were instrumental in his engagement with the multi-linguistic and multi-alphabetical intellectual sphere of the Empire. French, Ladino, and Turkish[44] are common languages that we see in his documents. Moreover, a variety of notes or correspondences written in Arabic, English, German, Hebrew, and Italian are also present within his files. This is indeed an impressive richness of languages and alphabets for the documents of a single intellectual.

Galanti's command of various languages reflects the complexity of his intellectual efforts and, partially, the circumstances of the late Ottoman Empire. When he started learning Turkish at age eleven, he already knew Ladino, French, and Hebrew. Later, Turkish, French, and Ladino became his main languages for research and intellectual production. In his multilayered sociopolitical and intellectual efforts in the late Ottoman period, Galanti used these languages in his written works according to the audience that he was aiming to reach. Ladino was his mother

---

Aviv University, accessed 21 July, 2020, https://jewishturkstones.tau.ac.il. For a further discussion of the topic, see the introduction of this volume.

44 Turkish refers both to Ottoman and Modern Turkish. Following the sources, and for the sake of simplicity, I refer to both as Turkish.

tongue and the most common medium of communication in the Jewish press at the time. On the other hand, he used Turkish to reach a broader audience in the Empire. It was also a source of income for him. Thanks to his fluency in Turkish, Galanti was able to secure positions in various Ottoman institutions throughout his career. His work in French might be seen as an attempt to connect with educated citizens of the late Ottoman Empire, for whom French was a common language. Moreover, he utilized French to communicate with Jews in Europe in the context of the gradually increasing influence of the Alliance Israélite Universelle on the sociocultural life of the Ottoman Jewry.

While the importance of Ladino, Turkish, and French were central for Galanti's intellectual pursuits, he continued expanding his knowledge of foreign languages throughout his career. He studied English, Greek, Arabic, and Persian. He actively benefited from his language skills to engage with the written worlds of different audiences within the Ottoman realm and beyond. For example, he learnt Greek to be able to read writings about blood libels in the Greek press.[45] Also, languages like English and Arabic were essential for him to research a variety of topics.[46] Lastly, extensive language skills enabled him to be a part of broad networks that extended to different parts of the world. Documents in CAHJP and ADNLI show that, particularly in his years in Cairo, his networks, which spanned from the center of the Empire to the peripheries and beyond, were essential for him to promote his sociopolitical agenda and to exchange information.

These multi-linguistic pursuits of Galanti push us to think of the possible breadth of his intellectual connections, exchanges, common grounds, and tools that are not necessarily appreciated or acknowledged by the nationalist historiographies of the twentieth century. The emergence of nation-states with the collapse of the Empire was accompanied by the promotion of different nationalist historiographies which analyzed the new state's Ottoman past as per its nationalist discourses. A consequence of this development was the compartmentalization of the intellectual, social, and cultural history of the Empire, rather than approaching it as a whole. This teleological reading of the past did not necessarily help us to detect intellectual

---

45   Kalderon, *Abraham Galante*, 22.

46   Galanti was able to write and read English decently. He used English in his private correspondences and documents. He, however, did not prefer writing in English for published materials. For example, in a letter that Galanti wrote in English in 1931 and sent to the literary editor of the *Standard Jewish Encyclopedia*, he informs the editor that he would write an article entitled "Turkey" for the encyclopedia. However, he remarks that he would write his piece in French, as it was easier for him. CAHJP P/112, F.40.

and cultural encounters between different ethnic and religious groups in Ottoman society. In the last few decades, a gradually increasing number of studies have shown us how deficient these exclusivist narratives are in comprehending the dynamics of the late Ottoman intellectual context.[47] As a polyglot member of the late Ottoman intellectual sphere, Galanti's efforts and documents also encourage us to emphasize the need to approach late Ottoman intellectual history with a more inclusive perspective. As discussed above, through different languages, Galanti interacted with different intellectuals and audiences. Moreover, the usage of different languages and alphabets, sometimes even in the same pages of his notebooks, shows that different cultures were in constant interaction in his own mindset. He was both a product of this multi-linguistic intellectual sphere and an agent that promoted its dynamics. To understand the mindsets of Galanti and figures like him, an inclusive perspective that approaches the intellectual milieu of the Empire as a whole in the context of the period's sociocultural dynamics is necessary.

However, we should also note that the utilization of inclusive lenses comes with several difficulties. Firstly, the late Ottoman intellectual milieu included an extensive geography with active connections in different parts of the world. This means an inclusive approach requires dealing with abundant sources dispersed across various libraries, archives, and private collections. The case of Galanti is a good example. He spent most of his life within the borders of current Turkey, yet his personal papers are in Israel. While these documents are invaluable, they are not a complete set of documents that would help us to understand Galanti's pursuit entirely. Instead, they provide traces to pursue further research in the collections of different institutions and individuals located in different parts of former Ottoman lands and beyond. Some of these traces could lead us nowhere, due to the inaccessibility or disappearance of actual sources.[48] For example, different accounts mention a series of articles that Galanti published in the *Hizmet* (Service) newspaper with the title "Maarifimiz

---

47   For example, see Johann Strauss, "Who Read What in the Ottoman Empire (19th-20th centuries)?," *Middle Eastern Literatures: Incorporating Edebiyat* 6, no. 1 (2003): 39–76; Johann Strauss, "Linguistic Diversity and Everyday Life in the Ottoman Cities of the Eastern Mediterranean and the Balkans (late 19th– early 20th century)," *The History of the Family* 16, no. 2 (2011): 126–141; Evangelia Balta and Mehmet Ölmez, eds., *Turkish Speaking Christians, Jews and Greek Speaking Muslim and Catholics in the Ottoman Empire* (Istanbul: Eren, 2011); Evangelia Balta, ed., *Cultural Encounters in the Turkish-Speaking Communities of the Late Ottoman Empire* (Istanbul: The Isis Press, 2014); Murat Cankara, "Rethinking Ottoman Cross-Cultural Encounters: Turks and the Armenian Alphabet," *Middle Eastern Studies* 51, no. 1 (2015): 1–16.

48   Tınaz, "An Imperial Ideology," 22–23.

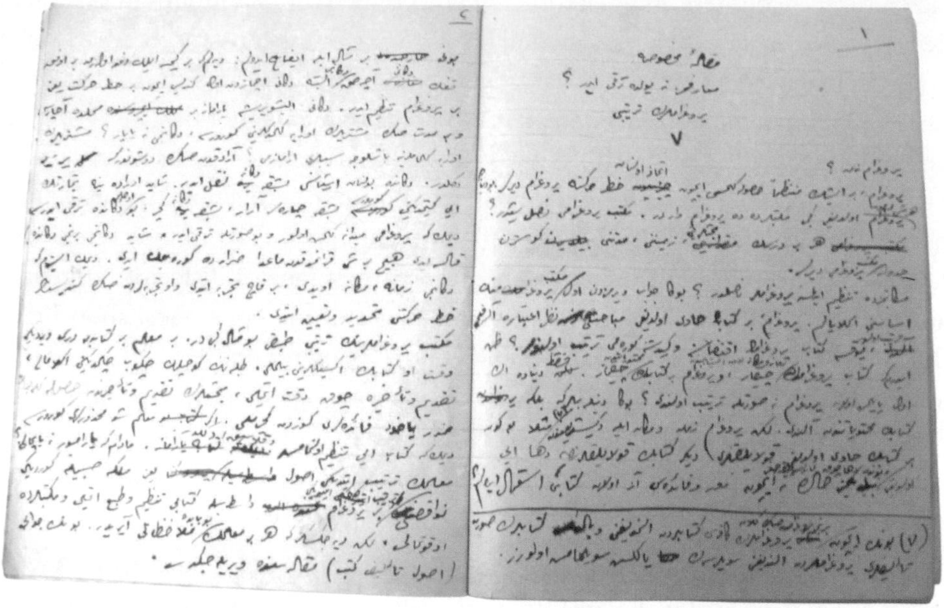

FIGURE 8.4. A page from Galanti's notebook which includes the draft copies of a series of articles titled "Maarifimiz Ne Yolda Terakki Eder?". CAHJP.

Ne Yolda Terakki Eder?" (How Would Our Education Progress?).[49] As one of my concerns was to understand Galanti's ideas on education as a part of my research, it was important for me to access these sources. Yet the secondary sources did not provide any details regarding the publication, except that the series consisted of 19 articles and that Galanti wrote them during his years in Rhodes (1894–1902). Founded by Halit Ziya Uşaklıgil and Tevfik Nevzat in 1886, *Hizmet* was one of the long-lasting newspapers in Izmir. While I was conducting research in different libraries in Turkey in 2014, I found various copies of the newspaper, yet none of the available issues were published in the years between 1894–1902. Finally, I was able to discover draft copies of eight articles written under the broader title "Maarifimiz Ne Yolda Terakki Eder?" in one of Galanti's personal notebooks located in CAHJP. The other eleven articles from the series, however, remained inaccessible. Another apparent difficulty is the variety of languages that a researcher needs to deal with to study figures like Galanti, as discussed above or, more generally, to understand, inclusively, the Ottoman intellectual milieu. However, these difficulties shall not lead us to pessimism. In recent years, the works of polyglot researchers or volumes that benefit from the collective efforts of historians with varying specialties and

---

49   See Elmaleh, *Le professeur Abraham Galante*, 73; Kalderon, *Abraham Galante*, 18; Bali, "Avram Galanti'nin Hayatı," 6.

skills have showed us that technical difficulties can be transcended.[50] Furthermore, numbers of translations and transliterations of texts from the late Ottoman period gradually grow, and the accessibility to sources and materials increases thanks to digital initiatives in the field. These are indeed developments that support researchers' efforts to study the period inclusively.

Lastly, while my focus in this chapter has been the story of Galanti's papers and some of the questions derived from its study, it would also be beneficial to discuss here the content of Galanti's documents and their significance, however briefly. Galanti's existent materials in Israel are essential for any researcher wanting to explore Galanti and his world. Firstly, the documents include most of the primary sources that Albert Kalderon benefited from while writing his work on Galanti. While Kalderon's work helps us to contextualize or understand some of these sources, they similarly aid us in evaluating Kalderon's approach to Galanti and allow us to extend our perspective on Galanti's ambitions and works. Furthermore, existent analysis on the content, context, and motivation of his pursuits in the early period of his career are deficient, due to the technical and historiographical factors discussed above. In this context, his documents in Israel provide us with angles to partially redress the gap. Pieces inside his notebooks and his private correspondences with different individuals, intellectuals, and institutions help us to grasp his position on affairs pertaining to education within the Jewish community and the Empire, its internal politics, as well as broader political issues concerning Jewish status in the Empire and beyond. Similarly, notes, manuscripts of letters, and reports allow us to examine his activities as an education inspector in the Ottoman Archipelago, a young Ottoman Jewish intellectual trying to find his path, earn his living, and make a name among different circles in the Empire and beyond, and an educator aiming to contribute to the educational life of his community specifically and, in general, the Empire. Last but not least, the documents partially allow us to observe the evolution of his career, along with his sociopolitical stance in the course of his

---

50   For example, see Balta and Ölmez, eds., *Turkish Speaking Christians, Jews and Greek Speaking Muslim and Catholics in the Ottoman Empire*; Christine Isom-Verhaaren and Kent F. Schull, eds., *Living in the Ottoman Realm: Empire and Identity, 13th to 20th Centuries* (Bloomington: Indiana University Press, 2016). Irvin Cemil Schick, in his review of a conference on Jews in the Ottoman Empire conducted in 1987 in Brandeis University, highlights the need to undertake collaborative projects in the face of an abundance of sources in the field. Clearly, Schick's conclusion still preserves its validity. Irvin Cemil Schick, "'Osmanlı İmparatorluğu'nda Yahudiler' Bir Uluslararası Konferansın Ardından," *Tarih ve Toplum* 43 (Temmuz 1987), 49.

life. Thus, they help us to evaluate the continuities and breaks in his career, visions, and sociopolitical expectations in the context of two different political orders.

Conclusion

The story of Galanti's private documents is both an integral part of his personal story and a channel that sets the limits of our understanding of his life. It is an integral part because the fate of his papers echoes Galanti's efforts in his lifetime, as well as providing us with additional insights to examine the endeavors and legacy of Galanti. On the other hand, the story's implications defined the limitations to our discovering the elements of his intellectual pursuits. The poor preservation conditions, and consequently loss of some of his documents, had direct consequences on historians' capacity to analyze and narrate the subject. This brings us back to this volume's emphasis on the importance of community archives or similar initiatives in preserving socio-cultural memories, documents, and materials. Clearly, the lack of such actions harms historians' perspective on the past. To comprehend the extent of this damage, Galanti's documents are useful on two complementary levels. On the first level, the fact that his documents could not be appropriately preserved help us to evaluate the severity of problems regarding such initiatives in twentieth century in Turkey. On the second level, the angles that his available documents provide show the scope of the essential role that such initiatives might play in extending our understanding of the past.

Bibliography

Archives Department, National Library of Israel, Jerusalem: ARC. Ms. Var. 411 Abraham Galanté Collection.

"A World Beyond: Jewish Cemeteries in Turkey, 1583–1990." Goldstein-Goren Diaspora Research Center of Tel Aviv University, accessed 21 July, 2020, https://jewishturk-stones.tau.ac.il.

Alhadeff, Ty. "Wisdom for Politicians from a Ladino Poet: Avoiding a Nuclear Inferno." Stroum Center for Jewish Studies, University of Washington, 1 November 2016, https://jewishstudies.washington.edu/digital-sephardic-treasures/avoiding-a-nuclear-inferno/.

Baer, Marc David. "Turkish Jews Rethink 500 Years of Brotherhood and Friendship." *Turkish Studies Association Bulletin* 24, no. 2 (2000): 63–73.

Bali, Rifat N. "Avram Galanti'nin Hayatı ve Eserlerinin Bibliyografyası." In *Arabi Harfler Terakkimize Mani Değildir*, by Avram Galanti, 3–30. Istanbul: Bedir Yayınevi, 1996.

——— "Osmanlı/Türk Yahudiliği Tarihi ile İlgili Yayınlar ve İçerdikleri Tarih Söylemi – II." *Tarih ve Toplum* 33 (September 1996): 57–62.

——— *Cumhuriyet Yıllarında Türkiye Yahudileri Bir Türkleştirme Serüveni (1923–1945)*. İstanbul: İletişim Yayıncılık, 2010.

——— *Model Citizens of the State: the Jews of Turkey During the Multi-party Period*, translated by Paul Bessemer. Madison: Fairleigh Dickinson University Press, 2012.

——— "Osmanlı Türk Yahudileri Araştırmaları: Engeller, İmkanlar, Kaynaklar." In *Toplu Makaleler - I Tarihin Ufak bir Dipnotu: Azınlıklar*, 465–471. İstanbul: Libra Kitapçılık ve Yayıncılık, 2013.

——— "Unutmayı Tercih Edenler: Türk Yahudi Cemaati." In *Toplu Makaleler - I Tarihin Ufak Bir Dipnotu: Azınlıklar*, 295–303. İstanbul: Libra Kitapçılık ve Yayıncılık, 2013.

Balta, Evangelia, ed. *Cultural Encounters in the Turkish-Speaking Communities of the Late Ottoman Empire*. İstanbul: The Isis Press, 2014.

Balta, Evangelia and Mehmet Ölmez, eds. *Turkish Speaking Christians, Jews and Greek Speaking Muslim and Catholics in the Ottoman Empire*. İstanbul: Eren, 2011.

Cankara, Murat. "Rethinking Ottoman Cross-Cultural Encounters: Turks and the Armenian Alphabet." *Middle Eastern Studies* 51, no. 1 (2015): 1–16.

Cohen, Julia Phillips ve Sarah Abrevaya Stein, der. *Sephardi Lives: A Documentary History, 1700–1950* Stanford: Stanford University Press, 2014.

Elmaleh, Abraham. *Le professeur Abraham Galante: sa vie et ses oeuvres*. İstanbul: Kağıt ve Basım İşleri AŞ, 1947.

Ender, Rita. *Aile Yadigârları*. İstanbul: İletişim Yayınları, 2018.

Galanti, Avram. *Arabi Harfler Terakkimize Mani Değildir*, transliteration by Fethi Kale. İstanbul: Bedir Yayınevi, 1996.

——— *Vatandaş Türkçe Konuş*, transliterated by Ömer Türkoğlu. Ankara: Kebikeç Yayınları, 2000.

——— *Türklük İncelemeleri*, edited and transliterated by Önder Kaya. İstanbul: Yeditepe Yayınevi, 2005.

——— *Türkiye Büyük Millet Meclisi Mebusları İçin Tercümeihal*, TBMM Sicil Arşivi, Dosya no. 1272.

Gerez, Yusuf [Josef] Habib. "Bir Dost Gözü ile. Prof A. Galante," *Şalom Gazetesi*, 27 February 1985, *Yaşam Dergisi* (Newspaper Supplement), 8.

——— "Okuyucu ve Yazar [originally published in *La Luz De Turkiya*, 27.06.1956]." In *Örneklerle Türk Musevi Basınının Tarihçesi*, edited by Nesim Benbanaste, 73–74. İstanbul: Sümbül Basımevi, 1988.

——— "Sanatkarı Teşvik Babında [originally published in *La Luz De Turkiya*, 14.11.1956]." In *Örneklerle Türk Musevi Basınının Tarihçesi*, edited by Nesim Benbanaste, 75–76. İstanbul: Sümbül Basımevi, 1988.

———— "Türk-Yahudileri Hakiki Vatandaşlıklarını Türkçe Eser Vermek Suretiyle Göstermelidirler [originally published in *La Luz De Turkiya*, 21.09.1955]." In *Örneklerle Türk Musevi Basınının Tarihçesi*, edited by Nesim Benbanaste, 71–72. Istanbul: Sümbül Basımevi, 1988.

———— "Sunuş." In *Türklük İncelemeleri*, by Avram Galanti, 9–11. Istanbul: Yeditepe Yayınevi, 2005.

Güleryüz, Naim A. *Bizans'tan 20. Yüzyıla Türk Yahudileri*. Istanbul: Gözlem Gazetecilik Basın ve Yayın A.Ş.

Isom-Verhaaren, Christine and Kent F. Schull, eds. *Living in the Ottoman Realm: Empire and Identity, 13th to 20th Centuries*. Bloomington: Indiana University Press, 2016.

Kalderon, Albert E. *Abraham Galante: A Biography* (New York: Sepher-Hermon Press, 1983), 25–37.

Landau, Jacob M. "Due progetti per la colonizzazione del Sudan al principio del secolo XX," *La Rassegna Mensile di Israel* 21, no. 6 (1955): 210–237.

Levi, Avner. "Kahire'de Gazetecilik Yılları ve Avram Galanti." *Tarih ve Toplum* 26, no. 153 (September 1996): 13–22.

Meseri, Raşel and Aylin Kuryel. *Türkiye'de Yahudi Olmak Bir Deneyim Sözlüğü*. Istanbul: İletişim Yayınları, 2018.

Mignon, Laurent. *Ana Metne Taşınan Dipnotlar: Türk Edebiyatı ve Kültürlerarasılık Üzerine Yazılar*. İstanbul: İletişim Yayınları, 2009.

Schick, Irvin Cemil. "'Osmanlı İmparatorluğu'nda Yahudiler' Bir Uluslararası Konferansın Ardından." *Tarih ve Toplum* 43 (Temmuz 1987): 49–56.

Strauss, Johann. "Who Read What in the Ottoman Empire (19th-20th centuries)?" *Middle Eastern Literatures: Incorporating Edebiyat* 6, no. 1 (2003): 39–76.

———— "Linguistic Diversity and Everyday Life in the Ottoman Cities of the Eastern Mediterranean and the Balkans (late 19th–early 20th century)." *The History of the Family* 16, no. 2 (2011): 126–141.

The Central Archives for the History of the Jewish People Jerusalem: P/112.

Tınaz, Kerem. "An Imperial Ideology and Its Legacy: Ottomanism in a Comparative Perspective, 1894–1928." PhD dissertation, University of Oxford, 2018.

Yıldız, Süheyla. "Asimile Olma, İçe Kapanma, Kimliklenme Cumhuriyetten Bugüne Türkiye Yahudilerinin Kimlik Stratejileri," *Alternatif Politika* 7, no. 2 (June 2015): 257–290.

CHAPTER NINE

Galante's Daughter: Crafting an Archival Family Memoir[1]

HANNAH S. PRESSMAN

"Galante's daughter!"

Someone was calling to me as I walked into the crowded auditorium. It was the first night of Hanukkah in Seattle. People were gathering at the University of Washington campus for Ladino Day 2018, an annual celebration of Judeo-Spanish and Sephardic culture. The mood was festive, the anticipation high, hugs and handshakes flowing.

"Galante's daughter!"

I turned around, not sure if I was the intended recipient of this name. Finally, I spotted Selim S. Kuru, chair of Turkish and Ottoman Studies—it was he who had bestowed my new nickname. I grinned and waved back at him while trying on the identity in my head. *Galante's daughter.*

Was she—me?

* * *

In this essay, I will provide an overview of my approach to archival memoir writing, as well as a window into the world I am reconstructing. My work-in-progress, "Galante's Daughter: A Sephardic Family Journey," draws upon my private family collection, as well as the records available through institutional archives, scholarship, and genealogical research. To illustrate the range of sources that combine to tell my family's story, this essay will include capsule histories of my great-grandparents, Estrella and Haim Galante, Sephardic Jews who grew up in the waning decades of the Ottoman Empire and built new lives in Africa. I portray their life in dialogue with that of Haim's older brother, the eminent Turkish historian Abraham Galante. I will also offer reflections on the process of researching and writing about family history. Thus, this essay, like my overall memoir project, integrates different discursive layers: personal, intellectual, artistic, and historical.

---

1   All photographs in this article are courtesy of Hannah S. Pressman's private collection.

"Galante's Daughter" seeks to read my Sephardic great-grandparents' lives as a text laden with meaning. In reconstructing their past, and that of their family and community, I pay close attention to the quotidian details and anecdotes, generously provided via oral history interviews, that bring to life the unique texture of their environment. Grassroots sources like synagogue bulletins and cookbooks help me further understand how the Jewish community of colonial Rhodesia narrated and commemorated their own story. Material culture plays a large role in this exploration: my manuscript addresses many of the items that have made their way into my hands, mapping tangible elements like tablecloths, kiddush cups, and passports against the historical narratives that my research has uncovered. These personal belongings serve as rich points of departure wherefrom the literary text becomes a meditation on memory, identity, and family history.

I call my project a "multi-vocal memoir" because it weaves together different life stories in the pursuit of a broader narrative about modern Sephardic identity. On one level, for example, I reveal the voice of Estrella Galante, my great-grandmother, a woman whose history of changing countries and languages can teach us about the choices that Sephardic women of her generation faced. At the same time, however, the memoir tracks how roots research has impacted my identity as a Jewish woman, now raising a family in Seattle, one of America's most vibrant enclaves of Sephardic Jews. Here, through the University of Washington's Sephardic Studies Program (SSP), a genuine movement for Sephardic historical and linguistic preservation has taken root, forming a natural support base for my project. As the SSP archivists recognize, members of younger generations face considerable challenges when trying to learn about our Sephardic heritage. My project articulates the emotional tension of researching at a vast geographical, cultural, linguistic, and temporal remove from familial homelands. Why, despite all of the obstacles, do we still feel nostalgia's profound pull towards these places?[2]

I grew up with only a vague awareness that part of my family was Sephardic. At home, my siblings and I heard mostly about my father's roots in a Lithuanian *shtetl*, as small Eastern European market towns were called; my mother's Sephardic background

---

2   Regarding the powerful function of nostalgia for those born after emigration, Dario Miccoli aptly observes: "Especially for the second and third generations, the juxtaposition between *ici* and *là-bas* – before and after the migration – signals the desire, not so much for the real ancestral homeland, but for an imagined land that only exists beyond the boundaries of history *stricto sensu* and whither it is impossible to go back." See Miccoli, "'I come from a country that is no more': Jewish nostalgia in the postcolonial Mediterranean," *Ethnologies* 39, no. 2 (2017): 56.

was acknowledged more subtly. Living in central Virginia in the 1980s, simply being Jewish felt different enough from the Southern culture around us. Besides, mainstream American Judaism didn't offer any kind of vocabulary to articulate non-Ashkenazi identity. Mizrahi, Ottoman, Spanjoli, Rhodesli, Levantine, Ladino: these words were not readily available to me. I did not see "other" Jewish narratives reflected in my modern Orthodox religious school or in books that claimed to catalogue Judaism past or present. As a result, the space around my mother's family story was fuzzy and dark, and I could not locate where being part-Sephardic fit into my Jewish sense of self.

The aspect of our family background that actually predominated, beyond particularities of Jewish lineage, was the fact that my parents both grew up in Zimbabwe, when it was known as Rhodesia. From their accents to the tea they drank, the pale blue air letters that arrived in the mail to the baskets and beadwork displayed around the house—it all connected to their experience living in a British crown colony until their twenties, when they emigrated to the United States. I knew that my parents had left family and friends behind in Africa, and when I was very young, our family made the long trip back to visit. I still have memories, or memories of memories, of a few places—Victoria Falls, a game reserve where we watched animals stalking in the distance, the beach by Cape Town where hawkers called out "ice cream a-lolly!" and handed over delicious granadilla popsicles.

During college I began to probe my family's history and delve into my Sephardic roots in earnest. Two figures, siblings born into the Leon clan on the Mediterranean island of Rhodes, captured my attention immediately. My maternal great-grandmother, Estrella Galante (1898–1978), was an elegant and imposing woman who had studied in Paris with the Alliance Israélite Universelle. She briefly returned to the island to teach French before leaving for an arranged marriage in Africa in the early 1920s. Estrella's older brother, B.S. (Behor Samuel) Leon (1889–1963), was one of the earliest Rhodesli immigrants in southern Africa, arriving around 1908 and amassing a network of farms and properties. A prominent philanthropist and community leader, B.S. leveraged his resources to arrange safe transport for Jews out of Rhodes in the years leading up to World War II. He also supported the Royal Air Force during the war and was made a Member of the Order of the British Empire (M.B.E.) in 1952.

Estrella's husband, an Ottoman Jew named Haim Galante (1890–1980), was not the subject of many family stories growing up. Instead, we heard about the significance of his brother, Abraham Galante (1873–1961). I remember going through my mother's cache of family memorabilia and finding scholarly books he had published in French, as well as a biography of him written in Hebrew, part of a series featuring "great figures in Judaism." I have since learned a lot about Professor

FIGURE 9.1. Rhodes-born siblings B.S. and Estrella Leon, ca. 1920s, Salisbury, Rhodesia.

Galante, my great-granduncle. Born in the Turkish coastal town of Bodrum, he was a pioneering Sephardic intellectual who, during his long career, was a teacher, journalist, activist, deputy in the Turkish Grand National Assembly, and professor of Semitic languages and history of the Ancient Orient at the University of Istanbul. He wrote definitive histories of Mediterranean Jews, including the nine-volume *Histoire des Juifs de Turquie*, and scores of articles on topics ranging from language reform to ineffective communal leaders to Jewish settlement in the Sudan.[3] No less a titan of American Jewish historians than Salo Baron wrote to Galante in the mid-1930s, soon after assuming his chair at Columbia University, asking, "I hope that you will continue sending me your publications in any phase of Jewish history and literature as soon as they appear."[4]

---

3   Two biographies give insight into Galante's life: Abraham Elmaleh's *Le Professeur Abraham Galanté: Sa Vie et Ses Oeuvres* (Istanbul: Kağıt ve Basım İşleri A.Ş.), which appeared in French in 1946 and in Hebrew in 1954; and Albert Kalderon, *Abraham Galante: A Biography* (New York: Sepher-Hermon Press, Inc., 1983). For a contextualization of Galante's place in the genealogy of modern Sephardic scholarship, see Julia Phillips Cohen and Sarah Abrevaya Stein, "Sephardic Scholarly Worlds: Toward a Novel Geography of Modern Jewish History," *Jewish Quarterly Review* 100, no. 3 (Summer 2010): 349–84. For further analysis of Galante's legacy, see Kerem Tinaz's chapter in this volume.

4   Letter from Salo Baron to Abraham Galante, dated April 24, 1936. In *Sephardi Lives: A Documentary History, 1700–1950*, ed. Julia Phillips Cohen and Sarah Abrevaya Stein

Although Abraham continues to loom large in the Sephardic family mythos I have built for myself, I have gradually come to understand more about Haim and appreciate his narrative on its own terms. Haim and Estrella's Cape Town wedding in 1922 set in motion my family's sojourn in Africa that lasted two generations. Over the last decade and a half, I have interviewed several people who knew my great-grandparents, combed through books, searched online archives, and gradually pieced together their life stories. However, the largest source of information is my own collection of family photographs, documents, and heirloom objects, most of which my mother—following some kind of preservationist instinct—brought back from Zimbabwe to the United States following her mother's death in 1991.

As I have broadened out from Estrella's story to explore that of her husband Haim and her brother-in-law Abraham, my focus has expanded from the island of Rhodes to the Ottoman Empire as a whole. In focusing my attention on the Bodrum-born Galante brothers, I have discovered ways their lives both overlapped and radically diverged in the years following the Ottoman Empire's dissolution. Tracking the threads that connected the brothers across continents and decades has proven to be both fruitful and devastating. Sometimes I find myself leaning on the biography of the more famous brother, Abraham, to derive information about the more quietly accomplished Haim. Moreover, I now realize that I will need the official histories Abraham wrote to map out the Sephardic family past that I so desperately long to understand. If I am ever to fully grasp what it means to be an American descended from Ottoman Jews, to reckon with having family who lived in communities that no longer exist, to knowledgeably locate myself in a Sephardic discourse that has been either placed at a remove or simply ignored by most modern Jewish institutional mechanisms and narratives—to achieve these things, I will have to become a reader of my great-granduncle's work.

For now, though, I will share the story of Estrella, Haim, Abraham, and their journeys. On a technical level, these capsule histories show how crafting a family memoir is a process that integrates both personal and public archives. On a narrative level, my relatives' stories encompass major threads of twentieth-century Jewish history: migration, national identity, changing roles for women, language politics, political upheaval, and the Holocaust. On an emotional level, the tales that follow comprise an effort to build a bridge from America to the Sephardic past the best way I know: through writing.

*   *   *

(Stanford: Stanford University Press, 2014), 412–13.

Estrella Leon: A *Savante* Turned Colonial Wife

Estrella Leon Galante was born on the island of Rhodes in 1898, one of eight children born to Samuel (Shmuel) Leon and Rebecca (Rivca) Alhadeff. Across the Jewish Mediterranean, Rhodes enjoyed a reputation as *La chica Yerushalayim*, or the Little Jerusalem, thanks to the island's *yeshivot* (rabbinic academies) that trained Jewish scholars. With its convenient location along seafaring routes, Rhodes proved a desirable property for a series of occupying powers over the centuries. My great-grandmother grew up at the very end of the Ottoman Turkish rule over Rhodes, a reign that had lasted from Sultan Suleiman the Magnificent's conquest in 1522 until 1912. With their status as a *millet*,[5] the Jews enjoyed relative autonomy and religious freedom under the Ottomans. The Italian occupation of Rhodes from 1912 until World War II ushered in a series of drastic linguistic, cultural, and political changes, culminating in the tragic deportation of Rhodes' Jews to concentration camps in 1944. Estrella's mother, Rebecca, was among those who perished.

As a child, Estrella was a resident of La Juderia, the Jewish quarter of the ancient walled city of Rhodes. La Juderia was located on the city's eastern side, close to the port where giant cruise ships dock today. The quarter's architecture of massive arched gates and thick stone walls dates back to the medieval period, when a religious order affiliated with the Crusaders, the Knights of St. John, ruled the island. Historians believe that Rhodes' Jews, who have had a continuous presence on the island since antiquity, have inhabited the Old City's eastern pocket at least since that period. UNESCO added the medieval city of Rhodes to its list of protected World Heritage Sites in 1988.

My great-grandmother grew up on *Calle de la Eskola* (the street of the school), with only the medieval stone wall standing between her house and the sea. The street, called Kisthiniou Street today, is densely packed with squat stone houses. However, the Leons' bright white house stands out, its height, ornamentation, and extra room on top distinguishing it from neighboring homes. Estrella's father Samuel Leon made a comfortable living as a winemaker and was known to be charitable to less fortunate Jews in the community. As one illustration of this status, while *Papu* was the commonly used Ladino word for grandfather, Leon family members called Samuel by the Italian *Il Signore* (the lord, or Sir), reflecting the frequent petitions he received from the needy.

---

5   On the complexity of applying the term "millet" to the different groups living under Ottoman authority, see Heather J. Sharkey, *A History of Muslims, Christians, and Jews in the Middle East* (New York: Cambridge University Press, 2017), 81–88.

FIGURE 9.2. Samuel Leon (seated center) with wife Rebecca Alhadeff (right) and cousin Vida Bonomo (left). Island of Rhodes, undated.

Estrella's early life in La Juderia was lived within a very small circumference. Her family worshipped at the synagogue just around the corner, known as Kahal Grande or Kehila Grande (the great congregation). Almost directly across from their house was the school that gave the street its Ladino name. The building was constructed in 1904 to house Rhodes' newly launched Alliance Israélite Universelle school. Established in 1860 in Paris, the Alliance was a philanthropic organization with a civilizing mission that sought to bring "moral progress" and "regeneration" to Levantine Jews. French language and culture anchored the rigorous curriculum for the schools that the Alliance built around the Mediterranean, which by the start of World

FIGURE 9.3. Estrella and Haim Galante with their twin daughters, Rhodesia, 1924.

War I enrolled thousands of students in places ranging from Istanbul, Salonica, and Teheran to Aleppo and Tripoli. My great-grandmother studied at Rhodes' Alliance school and was then recruited to study at a teachers' seminary in Paris, a prestigious honor that required graduates to teach for the Alliance and continue spreading the message of French culture to their community. As Aron Rodrigue has pointed out, turn-of-the-century Sephardic Jewish society tended to be quite conservative, so it was a major paradigm shift for the community to allow young women to study for a professional degree outside the home—and not only that, but these women were called *savantes* (learned ones) when they finished their training.[6]

I am fortunate to have incredible primary sources upon which to draw for this angle of my research: my grandmother and mother preserved the notebook that Estrella used from 1913–1916, precisely the period when she left the Alliance Israélite Universelle school on Rhodes and began her studies in France. Full of poems, popular songs, literary excerpts, vocabulary lists, and more, the notebook reflects

---

6   See Aron Rodrigue, *Images of Sephardi and Eastern Jewries in Transition: The Teachers of the Alliance Israélite Universelle, 1860–1939* (Seattle: University of Washington Press, 1991); also, Frances Malino, "Prophets in Their Own Land? Mothers and Daughters of the Alliance Israélite Universelle," *Nashim* 3 (2000): 56–73.

the curriculum that Estrella absorbed as a teenaged student. Interestingly, while nearly all the entries are in French, there are a few interpolations in Italian, Turkish, and English—the latter being the lyrics to "God Save the Queen"! I can't shake the feeling that this written object, while on its surface a perfunctory chronicle of classroom exercises, generates a significant memoir between the lines.

In addition to the notebook, my memorabilia collection includes a teaching certificate, postcards written in French, and photographs from Estrella's school years. With Aron Rodrigue's assistance, I have also acquired scanned pieces of correspondence between the central Alliance office in Paris and the head of the Rhodes school, pertaining to Estrella's brief employment there in 1919 after she finished her training. The Alliance's online archive has helped to confirm the facts of Estrella's involvement.[7] These combined archival resources, the personal and the institutional, facilitate the reconstruction of Estrella's experience as she participated in the Alliance network as both a student and teacher.

Estrella pursued her Alliance career precisely during the period wherein Rhodes changed hands from Ottoman imperial to Italian colonial status—a dramatic transition that would, by the end of World War II, lead to irrevocably tragic consequences for Rhodes' Jewish community, which was deported in July of 1944. Estrella and her seven siblings escaped this fate by emigrating to southern or central Africa in the 1920s, choosing, as did many of their compatriots, to seek opportunities for settlement and economic growth in Rhodesia or the Belgian Congo. For my great-grandmother, leaving Rhodes meant leaving behind her career as a community *savante* and ambassador of French culture; once married and living in Rhodesia, she never again taught French.

Haim Galante: From Bodrum Boy to Rhodesian Businessman

The man for whom Estrella broke her teaching contract and left behind the Levantine lifestyle that had cradled her family for generations was named Haim Galante. Born in 1890 in the coastal town of Bodrum, Turkey, Haim was one of thirteen or fourteen children born to Joya Codron and Moshe Galante,[8] a scion of a legendary Sephardic

---

7   Information about the Alliance archives is available at https://www.aiu.org/en/archives-0. Thank you to Christina Sztajnkrycer for personally inquiring about Estrella's file when she visited the Alliance headquarters in Paris, as well as providing translations of selected notebook excerpts and letters, a detailed catalogue of the notebook's contents, and consultation about early twentieth-century French culture.

8   I have acquired a professional family tree based on the Rhodes Census records and private research, which include a twelfth sister, but she was not included in a hand-written list of the Galante siblings created by my grandmother.

clan that included the sixteenth-century Safed kabbalist Abraham ben-Mordocai Galante. Nearly all the siblings were born on Rhodes, Joya's own birthplace, but Abraham and Haim—the only sons—were born in Bodrum, which was relatively close to Rhodes via boat. As a young man, Haim studied at the Alliance Israélite Universelle's boys' school on Rhodes, learning Hebrew, Turkish, and French. (The up-and-coming pedagogue who co-established the school just happened to be his older brother Abraham.[9]) Haim then left for Egypt,[10] where he was joined by his friend B.S. Leon, whom he must have met during his schooling on Rhodes; Haim worked at the Deutsche Bank in Cairo, while B.S. worked at a tobacco and cigarette firm. Around 1908, the two friends made their way to the territory known as Southern Rhodesia, now Zimbabwe, where they launched various business enterprises.

Like immigrant Jews everywhere, Grandpa Galante, as he was known in our family, worked hard to make his way from the social, economic, and geographic margins to the center. He set up a trading station in the remote town of Gatooma, in a pattern to be repeated by other Sephardic immigrants in places like Umtali, Que Que, Chakari, and Penhalonga.[11] Conditions were not easy. In a recollection penned for his synagogue's 75th anniversary, Salvo Almaleh describes the existence of early Sephardic settlers like Haim: "Theirs was a lonely life, originally, being stuck out in lonely areas, where there was not a familiar face to be seen. We have an old Spanish saying, and it is very apt here—*andi se arapo il werko*—translated, 'where the devil shaves himself [in other words, to hell and gone].' It was a tough life, crossing swollen rivers, sleeping on bare store counters, with a blanket or two pulled out of the shelves, water from wells, outside toilets and paraffin lamps. And, of course, the added difficulty of having to cope with the language . . ."[12]

---

9   See Marc D. Angel, *The Jews of Rhodes: The History of a Sephardic Community* (New York: Sepher-Hermon Press Inc., 1978), 79.

10 It is possible that Haim went first to Cairo because Abraham was already there, editing the Ladino newspaper *La Vara* from 1904–09. See Kalderon, *Abraham Galante*, 28–39.

11 On early Sephardic immigration to southern Africa, see: Renée Hirschon, "Jews from Rhodes in Central and Southern Africa," *Encyclopedia of Diasporas: Immigrant and Refugee Cultures Around the World* Vol. 2, ed. Melvin Ember, Carol R. Ember, and Ian Skoggard (New York: Spring, 2005), 1–12; Yitzchak Kerem, "The Migration of Rhodian Jews to Africa and the Americas from 1900–1914: The Beginning of New Sephardic Diasporic Communities," in *Patterns of Migration, 1850–1914*, ed. Aubrey Newman and Stephen W. Massil (University College London, 1996), 321–34; Barry A. Kosmin, "A Note on Southern Rhodesian Jewry," *Jewish Journal of Sociology* 15, no. 2 (1973): 23–28.

12 Salvo Almaleh, "Down Memory Lane." In the *75th Anniversary Bulletin of the Sephardi Hebrew Congregation of Zimbabwe*, ed. Benny Leon, p.13. Accessed 21 February 2019

FIGURE 9.4. Lillian and Hilda Galante at University of Cape Town Graduation, 1945.

By the mid-1920s, Haim had partnered with J.N. Alhadeff and J.S. Benatar to manage several concession stores near the gold mines in the area of Shamva and Bindura. In what was clearly an arranged marriage, Haim wed Estrella Leon, a younger sister of his friend B.S., in 1922, meeting her boat when it docked at Cape Town. I found their marriage license via a wiki archive run by FamilySearch, which provides access to scanned records for people who lived in the Western Cape of Africa from 1792–1992.[13] My great-grandparents' signed and witnessed marriage certificate (*huweliksregister*, in the local Afrikaans dialect) bears the notarized date of January 10, 1922. Since there was no religious officiant in Rhodesia, they also arranged for a rabbi to marry them at a friend's house in Cape Town before heading up to Gatooma. Their identical twin daughters, Hilda and Lillian, were born in 1924; the girls would go on to become the first members of their family to graduate from college.

When business took a downward turn, possibly with the closing of the mines in the early 1930s, Haim left his family for a few years to start new ventures in the Belgian Congo, another African locus of Sephardic immigrants. He returned to Rhodesia with enough wealth to purchase a large house in the neighborhood of Highlands Township, in the capital city of Salisbury, now called Harare. (The stately building later became

---

on the website of the Zimbabwe Jewish Community, http://www.zjc.org.il/showpage.php?pageid=325.

13   www.familysearch.org/wiki/en/Western_Cape_Province,_South Africa Genealogy. Family-Search is a genealogy organization run by the Church of Jesus Christ of Latter-day Saints.

234 | HANNAH S. PRESSMAN

a residence for government officials and is now a Public Services Training Centre.[14]) Eventually, Haim ran his own business, the Anglo-African Shipping Company, which represented different brands in Rhodesia and arranged the import and export of goods all over the world. Nowadays, you can go on eBay and find envelopes stamped with the Galante name and the company's return address—tiny traces of a broad enterprise that extended to places like New York, Melbourne, and Stockholm.

When Haim and Estrella left the Highlands neighborhood, they bought a house on Pascoe Avenue in Salisbury, where two other Sephardic families, the Taricas and Alhadeffs, also lived. Jews from Rhodes—the country of origin of most, but not all, of the Sephardic Jews in Salisbury—often lived in the same neighborhoods, cousins growing up together, women gathering frequently to chat in Ladino and bake pastries for holidays and celebrations. The Sephardic community in Salisbury worshipped together at their own synagogue, called the Sephardi Hebrew Congregation. Beginning in the early 1930s, community leaders had begun organizing services with the tunes and liturgy familiar from their homeland, rather than attending the Ashkenazi-style services held at the more established Salisbury Hebrew Congregation. By the late 1950s, the Sephardic community had built their own hall, synagogue, and Hebrew school, the latter funded in large part by B.S. Leon and named in honor of Samuel Leon, Haim's father-in-law, the winemaker on the island of Rhodes.

The Galantes' Pascoe Avenue house was known for its garden and tennis court, which had required the purchase of a second plot of land next door. Haim let anyone in the neighborhood play on the court, reflecting the kindness that everyone I interviewed mentioned in regard to his personality; quietly philanthropic, Haim offered loans and jobs to those in need, such as two brothers who had lost their father at a young age.[15] The Pascoe house had a study with a wall full of books, including, I'm

---

14 An excellent photo essay of Harare, located at the website The Great Mirror, conveys a sense of Rhodesia's early colonial architecture and its contemporary urban landscape. Haim and Estrella Galante's house in Highlands Township is included towards the end of the essay: https://www.greatmirror.com/index.cfm?countryid=1469&chapterid=1448&picturesize=medium. The site is run by a geography professor at the University of Oklahoma, who has photographed and documented places in dozens of countries around the world.

15 A member of the Harare Hebrew Congregation (the Ashkenazi synagogue, known as the Salisbury Hebrew Congregation prior to Zimbabwe's independence) included the following observation within its 100th anniversary bulletin: "In 1931, there were enough Sephardi Jews to follow their own *minhag* and tradition. They had brought a wealth of culture and vitality to the new land and many were blessed with great business acumen. Among their members were some of the most philanthropic men; indeed, many struggling traders were grateful for a loan from B.S. Leon or Chaim Galante." Pat Baldachin,

told, all of the scholarly books his older brother Abraham published—though one relative reported, conspiratorially, that Haim's favorite genre was detective novels. Many people told me that he liked to retire to this room in the evenings with his pipe or a cigar and a glass of Scotch.

My mother, one of three children born to Estrella and Haim's daughter Hilda, lived around the corner and rode her bicycle to visit her grandparents every day. I ask my mother what she remembers about Grandpa Galante. She recalls him being very kind, wearing a jacket and tie, and smoking a pipe. His favorite evening snack was homemade yogurt or *soutlach*, a kind of rice pudding topped with cinnamon that was popular with Turkish Jews, accompanied by a drink that combined honey with apple cider vinegar. By his bedside, there were always piles of pale pink and yellow financial newspapers. The house also had a terrace that adjoined the first floor landing. Here, Haim would sit in a large armchair and take in the sun. My mother writes of "his hands stretched out on the wooden arms of the chair."[16] Hands that would one day hold me, his infant great-granddaughter from America.

*   *   *

Estrella Leon, Haim Galante, and their siblings were born in the waning decades of the Ottoman Empire. Until recently, I had no inkling about whether Haim clung to his Ottoman identity during his early struggles and later success in Southern Rhodesia. No one that I interviewed could remember his birthplace of Bodrum coming up in conversation. Looking through documents in the Galante file my mother has given me, I find a mysterious scrap of paper with a typed list of four men with addresses in Istanbul. I do not know if these were Haim's business associates (one, Rafael Torel, was a famous Turkish Jewish businessman and the subject of a biography) or perhaps colleagues of Abraham's that Haim planned to meet on a trip. As my research continues, I have to face that some family ephemera offer tantalizing clues that may never be solved.

Whereas Haim successfully integrated into British colonial life, his older brother Abraham spent his lifetime completely immersed in Turkish Jewish communal and public affairs, arguing passionately about issues emerging from Turkey's modern transformation while also diligently documenting the history of Anatolian Jews. Aside from some time abroad in his early career—five years in Cairo, where he founded the newspaper *La Vara* and got involved with the Young Turks movement,

---

"From Shtetl to Zimbabwe: Jewish immigrants find a new life," in *Our First 100 Years: The Proud Story of the Harare Hebrew Congregation, 1895 to 1995, 5655 to 5755*, 25.

16   Personal correspondence with the author's mother, 13 May 2019.

followed by a year each studying in London and Berlin—he primarily worked in Ottoman or Turkish locales like Izmir, Rhodes, Istanbul, and Ankara, and in this arena, he sought to have his greatest impact. Abraham even served as a Turkish government official: in the mid-1940s, he represented the province of Niğde at the Grand National Assembly in Ankara.

The divergent ways these two Galante brothers related to their national identities can be encapsulated by events of the 1930s. In 1934, the Turkish Surname Law, one of a slew of reforms passed in the new Republic of Turkey, required citizens to adopt an official Turkish-language surname.[17] Abraham took the surname Bodrumlu, which means "of Bodrum," in tribute to his birthplace on the Aegean coast. He had spent formative years there, studying in the Talmud Torah as a child and later in the Rüşdiye, the public middle school. Abraham would go on to write about his birthplace in his 1945–1946 work, *Bodrum Tarihi* (History of Bodrum).[18] To me, the choice of the surname "Bodrumlu" illustrates Abraham Galante's lifelong commitment to being a modern Turkish Jew, fully embracing both identities.

By contrast, Haim, though comfortably established in Rhodesia, found himself facing a difficult political situation by the late 1930s. With war looming, the community of Sephardic émigrés in Africa needed to become naturalized British citizens or risk being arrested and interned as enemy aliens. Jews from the island of Rhodes, or whose parents came from Rhodes, could have acquired Italian papers because of Rhodes' status as an Italian colony from 1912–1946; after providing protection and a legitimate European citizenship for several years, this identity imperiled them once it was clear that Italy would be fighting against England.[19] Through the United Kingdom's online National Archives, within a catalogue of Home Office records pertaining to the 1914 British Nationality and Status of Aliens Act, I am able to

---

17 See Marcy Brink-Danan, *Jewish Life in 21ˢᵗ-Century Turkey: The Other Side of Tolerance* (Bloomington: Indiana University Press, 2012), 66–73.

18 A new study, *The Bodrum Jewish Cemetery* by Siren Bora (Istanbul: Libra Kitapçılık ve Yayıncılık, 2017), documents the small community with photographs, maps, and translations of all the gravestone epitaphs, which bear fascinating linguistic and decorative elements. Several Galante tombstones are included in the book, though Abraham himself was buried in Istanbul. Bora discusses Galante's choice of surname in the book's Foreword.

19 As Sarah Abrevaya Stein notes in her excellent study of the complexities of Jewish citizenship, Rhodesli Jews in "émigré settings" like Rhodesia, South Africa, and the Belgian Congo "received Italian protection through local consuls and representatives despite having never [set] foot on the island in its Italian incarnation" (81). See Stein, *Extraterritorial Dreams: European Citizenship, Sephardi Jews, and the Ottoman Twentieth Century* (Chicago: University of Chicago Press, 2016).

find evidence that members of my family participated in the citizenship switchover process. Haim's close friend and brother-in-law, B.S. Leon, had received his British naturalization in 1931. Haim received his in August 1939, and Abner Leon, another brother-in-law, received his in September 1939, one week after Germany invaded Poland. All are listed as being "from Italy" prior to naturalization.[20]

Thus, in the same decade, Abraham reaffirmed his Turkish patriotism, while Haim cemented his British citizenship. Until recently, I thought this aspect of their divergent journeys was rather black-and-white, believing Haim must have left his Ottoman allegiance behind once he set out for southern Africa. Then, I discovered a trace of Haim Galante in history, a printed text that brought my great-grandfather into clearer definition: the Ladino newspaper *El Tiempo*, published in Istanbul from 1872–1931, ran an article about him in its issue of November 12, 1913. I found this source via a footnote in Abraham Galante's Hebrew-language biography, which has a brief section about Haim and his daughters. Eventually, I tracked down scanned copies of the original newspaper, now held at the University of Washington's Sephardic Studies Digital Library.[21]

Reporting out of Salisbury, the *El Tiempo* article describes how Haim Galante and two colleagues gathered donations from Jews and Indian Muslims in southern Africa to support the Ottoman navy. The impetus for the fundraising was the Balkan War, specifically the five-month siege of Edirne (Adrianople), which had a sizable Jewish population. Edirne's siege during 1912–1913 and eventual liberation during the Second Balkan War became, along with the Ottoman warship the *Hamidiye*, powerful symbols of Ottoman civilian and military resilience.[22] The *El Tiempo* article details how much money different constituents contributed and concludes by praising the "patriotic sentiment" of those who donated to support the Ottoman flotilla from afar.

An archive in Turkey now contains the letter, written in Ottoman Turkish, that my great-grandfather sent to accompany the donations he gathered. According to the scholar Halim Gençoğlu, who is based at the University of Cape Town, the letter praises the *Hamidiye* warship and the Ottoman navy and emphasizes Ottoman

---

20 The online archive is located at https://discovery.nationalarchives.gov.uk/.

21 Thank you to the UW Sephardic Studies Program for providing access to this article. *El Tiempo* issues from the years 1872–1904 are also archived and viewable online through the Historical Jewish Press website maintained by the National Library of Israel and Tel Aviv University, in association with Israel's National Authority for Ladino Culture. See https://web.nli.org.il/sites/JPress/English/Pages/ElTiempo.aspx.

22 See Eyal Ginio, *The Ottoman Culture of Defeat: The Balkan Wars and their Aftermath* (New York: Oxford University Press, 2016), especially 236–64.

Jewish gratitude and loyalty.[23] Haim was twenty-three when he led this fundraising initiative to unite Jews and Muslims in southern Africa. Can this effort be traced to his roots in Bodrum, where there was relative coexistence between the small Jewish population and their Turkish neighbors?[24] I also wonder whether it was, on some level, an attempt to connect with (or impress) his older brother from afar. Abraham had returned to Turkey from abroad in 1911, and by 1913, at age forty, he was well on his way to a multi-faceted career: he served as a translator in the Ministry of the Navy, translated and wrote articles for the Red Crescent, became an assistant instructor at the University of Istanbul, and published pathbreaking research on Dona Gracia and Don Joseph Nassi. Perhaps Haim wished to signal to his brother, family members, and colleagues that he, too, was invested in Ottoman security and socio-political causes.

The gesture of national solidarity recorded by *El Tiempo* adds to my growing understanding of Grandpa Galante's personal and political sensibilities at this formative stage of his life: single, struggling to establish a business presence in Africa, observing catastrophic world events from a distance, he asserted his ties to the Ottoman Empire and encouraged others in his sphere of influence to do the same.[25] The *El Tiempo* article provides a precious piece of evidence about his activism in a time of national duress. Moreover, it shows that Haim did not shed his Ottoman Jewish identity as soon as he emigrated. I marvel at how the brothers Galante, while embarking on very different paths in the early twentieth century, shared a commitment to their place of origin. In fact, when asking about Haim's Turkish identity in a recent discussion with someone who knew him well, I received this reply: "Haim was very proud of his brother's position in the Turkish parliament. Though he was generally a reticent man, this was something he liked to tell people about."[26]

* * *

23 Halim Gençoğlu, *Ottoman Traces in Southern Africa: The Impact of Turkish Emissaries and Muslim Theologians* (Istanbul: Libra Kitapçilik ve Yayincilik, 2018), 289–306. Gençoğlu's chapter about Haim Galante includes his original Ottoman letter and its English translation.

24 See Bora, *The Bodrum Jewish Cemetery*, 19–20, citing Abraham Galante's observations on the "amicable relations" between Jews and their neighbors in Bodrum.

25 Cf. Gençoğlu's point that relations between Sephardic Jews and the Ottoman Empire continued after they migrated to South Africa. Gençoğlu, *Ottoman Traces in Southern Africa*, 299.

26 Personal conversation with Henry Tarica, January 1, 2019. Mr. Tarica was Estrella and Haim's godson and neighbor, and he worked as Estrella's driver. His aunt, Deborah Tarica (née Galante, 1900–1958), was Haim and Abraham's younger sister. I am indebted to Henry for many hours of discussion about the Sephardic Jewish community in Zimbabwe.

FIGURE 9.5. Front and back of a small signed photograph that Abraham Galante sent from Turkey to his brother Haim in Rhodesia in 1958. The French inscription translates as, "To my dear brother H. Galante. 11/9/1958 Abraham."

I own two photographs that Abraham Galante sent to his younger brother Haim towards the end of his life; both are inscribed in French. In 1953, Abraham wrote, *"A mon cher frère Haïm, ainsi qu'à sa femme et ses enfants. Istanbule le 4/1/1953. Abraham"*—"To my dear brother Haim, as well as to his wife and children. Istanbul, January 4, 1953. Abraham." (I still do not know if he ever met Estrella, the twins, or the children born to the other Galante siblings who had emigrated to southern Africa.) Printed on a stiff postcard, the matte photo on the front is the same one you see when you search for Abraham Galante on Wikipedia: a serious-looking, bespectacled man in a long, striped suit coat that hangs a little loosely on him. The second, smaller photo, printed on shiny photo paper, is stamped with the production date of August 20, 1957. However, it took Abraham over a year to inscribe and send it.

The man in this picture is gaunt, but his eyes are fierce. He wears a three-piece suit and appears to be sitting outside a house. On the back, in larger, shakier handwriting, he has written simply, *"A mon chere frère H. Galante. 11/9/1958 Abraham."* By that point, the aging scholar, who never married, had been living in relative isolation on the island of Kinali, a forty-minute boat ride from Istanbul, for many years. He was in failing health and trying to organize his papers, aggrieved that his writings (many of which were self-published) had not found an audience with the younger generation of Turkish Jews.

I think about this man and his language politics, the fervency with which he publicly argued for acculturation and advocated that Turkish Jews speak the Turkish language, contrasted with these tender French inscriptions sent to his faraway brother and family. Despite his assimilationist ideology, the proud Turkish citizen still communicated in the Romance language he and his brother learned as schoolboys.[27]

It is through French, as well, that I read about the most devastating chapter in the Galante brothers' family history. One of Abraham's many publications in 1935 was *Histoire des Juifs de Rhodes, Chio, Cos, etc.*, considered a foundational history of Mediterranean Jews. In 1948, he published an appendix to this book: *Fin Tragique des communautés Juives de Rhodes et de Cos, Oeuvre du brigandage Hitlérien*. This text documents what happened to Rhodes' small Jewish community in July of 1944, when its 1,651 members, along with Jews from the nearby island of Kos, were deported to the Greek concentration camp of Haidary en route to Auschwitz. Only 151 people survived. Galante includes testimonials, letters, and poems written by survivors in French and Ladino, as well as a last note—an appendix to his appendix—where the source of emotion underlying the report becomes clear:

> *Laissez-moi, auteur de cet ouvrage, pleurer mes chers disparus, victimes du brigandage hitlérien. J'ai perdu:*
>
> Allow me, author of this publication, to mourn my dear departed, victims of Hitler's plundering. I have lost:

This strikingly first-person phrase, *J'ai perdu*, introduces us to the Galante siblings and loved ones who were murdered: Lea (born 1872) and Mazaltov (born 1886), who were living on Rhodes, and Rosa (born 1892), who was living on Kos. He also mentions his brother-in-law Ruben Codron (whose wife Rachel, the third-oldest Galante sibling, had passed away before the war) and their family. Abraham names and honors these relatives, who were, of course, Haim's as well.

J'ai perdu, "I have lost." Haim lost not only three siblings, but his mother-in-law as well: Rivca Alhadeff, Estrella's mother, was among those deported and murdered in 1944. Finding an Italian document referring to Rivca was my first real discovery that members of my Sephardic family were victims of the Holocaust, as well as my first inkling about the breadth of the catastrophe's Sephardic dimension, which my American Jewish education had not directly addressed in any way. Seeing these

---

27   Marcy Brink-Danan describes how being descended from Ottoman Jews, on one level, means inheriting a long tradition of "semiotic awareness," built by "[y]ears of education in multiple languages and the constant negotiation between religious laws and secular citizenship." See Brink-Danan, *Jewish Life in 21ˢᵗ-Century Turkey*, 22.

relatives' names in printed sources and then locating them in Yad Vashem's on-line archive[28] have been difficult but important steps towards understanding that Sephardic history is part of the broader narrative of the events of World War II.[29]

My sources tell me that the Holocaust was not openly discussed in the tight-knit community of Sephardic Jews living in southern Africa. There was a taboo on the subject after the war, stemming from the belief that talking about it might invite the evil eye. Survivors gradually made their way to the region, joined the community, married. I wonder if, like Abraham's other publications, his small book about the atrocities that befell Rhodes' Jews also made its way to Grandpa Haim's study on Pascoe Avenue. I imagine the unspeakable truths that Abraham Galante recorded for posterity sitting quietly on Haim's bookshelves, the names of their sisters—Lea, Mazaltov, and Rosa—present in print, not forgotten.

Tracing the twentieth-century history of a Jewish family inevitably means facing counterfactuals. *What if…would they have…if only.* What losses could have been avoided if a letter had been answered, a visa signed, a ship allowed to make land-fall. I feel a strange pull when I read that, in 1914, Abraham Galante was entreated to take on a leadership position uniting Sephardic Jews, who were then usually referred to as Oriental Jews,[30] in America. (Somewhat strangely, the nominating group referred to him as "Rabbi A. Galante," even though he had never obtained ordination.) My great-granduncle went so far as to meet with Henry Morgenthau, President Wilson's ambassador to the Ottoman Empire, in the summer of 1914. Ultimately, he turned down the position, deciding to stay in Turkey during the war.[31]

My mind spins out the scenarios if he had accepted the offer: would Abraham have convinced Haim, then only a few years into his African adventure, to give up and join him in New York? Might the brothers have persuaded other siblings to leave their homes and build a whole Galante outpost in the American melting pot? Could Lea, Mazaltov, Rosa, and the family of Rachel all have avoided their

---

28 Names are searchable in the Central Database of Shoah Victims' Names, located at https://yvng.yadvashem.org/.

29 I have explored this topic in more depth in my article about the Ladino letters written by my great-grandmother Rivca and sent to Africa in 1940. See "'I'd Like to Become a Bird,'" *Tablet Magazine*, August 21, 2017, https://www.tabletmag.com/jewish-life-and-religion/242352/ladino-letters-from-rhodes.

30 On the evolution of nomenclature for Sephardic Jews in America, see Devin E. Naar, "'Sephardim since Birth': Reconfiguring Jewish Identity in America," in *Sephardi and Mizrahi Jews in America*, ed. Saba Soomekh (West Lafayette, Indiana: Purdue University Press, 2016), 75–104.

31 Kalderon, *Abraham Galante*, 43–45.

tragic fate? The scenario plays out further: I imagine Estrella sailing from Rhodes to New York harbor instead of Cape Town, bringing her mother Rivca along; my grandmother Hilda attending CUNY instead of the University of Cape Town; my mother coming of age in New York public schools and parks instead of a British colonial private school. What if my family's time in Africa had ended before it even began?

*   *   *

In exploring the notion of Sephardic *yichus* (pedigree),[32] I have learned that Sephardim will ask new acquaintances, *De ken sos tu?* ("From whom are you?"), a question directly probing a newcomer's family tree. Additionally, in Ladino, a family name is *alkunya*, a word indicating lineage.[33] When I moved to Seattle twelve years ago and began meeting people in the city's sizable Sephardic community, I would mention that my mother's side had family from the Mediterranean island of Rhodes. Sure enough, I would then be asked which families I was related to; usually, I replied "Leon and Alhadeff," names that would ring a bell since many descendants of those Rhodesli clans ended up in Seattle. These two surnames were usually sufficient information to play Jewish geography and figure out our degree of cousin-hood. Afterwards, I would marvel at the novelty of meeting people for whom Sephardic identity was a given, the seamless fabric of their homes and community.

Sometimes, in these introductory chats with local Sephardim, I added that my Rhodesli great-grandmother married a Turkish man. This distinction matters

---

32 *Yichus* is based on the Hebrew root yud-het-sin, which connotes relation. In Tanakh, we find mentions of this word as far back as the Books of Nehemiah and Ezra, which use it in the sense of genealogical records: "I found the genealogical register (*sefer hayahas*) of those who were the first to come up" (Nehemiah 7:5). In that era, as the Jews who had been exiled to Babylonia began to return to the land of Israel, there was concern about priestly purity and that of the Jewish community as a whole; checking genealogical records was a way to ensure the maintenance of certain religious and social hierarchies. The Babylonian sages also emphasized elite lineage as a crucial source of rabbinic authority; see Jeffrey L. Rubenstein, *The Culture of the Babylonian Talmud* (Baltimore: Johns Hopkins University Press, 2003), especially Chapter 5, "Lineage and Rabbinic Leadership," 80–101. Centuries later in the lands of Ashkenaz, proving a potential match's *yichus* was essential for the business of Eastern European matchmakers. In the social web of the *shtetl*, *yichus* meant an acceptable pedigree, particularly descent from a prestigious family tree of rabbis and Torah scholars. Today, the word *yichus* retains that valence: not just family relations, but the right *kind* of relations. My thanks to Mika Ahuvia for clarifying the meaning of *yichus* in ancient Jewish contexts.

33 Thank you to Devin E. Naar for teaching me how these words function in Ladino.

in Seattle, where there are still two Sephardic synagogues: one for Rhodes-based Sephardim, the other founded by Jews from Turkey. "He was a Galante, from the coastal town of Bodrum," I would say, and then pause; if my interlocutor seemed interested to hear more, I would add, "In fact, my great-grandfather's brother was the historian Abraham Galante." Invariably, eyes would light up at this new information: "You're related to THAT Galante?" "Wow, that's real Sephardic *yichus.*" The excited reaction was the same in academic spheres when I met colleagues whose work connected with Ottoman Studies, Mediterranean history, or Jewish history; likewise, when I met anyone from Turkey. "Galante?" exclaimed a Turkish political philosopher visiting campus a few years ago. "I've always wanted to write a book about him!"

In a way, the Galante name has provided a security blanket as I've begun writing about my roots research and presenting my findings to others. As I lean further into my Sephardic identity, making space for something that is largely absent from the American Jewish mainstream, it feels reassuring to know that I am descended from a family that extends back to such interesting places and times. Accepting my friend's nickname of "Galante's daughter" makes me feel a part of the Sephardic story that I am still uncovering and claiming for myself. This validation is no small thing, given the challenges of researching family history. Even with all of the genealogical and archival technologies at our disposal, some questions remain mysteries. We follow leads until we reach what the memoirist Nicole Chung, a Korean adoptee who searched for her biological parents, evocatively calls "all you can ever know."[34]

Reconstructing my great-grandparents' narrative is an act of *kavod* (Heb. honor), of acknowledging the foremothers and forefathers who came before me. When I write about their journeys into and out of Africa, I offer an elegy for a vibrant, endangered Jewish community that, at a certain point in history, found a few decades of refuge in another country's colony before again dispersing elsewhere.[35] At the same time, I am trying to map myself onto the story of Levantine Jews who spent the late nineteenth and twentieth centuries trading in nationalities and languages. I am trying to see where I fit into the history of Ottoman Jews in diaspora, realizing that I am one drop in the waves of history recorded by my great-granduncle. I recognize that, by being born and raised in America, I am operating at a distinctly doubled remove—not just from the experience of growing up in a Jewish com-

---

34 Nicole Chung, *All You Can Ever Know* (New York: Catapult, 2018).

35 The group continues to evolve in the postcolonial era, as former members of the Zimbabwe Jewish community now living around the world stay connected through social media and virtual spaces.

munity in Africa, but also from the origin points of Rhodes and Turkey. Yet, if I have learned anything from the process of reclaiming my Sephardic identity, it's that our feelings of nostalgia, loss, and connection to the past don't always follow logical or geographical boundaries.

The research process has made manifest the difficulty of writing about geneal-ogy in a way that successfully navigates between personal history and collective history. Which version is the official version? Whose memory will be inscribed as true? Dario Miccoli suggests that, for post-migratory generations, "literature and the literary imagination" can provide "alternative repertoires of historical knowledge that complement those of the institutional archive."[36] Through my nostalgia for Rhodes and Turkey, places I have never lived but which are very important to me, a fruitful textual contribution can emerge. The "Galante's Daughter" of my book's title is me—an indication of my personal search to reckon with this inheritance, name it, and make it visible in an American Jewish discourse that has tended to privilege the stories and culture of Ashkenazi Jews.

I often find myself thinking about Samuel Leon's house on Rhodes, where my great-grandmother grew up with her seven siblings in the last decades of the Ottoman Empire. The fact that the house still stands at all is remarkable, given that British bombings towards the end of World War II caused significant structural damage on nearby streets. During my 2006 visit to the island, I kept returning to *Calle de la Eskola* and marveling at the house, touching its cool stone and peering inside its door. In the twenty-first century, such opportunities cannot be taken for granted, since for many Jews, all physical traces of their ancestors' homes have vanished forever. It is nearly impossible to go back to Eastern Europe and locate an ancestral *shtetl*; even if sites of former towns are marked, their structures were completely destroyed during World War II. We are forced to ask: what does it mean to go back to a place that has vanished? And for Rhodes' La Judería, I realize, the inverse question applies: what if the neighborhood still stands, but all of the Jews have disappeared?

Crafting an archival family memoir has helped me navigate the nearly-over-whelming sense of loss and rupture inherent in these questions. My goal to un-derstand, interpret, and record my family's history has involved a reimagining of the spaces where long-lost relatives lived—rebuilding fallen walls, repopulating empty hallways, hearing silent voices. This task would be daunting without the diversity of archival sources I have catalogued in this essay: the technological and

---

36   Miccoli, "'I come from a country that is no more'," 62.

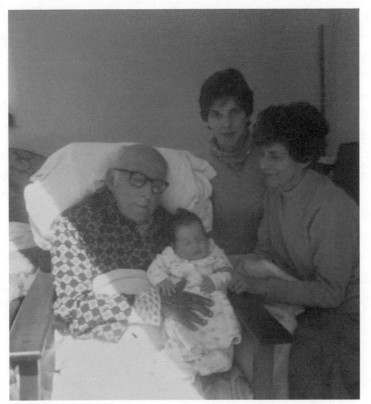

FIGURE 9.6. The author with her mother, grandmother, and great-grandfather, Harare, August 1979.

the human, the institutional and the communal, the public and the private, the textual and the material. The collection begun by my great-grandmother and preserved by her daughter and granddaughter—documents, photographs, and objects that have traveled the world, from Rhodes and Turkey to Rhodesia and the United States—is now, literally and figuratively, in my hands. There are so many Sephardic stories yet to tell.

* * *

A coda:

My great-grandmother Estrella died the year before I was born. I met my great-grandfather Haim once, when I was two months old. My mother's father had just passed away, and she brought me with her to Zimbabwe for an extended stay with my grandmother Hilda. A few months later, in April 1980, Haim too would pass away.

In this picture, Grandpa Haim, the import-export specialist, has pulled off quite a feat: importing his littlest great-granddaughter all the way from America. We are both wearing pajamas and snuggled in blankets, for it was the end of winter then. My shock of dark hair matches my mother's and grandmother's. All I knew at two months old was whether my mother's warmth was near, and maybe if the light was bright or dark. I couldn't know that this man holding me had journeyed from a town in Turkey, studied on Rhodes, worked in Egypt, and built a business and a life for his family in Rhodesia. I couldn't know that he was an Ottoman patriot who raised funds for the Ottoman navy from afar and ate *soutlach* to remind himself of home, a husband with a sophisticated wife, who gave up her teaching career for marriage, a kind man who let everyone in the neighborhood play on his tennis court, the younger brother of an important professor in Istanbul who sent him photographs inscribed in French, a man who mourned three sisters and many relatives who perished in the Holocaust, and now, as our family tree spreads roots into the twenty-first century, an ancestor of fifteen great-great-grandchildren.

I couldn't know any of what was or would be, but in the photograph, my hand rests on Haim's. Was it placed there, or did I instinctively put my hand on his? No matter: the arc of our lives had intersected for a little time on this earth. He held me in his chair, in the light of a sunny terrace in Africa.

Bibliography

Almaleh, Salvo. "Down Memory Lane." In *75th Anniversary Bulletin of the Sephardi Hebrew Congregation of Zimbabwe*, ed. Benny Leon, p.13. Accessed February 21, 2019 on the website of the Zimbabwe Jewish Community, http://www.zjc.org.il/showpage.php?pageid=325.

Angel, Marc D. *The Jews of Rhodes: The History of a Sephardic Community.* New York: Sepher-Hermon Press Inc., 1978.

Baldachin, Pat. "From Shtetl to Zimbabwe: Jewish immigrants find a new life." In *Our First 100 Years: The Proud Story of the Harare Hebrew Congregation, 1895 to 1995, 5655 to 5755.*

Bora, Siren. *The Bodrum Jewish Cemetery.* Istanbul: Libra Kitapçılık ve Yayıncılık, 2017.

Brink-Danan, Marcy. *Jewish Life in 21st-Century Turkey: The Other Side of Tolerance.* Bloomington: Indiana University Press, 2012.

Chung, Nicole. *All You Can Ever Know.* New York: Catapult, 2018.

Elmaleh, Abraham. *Le Professeur Abraham Galanté: Sa Vie et Ses Oeuvres.* Istanbul: Kağıt ve Basım İşleri A.Ş., 1946.

Gençoğlu, Halim. *Ottoman Traces in Southern Africa: The Impact of Turkish Emissaries and Muslim Theologians.* Istanbul: Libra Kitapçilik ve Yayincilik, 2018.

Ginio, Eyal. *The Ottoman Culture of Defeat: The Balkan Wars and their Aftermath.* New York: Oxford University Press, 2016.

Hirschon, Renée. "Jews from Rhodes in Central and Southern Africa." *Encyclopedia of Diasporas: Immigrant and Refugee Cultures Around the World*, Vol. 2, ed. Melvin Ember, Carol R. Ember, and Ian Skoggard, 1–12. New York: Spring, 2005.

Kalderon, Albert. *Abraham Galante: A Biography*. New York: Sepher-Hermon Press, Inc., 1983.

Kerem, Yitzchak. "The Migration of Rhodian Jews to Africa and the Americas from 1900–1914: The Beginning of New Sephardic Diasporic Communities." In *Patterns of Migration, 1850–1914*, ed. Aubrey Newman and Stephen W. Massil, 321–34. London: University College London, 1996.

Kosmin, Barry A. "A Note on Southern Rhodesian Jewry." *Jewish Journal of Sociology* 15, no. 2 (1973): 23–8.

Malino, Frances. "Prophets in Their Own Land? Mothers and Daughters of the Alliance Israélite Universelle." *Nashim* 3 (2000): 56–73.

Miccoli, Dario. "'I come from a country that is no more': Jewish nostalgia in the postcolonial Mediterranean." *Ethnologies* 39, no. 2 (2017): 51–68.

Naar, Devin E. "'Sephardim since Birth': Reconfiguring Jewish Identity in America." In *Sephardi and Mizrahi Jews in America*, ed. Saba Soomekh, 75–104. West Lafayette, Indiana: Purdue University Press, 2016.

Phillips Cohen, Julia and Sarah Abrevaya Stein. "Sephardic Scholarly Worlds: Toward a Novel Geography of Modern Jewish History." *Jewish Quarterly Review* 100, no. 3 (Summer 2010): 349–84.

Phillips Cohen, Julia and Sarah Abrevaya Stein, ed. *Sephardi Lives: A Documentary History, 1700–1950*. Stanford: Stanford University Press, 2014.

Pressman, Hannah S. "'I'd Like to Become a Bird,'" *Tablet Magazine*, 21 August 2017, https://www.tabletmag.com/jewish-life-and-religion/242352/ladino-letters-from-rhodes.

Rodrigue, Aron. *Images of Sephardi and Eastern Jewries in Transition: The Teachers of the Alliance Israélite Universelle, 1860–1939*. Seattle: University of Washington Press, 1991.

Rubenstein, Jeffrey L. *The Culture of the Babylonian Talmud*. Baltimore: Johns Hopkins University Press, 2003.

Sharkey, Heather J. *A History of Muslims, Christians, and Jews in the Middle East*. New York: Cambridge University Press, 2017.

Stein, Sarah Abrevaya. *Extraterritorial Dreams: European Citizenship, Sephardi Jews, and the Ottoman Twentieth Century*. Chicago: University of Chicago Press, 2016.

Contributors

Oscar Aguirre-Mandujano is Assistant Professor of History at the University of Pennsylvania. His research focuses on intellectual and cultural history of the early modern Ottoman Empire. He is currently working on his first monograph, which examines the relationship among literary composition, Sufi doctrine, and political thought in the early modern Islamic world.

Ty Alhadeff teaches Judaic Studies and World History at the Northwest Yeshiva High School. Previously, Alhadeff worked as the research coordinator, archivist, librarian, blogger, and social media strategist for the Sephardic Studies Program at the Stroum Center for Jewish Studies, University of Washington. Alhadeff received his BA degree from the University of Washington and a master's degree in Jewish Studies from the Hebrew University of Jerusalem

Benjamin Fortna is Professor and Director, School of Middle Eastern and North African Studies at the University of Arizona. His research focus is the late Ottoman Empire and early Turkish Republic. His books include *Imperial Classroom: Islam, the State, and Education in the Late Ottoman Empire* (Oxford University Press, 2002), *Learning to Read in the Late Ottoman Empire and the Early Turkish Republic* (Palgrave McMillan, 2010) and *The Circassian: A Life of Esref Bey, Late Ottoman Insurgent and Special Agent* (Oxford University Press, 2016).

Chris Gratien is an Assistant Professor in the Corcoran Department of History at University of Virginia, where he teaches courses on environmental history and the modern Middle East. His research focuses on the late Ottoman Empire, with an emphasis on the themes of ecology, disease, and displacement. He is also co-creator of the Ottoman History Podcast.

Maureen Jackson received her PhD in Comparative Literature from the University of Washington in 2008. She is an independent scholar and vocalist who conducts research on Jewish and multiethnic musical cultures in Ottoman and Turkish contexts as a lens for understanding cultural, economic, political, and immigrant histories. Jackson is the author of *Mixing Musics: Turkish Jewry and the Urban Landscape of a Sacred Song* (Stanford University Press, 2013), awarded the National

Jewish Book Award in Sephardic Culture. Her current research focuses on eastern Mediterranean music-making centered in late Ottoman Izmir, and ethnographic and archival projects in immigrant Turkish Jewish communities in the United States.

Laurent Mignon is Associate Professor of Turkish at the University of Oxford and a Fellow of the Middle East Centre at Saint Antony's College. His research interests range from minority literatures in late Ottoman Turkey to literary engagements with non-Abrahamic religions in a Turkish context. He is the author of, among others, *Hüzünlü Özgürlük: Yahudi Edebiyatı ve Düşüncesi Üzerine Yazılar* (A Sad State of Freedom: Writings on Jewish Literature and Thought, 2014) and, together with Katja Triplett, of *Et le papillon chanta: Orhan Veli, les "Haïkaï de Kikakou" et la genèse du haïku turc* (Paris, 2019.)

Devin Naar is the Isaac Alhadeff Professor of Sephardic Studies and Associate Professor of History at the University of Washington. Naar is the founder of the UW's Sephardic Studies Collection. He is author of the book *Jewish Salonica: Between the Ottoman Empire and Modern Greece* (Stanford University Press, 2016).

Sam Negri is a retired journalist who worked as a reporter for newspapers and magazines for roughly 50 years. His articles have appeared in the *New York Times*, the *Los Angeles Times* and numerous other publications. Over a period of more than 20 years he wrote numerous feature articles and books for *Arizona Highways Magazine*, and was a staff writer with *The Arizona Republic* (Phoenix) and the *Arizona Daily Star* (Tucson).

Özgür Özkan is a PhD candidate at the Henry M. Jackson School of International Studies at the University of Washington. His research focuses on the history of the military-society relations in Turkey and the United States.

Hannah S. Pressman received her PhD in Modern Hebrew Literature from New York University in 2012. Her writings on modern Jewish culture, religion, and identity have been published in a broad range of academic and journalistic venues. Pressman is currently at work on *Galante's Daughter: A Sephardic Family Journey*, a memoir that traces her family's travels from the Levant to southern Africa, while also exploring Sephardic identity in contemporary America.

Kerem Tınaz is Assistant Professor of History at Koç University where he teaches courses on the history of Ottoman Empire and Turkey. His research focuses on the intellectual and cultural history of the late Ottoman Empire with a particular interest in identity, ideology, and networks.

Index